How to Face Death without Fear

Helping our loved ones at the time of death
is the best service we can offer them, our greatest gift.
Why? Because death is the most important time of life:
it's at death that the next rebirth is determined.
—*Lama Zopa Rinpoche*

How to Face Death without Fear

A HANDBOOK BY
LAMA ZOPA RINPOCHE

COMPILED AND EDITED BY
Robina Courtin

Wisdom Publications
199 Elm Street
Somerville, MA 02144 USA
wisdomexperience.org

© 2020 Lama Thubten Zopa Rinpoche
All rights reserved.

No part of this book may be reproduced in any form or by any means, electronic or mechanical, including photography, recording, or by any information storage and retrieval system or technologies now known or later developed, without permission in writing from the publisher.

Library of Congress Cataloging-in-Publication Data

Names: Thubten Zopa, Rinpoche, 1945– | Courtin, Robina, compiler.
Title: How to face death without fear / Lama Zopa Rinpoche; compiled and edited by Robina Courtin.
Other titles: How to enjoy death
Description: Revised edition. | Somerville, MA: Wisdom Publications, 2020. | Includes index.
Identifiers: LCCN 2020001539 (print) | LCCN 2020001540 (ebook) | ISBN 9781614296874 (paperback) | ISBN 9781614296881 (ebook)
Subjects: LCSH: Death—Religious aspects—Buddhism.
Classification: LCC BQ4487 .T59 2020 (print) | LCC BQ4487 (ebook) | DDC 294.3/423—dc23
LC record available at https://lccn.loc.gov/2020001539
LC ebook record available at https://lccn.loc.gov/2020001540

ISBN 978-1-61429-687-4   ebook ISBN 978-1-61429-688-1

24 23 22 21 20
5 4 3 2 1

Cover photo: Statue in the courtyard of Jamyang Buddhist Centre, London. Sculpture, Nick Durnan; photograph, Natascha Sturny.

Cover design by Phil Pascuzzo.
Interior design by Gopa & Ted2, Inc.

Printed on acid-free paper that meets the guidelines for permanence and durability of the Production Guidelines for Book Longevity of the Council on Library Resources.

Printed in Canada.

Contents

Editor's Preface: How to Use This Book	vii
Introduction: We Must Prepare for Death	xi

PART ONE:
How to Think about Death and Reincarnation — 1

1. What Happens after Death? — 3
2. Everyone Dies, So There's No Need to Be Afraid — 9
3. Death Is Easy When We've Given Up Attachment — 13
4. Get Ready for Death by Living Life with a Good Heart — 19
5. The Best Way to Live and Die: Practice the Five Powers — 23
6. Pray to Be Reborn in Amitabha Buddha's Pure Land — 31

PART TWO:
How We Go from One Life to the Next — 37

7. What Happens at Death? — 39
8. The Twelve Links of Dependent Arising at the Time of Death — 43
9. The Stages of Death, Intermediate State, and Rebirth — 47
10. Death Is What the Yogis Have Been Waiting For — 57

PART THREE:
Practices to Do in the Months and Weeks before Death — 61

11. Helping Others at the Time of Death Is a Big Responsibility — 63
12. Create a Conducive Environment for a Peaceful Death — 67
13. The Practices: What to See and Touch — 69
14. The Practices: What to Think About — 75
15. The Practices: What to Hear — 81

16. The Practices: What to Meditate On — 89
17. The Practices: What to Do to Purify Negative Karma — 97
18. Finally, What to Do in the Hours before Death — 103

PART FOUR:
Practices to Do in the Hours and Days after the Breath Has Stopped — 109

19. The Practices: What to Do as Soon as the Breath Stops — 111
20. The Practices: If Your Loved One Is at Home when They Die — 115
21. The Practices: If Your Loved One Is in the Hospital when They Die — 121
22. The Practices: If Your Loved One Has Offered Their Organs — 125
23. The Practices: If Your Loved One Dies Suddenly — 131
24. If Your Loved One Has High Realizations and Is Meditating at the Time of Death — 135
25. Make Sure the Mind Has Left the Body before You Move It — 141

PART FIVE:
Practices to Do after the Mind Has Left the Body — 143

26. How to Prepare Your Loved One's Body for Cremation or Burial — 145
27. The Funeral Service — 147
28. How to Bless Your Loved One's Ashes and Include Them in Holy Objects — 149
29. Practices to Do During the Forty-Nine Days after the Mind Has Left the Body — 153

PART SIX:
The Practices in Numerical Order — 161

Hospice Services — 389
Picture Credits — 391
Glossary — 393
Index of Practices by Category and Their Numbers — 411

Editor's Preface
How to Use This Book

In this revised edition of this handbook, Lama Zopa Rinpoche gives a great deal of advice about how to help our loved ones before, during, and after death. As Rinpoche says in his introduction: "When suddenly one day one of your loved ones dies and you don't know what to do to help, you'll feel so confused, so lost. . . . knowing how to help others at the time of death is such important education to have."

From the Buddhist point of view, the consciousness of all beings, including animals, will just naturally take another rebirth after death. As Rinpoche points out, the causes of the next rebirth are activated during the time of death, not long before the breath stops. Given that the manner in which our loved ones die—peacefully or not— determines the type of rebirth, and given that most people live in denial of this natural event, our role in helping them navigate this process is crucial. Our loved ones need time to prepare for death, at peace and unafraid, so that they can confidently take a human rebirth, in which they can continue practicing their spiritual path, or rebirth in a pure land, such as Buddha Amitabha's, in which they can easily attain spiritual realizations—even achieve enlightenment.

Much of the advice can be adjusted to the needs of non-Buddhists— animals as well.

Part One: How to Think about Death and Reincarnation and **Part Two: How We Go from One Life to the Next** contain Rinpoche's teaching about what happens at death; how attachment is one of the worst obstacles to a good death; the death process itself; the role of the twelve links of dependent arising at the time of death; the need to pray to be reborn in Amitabha's pure land; and an inspiring chapter about how, for the great meditators, "Death is the moment they have been waiting for," because now they can access their subtlest level of mind, the clear light, which arises naturally at death, and use it to become enlightened.

Because for most of us death is a difficult thing to come to terms with—our loved one's or our own—working out which practices to do can be daunting. Therefore Rinpoche's actual advice, the things to do—contained in parts 3, 4, and 5, the heart of the book—have been identified as eighty-seven distinct practices, numbered and structured chronologically to help us know what to do when.

Fifty-nine of the eighty-seven practices are recommended in **Part Three: Practices to Do in the Months and Weeks before Death** and are divided into six chapters: what to see and touch; what to think about; what to hear; what to meditate on; what to do to purify negative karma; and, finally, what to do during the hours before death.

Part Four: The Practices to Do in the Hours and Days after the Breath Has Stopped contains the next seventeen practices, as well as many of the earlier ones, recommended for the hours or days that the mind is still in the body—it is said that it can take up to three days before the consciousness leaves the body. The advice covers five different scenarios in which our loved ones could die. The practices recommended are essentially the same for each situation, with some variations, but it's helpful to see them listed clearly for each scenario: if your loved one is at home when they die, if your loved one is in hospital when they die, if your loved one has offered their organs, if your loved one dies suddenly, and if your loved one has high realizations and is meditating at the time of death.

The remaining eleven practices, as well as, again, many of the earlier ones, are recommended for the weeks after the mind has left the body. **Part Five: The Practices to Do After the Mind Has Left the Body** has four chapters: how to prepare your loved one's body for cremation or burial, the funeral service, how to bless your loved one's ashes and include them in holy objects, and practices to do during the forty-nine days after the mind has left the body.

All the practices—many of which are recommended several times throughout the various stages—are listed together, numbered from 1 to 87, in **Part Six: The Practices in Numerical Order.**

The essence of the incredibly compassionate and wise advice given by Rinpoche during the past fifty years is here, for us to select from, according to the needs of our loved ones. Even if we choose to simply recite the Medicine Buddha mantra and nothing else, "understand the essential points," as Rinpoche advises throughout the book, "and do the best you can."

And of course, by helping our loved ones prepare for their death and rebirth, we are preparing for our own.

GRATITUDE

I am grateful to many people for their help: First of all, Ecie Hursthouse, who began the work on this book, and Gordon McDougall for the many excerpts of his editing of Rinpoche's teachings; as well as Yangsi Rinpoche; Geshe Tenzin Loden; Geshe Thupten Jinpa; Geshe Gelek Chodha; Ven. Yeshe Khadro and Ven. Losang Chodron of Karuna Hospice; Ven. Roger Kunsang; Ven. Chantal T. Dekyi; Ven. Holly Ansett; Ven. Tenzin Chogkyi; Ven. Ailsa Cameron; Ven. Joan Nicell; Ven. Pende Hawter; Ven. Steve Carlier; Gen Don Handrick; Nick Ribush; Valerie Tripp; Dinae Monro; Lennie Kronisch; Sue Johnson; Kathleen Surawski; Guillermo Haas-Thompson; Elise Strevel; Julie Cattlin; Sarah Brooks; Renate Ogilvie; Owen Cole; Garrey Foulkes; Eddie Peet; Tara Baltazar; Peter Griffin; and a Vietnamese nun in Sydney, Australia, Bikhuni Chân Phuoc Hai, and her mother, Hong Dieuhen, who offered $500 to help cover the costs of working on the manuscript.

And finally, I'm grateful to Tom Truty and his team at FPMT Education Services, including Carina Rumrill, and his predecessor Merry Colony and her team, including Gyalten Mindrol; Mary Moegenburg; and Daniel Aitken and his team at Wisdom Publications, especially David Kittelstrom for his editorial advice.

Robina Courtin

Introduction

WE MUST PREPARE FOR DEATH

Our Greatest Gift to Others

WHEN SUDDENLY one day one of your loved ones dies and you don't know what to do to help, you'll feel so confused, so lost. Recently a Buddhist student of mine told me that this is what happened for her when her father died unexpectedly. That made me think that knowing how to help others at the time of death is such important education to have.

As you get older, you'll definitely hear about people dying—your family will die, your friends will die (your enemies too!)—so you will need to be prepared to help. This doesn't just apply to people who work with the dying; everyone should learn how to help.

Helping our loved ones at the time of death is the best service we can offer them, our greatest gift. Why? Because death is the most important time of life: it's at death that the next rebirth is determined. By providing the right support, the right environment, you can help your loved one die peacefully, with virtuous thoughts, and thus have a good rebirth.

The Spiritual Needs Are Paramount

We need to deal with the physical needs of our loved ones at the time of death, of course, but the spiritual needs are paramount. To die with a happy mind, a peaceful mind, *that* is a spiritual concern. Some people are prepared for it, but most are not because they never think about death.

How to Help

Buddhist teachings explain that the best spiritual practitioners are joyful when they are dying, as if they're going home to see their family after a long absence. Less accomplished practitioners are happy and comfortable at the time of death and are fully confident that they will have a happy rebirth. And even the least accomplished practitioners die without worry or fear; death does not bother them at all.

Tibetan Mahayana Buddhism has so many powerful methods to help people before they die, while they are dying, and even after death.

There are two aspects to helping a dying person.

Help Your Loved One Be Peaceful. First, the most important thing is to help the person prepare psychologically so that they die with a positive and happy mind. To die without anger or clinging is vital for a happy death and a good rebirth, and so that should be foremost in our thoughts when we are around a dying person. The help we give can result in a better rebirth and a swift path to attaining all realizations and eventually enlightenment. This gift is absolutely priceless, more valuable than universes full of wish-granting jewels.

Practices That Help. And second, there are many spiritual practices that can be done before, during, and after death that can help your loved one die well and receive a perfect human rebirth or rebirth in the pure land of a buddha. I will explain what to do at each stage.

You don't need to think, "Oh, I don't know what to do." Remember, as a Buddhist, the foundation of all the practices is refuge: relying on Buddha, Dharma, and Sangha. At the time of death, for example, with strong faith you could visualize Buddha above the head of your loved one and pray strongly that they purify all their negative karma immediately and achieve a good rebirth. Even if you don't know any other practices, other sophisticated things, this would definitely help.

Helping Those Who Can't Understand

As for babies and small children or a person who has lost their capacity to understand because of coma or dementia—animals too—there is not much that they themselves can do. The least we can do is help them be peaceful and thus die with a happy mind.

But not only that. Receiving benefit from many of the practices, such as those in chapters 13 through 18, doesn't depend upon the person's or animal's understanding: merely hearing the sounds of mantras, prayers, and teachings or seeing holy images will leave positive imprints on their mind, which can activate virtuous karmic seeds at the time of death, allowing them to receive a good rebirth. This is our precious gift to them.

Before You Help Others at Death, You Need to Prepare for Your Own Death

Before you can help someone else you need to learn how to prepare for your own death. If you look at your mind and how much attachment you have, I think you will see that there is a lot of work to be done before you face death, and this is true for almost everybody. Have you freed yourself from attachment to your possessions? To your loved one and friends? To your career and reputation? Could you separate from your body happily tomorrow?

Write It Down!

So write down what you want to practice at the time of your death, how you want to die. Write it down in your diary right now! Whether you die gradually or suddenly, you need to know this. Otherwise, when death comes, or when the doctor tells you that you have cancer, you will have no time to prepare, and because of attachment to this life you'll panic. You will have no renunciation, only grasping at this life.

At the time of death, it'll be like, "You mean you didn't prepare anything? Nothing? You don't know what to do?" You didn't plan anything. You never thought about it. You haven't had a good, strong practice of Dharma: collecting extensive merits, purifying, meditating on the path to enlightenment, planting the seeds of the path in your mind.

If it's like that, at the time of death there will be no difference between somebody who doesn't know any Dharma at all and somebody who does know Dharma but didn't practice. How very, very sad.

So prepare now, write down now what you are going to practice, what you intend to do; then when the time of death comes, you will be able to do it easily. That's *very* intelligent, I would say; that's the action of a very, very intelligent person.

Don't Wait until Death Comes
But preparing for a happy death depends not just on practices at the time of death; a happy death depends upon how we live our life every day, every moment. Practicing patience when someone is angry with us or provokes us or disrespects us, for example, is practical preparation for death. Practicing like this every day protects us from creating negative karma, and that makes death lighter, less fearful. The future depends on the present.

Practicing every day and preparing for the time of your death is far more important than going to the hospital to check the body, because death can happen at any time—even for healthy people. Today, many people will die, healthy as well as unhealthy.

When you know how to die with full confidence that you won't be reborn in the lower realms; that definitely you will have a good rebirth, a good future; that death is just change; and that you're leaving this old, sick body for a new, healthy one—*then* you are qualified to help others who are dying. You will be able to explain things skillfully, according to their minds. You will create the right conditions so that it's easy for their minds to be transformed into virtue at the time of death. You will know how to help them die with a happy mind.

And not only that: once you're familiar with what to do, you can tell others what they can do to help you at the time of your own death.

The Sources
As a basis for the advice in this book, I use an explanation that Chöden Rinpoche gave at Land of Medicine Buddha, in Soquel, California, in July 2002. I mention just some of the things that Rinpoche taught so that you get the essence of Rinpoche's advice, which is extremely precious, very useful. I also give advice that I have received from some of my other lamas.

As well, I use a book called *Tibetan Ceremonies of the Dead*, written by Thupten Sangay and published by the Library of Tibetan Works and Archives in Dharamsala, India. (I don't think it has been translated into English.) It was written to educate the Tibetan people outside of their country about their traditions. It is very, very useful. It explains what to do at the time of death and immediately after the person has died; how to request a lama, a guru, to do the practice of transferring the consciousness of the loved one to a pure land (Tibetan: *phowa*); and how to make offerings to the lamas. It explains how to go about having astrological readings done after death, which determines what to do during the days before the body is removed; how to pack the body and remove it and whether it should be moved today, tomorrow, and so on; what offerings should be made to the monasteries, the holy objects, beggars, and the like. It also explains what to do during the forty-nine days that the mind is in the intermediate state between lives (Tibetan: *bardo*): what prayers and practices should be done during the first week, the second, and so forth, and finally, what to do on the forty-ninth day.

I don't go into all these details here. But I explain some of the most important points relating to the weeks and days before death, the time of death itself, and the days and weeks afterward.

Part One

How to Think about Death and Reincarnation

SHAKYAMUNI BUDDHA

"A happy death depends upon how we live our life every day, every moment."

1

What Happens after Death?

Our Mind Continues after Death

WHAT HAPPENS AT DEATH and afterward is such an important subject, yet few people seem to want to know anything about it. We will definitely die, but unwilling to acknowledge that fact, we ignore it. It is as if we have all the symptoms of cancer but we never consult a doctor because we fear knowing the truth. Unless we face death with facts, we will just be terrified for no reason.

What *does* happen after death? We know what happens to the body. We can see that the breathing stops, the heart stops, the organs cease to function, and the body begins to decompose. Is that the end of us? If we did not have a mind that is separate from the body, that would be the end. But according to the Buddha, our mind, our consciousness, is not the body: it is nonmaterial energy. The simple fact is that the mind connects with a body for a certain period of time, and when the person dies, the mind continues. Because of karma—a person's past actions, which leave seeds in the mind that ripen as future experiences—the mind goes to another body. This is what is called *reincarnation*.

Even though the body completely disappears until not even a single atom of what we once called "my body" can be found, our consciousness continues. Because of our deep craving for the physical, we enter an intermediate state—a state between lives—and then take another body, pushed into whatever rebirth in samsara our karma dictates. (See chapters 7, 8, and 9.)

Before giving his explanations about what to do at the time of death, Chöden Rinpoche explained that *samsara* is the continuity of these aggregates—our body and mind joining to the next life's aggregates—caused by karma and delusion. Another meaning, Rinpoche said, is cycling from birth to death to the intermediate state, and again birth, death, and intermediate state, continuously circling like this.

We ordinary beings have no control over where we are born. Highly realized beings such as *arhats* and higher bodhisattvas, however, have completely ceased even the seed of the fundamental ignorance that holds the self and everything else as existing from its own side, which is the root cause of repeated birth in samsara. (See chapters 10 and 24.)

Reincarnation Is Not Just Some Asian Superstition
Western society does not have a culture that accepts reincarnation, so Westerners often presume it is an Asian superstition. Because it is not talked about, they think it can't be real. It is like the reluctance of Westerners to accept acupuncture when it was first introduced in the West. People found it impossible to believe that sticking a needle in one part of the body relieved the pain in another part, just because they had no knowledge of the wind energies that flow throughout the body. These days, acupuncture is more accepted, mainly because it has been shown to be effective. Similarly, people in the West are hearing more about reincarnation, and some are even starting to accept it, or at least not write it off as a primitive religious superstition.

There is a meditation where you observe that this present moment of mind is the direct result of the moment of mind that immediately preceded it, that the previous moment of mind is the direct result of the moment of mind before that, and so on. Because there can be no result without a cause, and because the main cause of a moment of mind must be its preceding moment, we can trace these moments of mind back to last week and last year and twenty years ago, right back to the moment of mind at birth, which must have been caused by the moment of mind at the last moment in the womb. Then we look even further, to the first moment of life at the time of conception. This first moment of mind in this life must have had a cause, and that cause must have been a previous moment of that mind, the mind of the last moment of the intermediate state. That can be traced back to the last moment of the previous life, and so forth.

Reincarnation Hasn't Been Disproved
We can't remember our previous lives because our minds are too clouded, not because there was no previous life. In the West this is not

widely studied. Universities grant degrees for studying how organisms function, but the process of death and rebirth is unknown to them; it's like a big, black hole. Scientists can explain how the cells break down and the brain stops functioning but can never seem to get beyond that to address the question of what actually happens to us at death.

They can show that we were once in a womb—but what caused us to enter our mother's womb? They explain things at a physical level, but there is no scientific explanation of the mind leaving one body and taking another. There is no mechanism that measures our mental experiences in this life, so of course they cannot deal with past and future lives and how they are connected.

We need to really investigate this, because accepting karma and reincarnation goes against a lot of contemporary scientific thinking. If a consciousness separate from the body does not exist, what is it that experiences pleasure and pain, what creates the causes of happiness and suffering? If this consciousness doesn't exist, what is the basis of this sense of self that we feel so strongly? If we deny the mind we deny the universe, because it is only through the mind that the universe exists. If nothing exists, then nothing matters.

Without Understanding Karma and the Nature of Mind, Science Is Incomplete

We are often skeptical when we shouldn't be and not skeptical when we should be. What we need to do is escape from ignorance and thus free ourselves from suffering, and skepticism about past and future lives does nothing to help us do this. We cannot properly understand physical evolution without fully seeing mental evolution. They are not one, but they are nevertheless related. That's why what is explained in science books is incomplete. Science explains that the first conscious entities emerged from the oceans and slowly evolved into animals, one of which is the human being, but there is no explanation of *why* this was happening. It is a wonderful account of the physical evolution of life, but it ignores the mental aspect—and the mental aspect is primary. The explanation of evolution is incomplete without acknowledging the existence of nonmaterial consciousness.

The deeper explanation of life on this planet needs an explanation of karma, how suffering is created by negative actions and happiness by positive actions. Even if scientists could photograph and record the various realms of existence—the higher realms of the gods, the lower realms of the hell beings, and so forth—this would still not explain that mind caused them. To avoid suffering and achieve happiness we need to accept this explanation, but it is very subtle and beyond our current capacity to know beyond the superficial level.

We Need the Explanations of the Buddha
This is not something to take lightly. We need to determine whether the Buddha is a reliable source. The more convinced we are by the words of the Buddha, the more faith we will have in his teachings, and the more we will be able to transform our mind. When we investigate, either through our own analysis of his teachings or through the fact that countless practitioners have been led from suffering to full enlightenment using his guidance, we will see that the Buddha is the perfect guide. Just look at great practitioners like His Holiness the Dalai Lama: what they know is faultless and based entirely on the wisdom of the Buddha. To feel that we know more than these highly realized beings is not only arrogant, it is self-defeating—we can cause ourselves so much suffering by going against their advice.

As the great practitioners of the past progressed along the path to enlightenment, their understanding of reality increased, and they saw things we can't imagine. This was all the product of the mind, not machines. Great bodhisattva yogis like Milarepa, who lived in Tibet in the eleventh century, had minds so powerful that they could influence their bodies, being able to fly, for example, or take on different forms.

The Great Bodhisattvas Remember Their Past Lives
Such great beings could also see past and future lives just as we can see a table in front of us, and they could see the different realms of existence. To them these were not mere logical possibilities but actual objects of knowledge, things that they experienced as real with their own minds. They could also control where they reincarnated and so could choose the future rebirth most beneficial to others. Everything they experienced confirmed the truth of the Dharma that the Buddha taught.

If you still find it hard to accept the logic of reincarnation, there are plenty of accounts of people who have actually remembered past lives. As a two-year-old, His Holiness the Dalai Lama immediately recognized his attendant from when he was the previous Dalai Lama the first time he saw him, even remembering his name. People like His Holiness rarely like to talk about remembering their past lives because it is more skillful to appear in the aspect of an ordinary monk. I remember one time at the center of Geshe Sopa in Wisconsin, when talking about *bodhichitta*—the wish to attain enlightenment in order benefit each and every sentient being—His Holiness said, "I have absolutely no realization of bodhichitta, but I have great devotion for bodhichitta, and I have absolutely no realization of emptiness, but I have strong faith in emptiness." This is typical of His Holiness's humility.

Afterward, in a private audience with the organizers of the event, one person said that if His Holiness has no realizations, then it is hopeless for the rest of us. His Holiness, with his great compassion, couldn't bear this person thinking that it's hopeless so felt he had to say something. His Holiness admitted that he could actually remember when the Buddha was in India. This casual remark is amazing: His Holiness was around at the time of the Buddha, and he could still remember it!

It seems that there was a bodhisattva to whom the Buddha predicted that if he recited certain prayers, he would be reborn in the snow lands of Tibet and become the Compassion Buddha, Chenrezik (Sanskrit: Avalokiteshvara), to spread Buddhadharma in Tibet and guide all the Tibetan sentient beings. Evidently, all the Dharma kings of Tibet are also manifestations of this bodhisattva, and each was instrumental in starting and spreading the Dharma in Tibet. This is why the Tibetan people have such a special connection with the Compassion Buddha.

Now, of course, His Holiness's influence has spread well beyond Tibet, and he is able to benefit the sentient beings of the entire world, traveling constantly to many countries, giving teachings and initiations, and being a living example of bodhichitta.

If His Holiness can remember a life that happened over 2,500 years ago, then there is no question that other highly realized practitioners can also remember previous lives.

Ordinary People Remember Their Past Lives
Besides the high lamas who can remember past lives, ordinary people have also been known to remember them. Many of these accounts have been verified. For example, a girl in the Punjab, in India, could

clearly remember things about her previous life: the town she lived in, her house, her parents, and so forth. One day the memory just came to her, and she led her present-life parents to a village not far from where she lived and showed them a house, saying that she had lived there in her last life. On seeing the people living there, she recognized them as her previous parents, although of course they were older and more wrinkled, and she knew their names. She knew each of the rooms in the house and could tell when something had been moved or changed. For many years I kept a photo of her and her two sets of parents, a precious photo. His Holiness the Dalai Lama heard about this girl and sent somebody to visit her.

There are many examples like this. But of course most of us can't even remember our birth, let alone what happened before that. I think the reason most of the people who remember previous lives are Asian is because Asian society is a lot more open to reincarnation than Western society. Even if a Western child did remember something, their parents would probably presume it was some strange fantasy and not investigate.

We Need to Question Our Assumptions about Reality

It is interesting to analyze the society we live in and the unquestioned beliefs of that society. When we analyze, we see the cracks in what seems to be the truth. Many Westerners believe in neither reincarnation nor the Christian heaven. When you die everything finishes; it's just a big blank nothing. The body and the mind both cease to exist. Is that what really happens? It's good to check what beliefs we have and see whether they are based on a firm understanding or on the assumptions of our society.

2

Everyone Dies, So There's No Need to Be Afraid

We Will Die, but We Don't Believe It

ONE THING we can be sure of is that we will die. But we have this feeling that we won't die. It might not be spoken, it might be quite unconscious, but we live with this belief all the time. We say to our friends, "See you next week!" and the assumption is "I won't die." We work one more hour in order to get our pay assuming we will still be alive on payday. Every day we live with this belief we won't die. Right up until the day we die, we carry around this belief in permanence like a heavy weight, which totally deceives us, blinding us to reality.

Death Believes in Equal Opportunity

Nobody escapes death. It is not a class thing, or a race thing, it does not depend on where we live, what education we have, or how much money we have in the bank. Death believes totally in equal opportunity. A president or a rich executive is as likely to die as a beggar; a college professor is as likely to die as an illiterate farmer.

Think of the people you know who have died: your friends, your parents, your aunts and uncles, your grandparents and great grandparents, perhaps even your children or grandchildren. Go back through your family tree, as far back as you can. Generation upon generation of your family have come before you, hundreds of people, and yet how many survive now? Four? Five? Not many, I am sure.

Of the family members remaining, whose turn will be next? Nobody knows. You may have a rich parent or grandparent and expect to inherit their money and property. Don't count on it! Maybe you have a ninety-year-old grandmother, but she might have to attend your funeral.

Nothing is certain except that in a hundred years or so, no one currently in your family will be alive.

In the history of this world, not one person has ever escaped death. If we think of the billions of humans who have lived on this planet since humans first appeared, we will see that not one has been able to stay alive. A few have been able to prolong their lives a little, many have shortened theirs a lot, but all have had to die. Not one human being, not one sentient being since the evolution of life began, has been able to hold on indefinitely to that most precious thing called life.

Nowhere to Hide
Nobody escapes death, and there is nowhere in the world or beyond the world we can go to escape death. Not even Disneyland! We can go to Disneyland to stay forever young, but we will still age at the same rate and we will still die.

We can build the deepest, thickest fallout shelter to protect ourselves from the nuclear bombs that could destroy us, like so many Americans did in the middle of the last century, but we cannot escape death. None of those Americans died from an atomic bomb strike, but most have died, and those still alive will die one day.

We can bury ourselves in the middle of a huge mountain made of diamond, something so solid and indestructible, but that will not stop death. There is no sanctuary that can protect us from death.

Even if we leave the Earth, we won't leave death behind. If we buy a ticket on a rocket that takes us to other planets or even out of the solar system, maybe even to another galaxy, death will be waiting for us when we arrive.

Life Is Slipping Away Every Day
And the reality is that with every passing second we are getting closer to death. In *A Guide to the Bodhisattva Way of Life*, Shantideva says,

> Remaining neither day nor night,
> life is always slipping by
> and never getting any longer.
> Why would death not come to one like me?

In Fact, We Could Die Today

Not only is our death definite, the time of our death is most uncertain. Death can happen at any moment, from our next breath to many years from now. We simply don't know. If we think about all the "certainties" in life—our next birthday, tonight's dinner, our favorite television program on Friday—we will see that they are just assumptions, because no matter how likely they are, we may very well not be here to experience them.

Whether we say it or not, we have the thought that we are healthy and young—and that's even if we're sixty—and that life is pretty good and will continue just like this. To feel we won't die is dangerous, and to assume that we won't die soon because we are not old or sick is wrong. Young, healthy people die all the time. Babies die, teenagers die; at any age, for countless reasons, our life can suddenly cease.

When We Prepare for Death, There Is Nothing to Fear

Living in denial of the fact that we will die causes so many of our problems. If we don't prepare for death, our life will be full of dissatisfaction. Elvis Presley was rich and loved by millions, and yet when he was close to death, he was crying and miserable because he knew he had wasted his life. He had made so many records, and he was better known than anybody else in the world at that time, but he felt deeply how empty his life had been. It is tragic, but this is the story of so many people, both famous and unknown.

If we can't stop death, then the only thing we can do is prepare for it. When we die, our consciousness will not cease to exist. That is a basic fact of karma. Our consciousness existed before this human life—it is beginningless—and will continue to exist after our body is destroyed.

Right now we have the freedom to think about what is worthwhile in life and to change our life so it is truly meaningful. Then we will be ready to die with a happy mind, to die with satisfaction.

3

Death Is Easy When We've Given Up Attachment

Attachment Makes Death So Difficult

DEATH ITSELF is not what causes fear. It is simply the consciousness leaving the body; we label "death" on that event. There is no terrifying death from its own side; the terrifying death is made up by our mind. We have made death terrifying.

What causes the worry and fear, what makes death so difficult, is attachment, desire, clinging: to this life, to our body, possessions, family, friends, and so on. This clinging makes death difficult, bringing so much worry and fear. And we cause this ourselves.

Attachment makes our mind not free. Not wanting to be separated from these things, we can't let go, we don't want to die. Attachment tortures us. And then this stirs up so much worry and fear in the minds of family and friends, who can do nothing to help.

If we die without having let go of attachment, our past negative karma will cause us to be reborn in an unfortunate realm as a hell being, hungry ghost, or animal. The most harmful thing at the time of death is attachment.

The basic method, the main thing to do, to ensure that our mind is free at the time of death—to have no worries, no fears, nothing that ties our mind; to not be like the bird who has such a strong wish to fly, to be free, but cannot because its legs are fastened by a rope that is bolted to the rock face—the main thing to do is give up attachment.

Attachment to the Body

Our greatest attachment is to our body, and so the greatest suffering at the time of death is when we are about to be separated from it. At the time of death, a kangaroo, a slug, a human—whatever the being is—

feels so much fear: we can't stand the thought of dying, of leaving this body, no matter how much suffering it has caused us.

What is the body? It's a skeleton plastered over with bits of flesh and muscle. Inside there are the organs, veins, blood, and other fluids; a layer of skin covers it, and it is adorned with hair, nails, and teeth. Taken individually, none of these things is attractive. The body is filled with filthy and smelly substances, and what comes out of the body is also unappealing. Why be so attached to this body and cause yourself so much suffering?

Clinging to the body at the time of death creates unimaginable suffering. To die with a peaceful and happy mind, you must break this attachment. Understanding this can help anybody, whether Buddhist, Christian, Hindu, Muslim, or Jewish. Even somebody who believes that there is only one life and that they will soon cease to exist entirely can benefit from understanding this. Even a person who has suffered greatly in life will die peacefully if we help them understand this important point.

What happens if you don't let go of this attachment? Chöden Rinpoche told a story about a woman who was very attached to her beautiful body. She was on a boat that sank, and her body washed up on the shore. Because of her attachment, she was reborn as a snake that lived in the corpse, slithering in and out of the mouth and the lower orifices, totally attached to it.

Laugh at Samsara
One day Buddha's heart disciple Shariputra, who excelled in wisdom, passed the house of some villagers on his alms round. He looked in and saw a man eating his lunch, with his son on his knee and his dog at his feet, which he was hitting. Shariputra thought to himself:

> He eats his father's flesh and beats his mother.
> The enemy he killed sits on his knee.
> A wife gnaws her husband's bones.
> What a farce samsara is!

Because of his clairvoyance Shariputra could see that the man's father, who had died, would always eat fish from a pond behind the house so was reborn as a fish there. The mother had been very attached to the house so after she died she was reborn as the man's dog. The man himself had killed an enemy for raping his wife, and because the enemy was so attached to her, he was reborn as her son. In other words: while the son eats his father's flesh, his mother, the dog, eats the bones of her husband, the fish, and is being beaten by her son. His enemy, his own child, is sitting on his knee.

Attachment Is the Main Push behind Samsara
When talking about the cessation of suffering and its causes in relation to taking refuge in the Dharma, the refuge prayer mentions "the supreme cessation of attachment." It doesn't say cessation of anger, it doesn't say cessation of ignorance, it doesn't say cessation of pride—there are many delusions. Why attachment in particular? Because attachment is the main push behind samsara, this cycle of death and rebirth—the main cause.

There is the attachment that motivates negative actions, which cause rebirth in the lower realms. Then there is the attachment that clings to rebirth in the human realm, for example, which makes us create the virtuous karma that causes such a rebirth.

Then, at the time of death, craving and grasping—strong attachment, in other words—arise and nourish the seed that was left on the mind by the past karma, driven by the root ignorance, making it ready to produce the next life. (I describe the process of the twelve links of dependent arising at the time of death in chapter 8.)

So you can see that even the nearest cause of the next rebirth in samsara is this attachment at the time of death. It is what ties us to samsara continuously, has been tying us to samsara continuously, and will continue to tie us to samsara. Our consciousness has existed since beginningless time and will continue to exist forever. Until we cut the causes of samsara, body after body will keep coming, like the assembly line in a factory.

Give Up Attachment, Enjoy Death
Therefore we need to cultivate renunciation of samsara by meditating on, or thinking about, the shortcomings of samsaric happiness. When we investigate the nature of this kind of hallucinated happiness, we find

that it is only suffering. Once we do that, we can cut this emotional pain, free our mind from attachment, and die with a happy mind.

Don't wait until you're close to death to practice renunciation. If you practice in your daily life, freeing your mind from the bondage of the emotional pain of attachment, your mind will be trained. You'll be like the military, prepared to defeat the enemy whenever he attacks.

By practicing in daily life, you've trained your mind to know not only that death is definite but also that it can occur any year, any month, any week, any day, even in this moment. If death comes suddenly, right now, you will be well prepared. There will be nothing to bother you, nothing to be upset or angry about, nothing to regret, no reason for sadness. For you, death will be easy; you will be able to guide your consciousness to the pure land of a buddha or a good human rebirth.

For the person who has practiced like this, who has lived a sincere, ethical life, who has not harmed others and has been kind and treated them with compassion and a good heart—for this person there will always be a good result, a good ending to life. This is logical. During their life, there is more peace and happiness, more satisfaction, more fulfillment in their heart, therefore at the time of death, there will be no worries; death won't frighten them, even if they don't believe in reincarnation. For them there is no fear, no guilt; they are satisfied, confident, relaxed, peaceful. It's just another change, a change of life.

A few years ago, when I was in Adelaide, Australia, I heard in a radio interview a lady say that she was not afraid of death. "I know where I'm going," she said. I really hoped that the interviewer would pursue it, would go further, but he didn't. I think for him her comment was unexpected; it obviously wasn't a normal thing to talk about. There are people like her in the West: the way they've lived their life reflects in the way they approach death; it shows.

The way you live your life is like a test, an examination. If you have created many problems, harmed sentient beings, been immoral, unethical, very selfish, not only will there be a lot of suffering in your life but also a lot of fear at death: a feeling that you're going toward a great, frightening darkness.

At the moment, given that we're still in samsara and can't stop death, we can at least learn to enjoy death, to go through the process with a happy mind. To accomplish this we must make the effort to meditate on the methods to free ourselves of attachment, to let go. This is the main thing. Then our mind will be free—like releasing the bird whose legs were fastened: now it can fly. Now we can have a peaceful, happy death and a good rebirth.

THE COMPASSION BUDDHA

"If the only thing your loved one knows is the mantra of the Compassion Buddha and, free of attachment to this life, has spent their life chanting it, that is enough."

4
Get Ready for Death by Living Life with a Good Heart

The Purpose of Our Life Is to Help Others

THERE ARE many Buddhist practices, but the very essence is developing a good heart: love and compassion. This means we want to help sentient beings as much as possible and not harm them in any way. This is the basis of morality, of ethics, and within that lies the whole of the Dharma. Within that there are all the beneficial attitudes that we need to cultivate: equanimity, generosity, patience, loving kindness, and especially bodhichitta.

Living every day of our life with a good heart is so important for the happiness—both temporary happiness and the ultimate happiness of enlightenment—of the sentient beings of the six realms: hell beings, hungry ghosts, animals, human beings, gods, and demigods, as well as the intermediate-state (*bardo*) beings. Your good heart is so important for the happiness and peace of the numberless beings of this world, both people and the animals. It is essential for the happiness of your country, your family, your society, your workplace. Their happiness depends upon your good heart, comes from your good heart. This is the most important thing in life.

A good heart is the very meaning of life. If we can hold the welfare of all beings in our heart in whatever we do, we will never harm others again. Wherever we are, whatever we do, whoever we are with, if we maintain awareness that the purpose of our life is to help others, to give happiness to others, we will never create the causes of suffering, either for ourselves or others. Then we become the source of happiness for everybody around us—every being—and they become the cause of our enlightenment.

Everything we do in our daily life should be fueled by the wish to make others happy. When we meet people, we should feel that our job in meeting them is to make them happy. When we eat, we should feel we are eating to get the energy to help others. When we work, we should feel our job is to benefit others. When we walk, every step is to benefit others.

Whenever we see an insect, we should think that we are here to give happiness to that insect. Whenever we hear a bird, we should think that we are here to give happiness to that bird. Whenever a friend phones, we should think that we are here to give happiness to that friend. Whenever we have a confrontation at the office, we should think that we are here to give happiness to the person who is confronting us.

Whatever we do, we should think, "I am doing this to make others happy. This is my job; this is my purpose in life." From the moment we wake up to the moment we go to sleep, this should be the motivation for every action. With a good heart, with a mind sincerely wishing to benefit others, our life will make sense.

With a Good Heart, We Are Brave in the Face of Problems
When we have a heart full of loving kindness and compassion, then rather than becoming upset or depressed when problems arise, we remain happy. Even if there are serious problems in our life, we won't be bothered by them. Even if our business fails or we are diagnosed with cancer, since our focus is on the happiness of others, we will remain joyful amid dealing with our problems. When somebody becomes angry with us, because all we are concerned about is that person's happiness, we won't react with anger or indignation; we will do whatever is necessary to help them.

With a Good Heart, Our Own Wishes Are Fulfilled
Helping others subdues our own mind, making it softer and softer, more and more patient, more and more tolerant, more and more compassionate, more and more loving and kind. Thus everything we do for others becomes a cause for our own happiness. Without expectation or desire for it, we effortlessly achieve whatever we need in this life: comfort, health, leisure, protection, money—what normal people fight

for all their lives. And then when we get these things, we use them not for ourselves but for serving others.

And we don't only get what we need now. Helping others gives us a better future rebirth and eventually leads us to liberation from samsara and the peerless happiness of enlightenment.

With a Good Heart, Death Is Easy

What makes death easy is not being a scholar of Buddhist philosophy; that alone cannot help you stop fear at the time of death. What helps most at the time of death is a good heart. Being learned, being wise, doesn't help. Pure morality can help, but pure morality comes naturally when there is a good heart.

There was an older monk at one of the monasteries, not learned but with a very good heart. He went to see his guru, Geshe Urgyen Tseten, one of the main teachers there, and said he wanted to do a three-year Vajrayogini retreat. Geshe Urgyen asked him, "Do you know what the three principal aspects of the path are?" He didn't know, he couldn't say; he could not inform his teacher of these: renunciation, bodhichitta, and emptiness. Geshe-la said, "How can you do a three-year retreat? You don't even know the three principal aspects of the path!"

Nevertheless, the monk did the retreat. And when he died, he died in meditation. He didn't even know the essence of Buddhism, he couldn't tell his teacher when he asked him, but he finished the retreat and died in meditation. Can you imagine?

The point is, he lived a normal life with a very good heart—as well as guru devotion, of course. There are many monks in the monasteries like this, who don't have a reputation for being learned but who die in meditation or in the lion position, like the Buddha when he passed away (discussed in practice 55).

Among being learned, keeping pure morality, and having a good heart, the most important is to have a good heart. I'm not saying that if you're learned you'll have a hard death—I'm not saying that at all. But a good heart is the main thing we should practice. For even if you have no education but you have a good heart, your mind will be happy. You have real happiness, real peace. Whereas if you have everything else but not a loving heart, your life will be full of problems.

With a Good Heart, We Will Die without Fear

When we live with love and compassion, we live our life in the best possible way, and we can be confident of dying with compassion, with a happy, peaceful mind, and thus taking a good rebirth.

Living life with a good heart means we will die free from guilt and fear. We will be satisfied with our life, with no sense of things left undone. Even though we have enjoyed our life and lived it to the full, we will experience no regret at having to leave it. Because of our selfless attitude, we have not clung to the objects of attachment of this life, and so at the time of death, we accept that we must leave everything behind. As we have seen, attachment to this life is what brings fear at the time of death. For somebody who believes in reincarnation, death is just a transition from one happy state to another. And even for somebody who doesn't believe in reincarnation, one effect of having led a sincere and compassionate life is to die without fear or regret.

It is natural to look back on our life as we are dying. It will be a bit like a school exam. We will be forced to honestly examine just what our life has meant. If it has been a life of selfishness, during which we have always placed our own interests before the interests of others, causing problems for others and harming them, it will become very clear that our life has been a complete waste of time.

Morality isn't some system of behavior imposed by a religion; it is a natural understanding of the right thing to do. We don't need a lama or a priest to explain we have harmed others because of our selfish concerns. We know this, whether consciously or not, and at the time of death our mind will be filled with dread and fear, with great regret that it has all been pointless. We'll feel that our life has been futile and that a terrible darkness awaits—I have heard people express this many times.

Whether or not you believe in a religion, whether or not you think there is something after death, compassion and a good heart will give you a special sort of courage. You will die with a calm and happy mind, and peace will radiate from you. Everybody around you will be aware of this very special quality, and your death will be a great lesson for others.

5
The Best Way to Live and Die: Practice the Five Powers

THE FIVE powers are five ways to strengthen our life and prepare ourselves for death. It's a practice in the tradition of *mind training*, or *thought transformation* (Tibetan: *lojong*), in Tibetan Mahayana Buddhism. The Seven-Point Mind Training practice says, "The Mahayana instruction for transference of consciousness [after death] is only the five powers. Therefore cherish this practice!"

The texts in this tradition list the five powers in two different orders: one to practice in life and one to practice close to the time of death. The *power of training* gets moved to the end of the list because at the time of death it refers to the way we die. The five at the time of death direct our mind to our next rebirth.

The Five Powers at the Time of Death
The five powers in life are: intention, training, the white seed, blaming the ego, and prayer. The order at death is different:

1. The power of the white seed
2. The power of planning, or intention
3. The power of blaming the ego
4. The power of prayer
5. The power of training

The Best Way to Transfer Your Consciousness
The tantric teachings, or Vajrayana, present a special method called *phowa* for transferring your consciousness to a pure land after death (see practices 48, 62, and 81). However, even learning this method by heart doesn't mean that it will work when you practice it at the time of

death, that you won't encounter obstacles to rebirth in the pure lands. Without a proper foundation—renouncing this life and future samsara and cultivating bodhichitta—merely knowing the technique of phowa will not be enough.

There's a story about an old monk in Tibet who knew the technique very well and was trying to shoot his consciousness into Tushita, the pure land of Buddha Maitreya. But he wasn't having any success. His guru, who was nearby, could see that the monk's attachment to his butter tea was causing him difficulties, and he immediately sent a young monk with a message that the butter tea is better in Tushita. As soon as the young monk whispered the message in his ear, the old monk was able to let go of this one last thing, his consciousness was released, and he was reborn in Tushita.

In Tibet, you see, there weren't too many enjoyments for the monks in the monasteries—only their tea, which is made with butter and salt. They really prized the butter in the tea, which would float on top and would then remain at the bottom of the cup when the tea was finished. Tibetans call this *shakh*—there are many kinds of *shakh*, such as thick *shakh* and so on. I think the equivalent for Westerners must be ice cream or chocolate!

Anyway, an even better way to guarantee that you transfer your consciousness to a pure land or a good rebirth, a safer approach to phowa and a method that you can have confidence in, is the five powers.

Bodhichitta Is the Heart of the Five Powers

With the five powers you make your heart practice bodhichitta; you split yourself off from self-cherishing and live your life with bodhichitta. If you are able to do this, then, no question, you will be able to practice the five powers when the moment of death arrives. There will be no obstacles to going to a pure land or receiving a perfect human rebirth—whatever you wish. Many things can be explained to help us perform this practice in daily life, but this is its essence.

We need to know the order of both sets of the five powers. The order here is for those at the time of death.

1. The Power of the White Seed: Give Away All Your Possessions before You Die

The first power is to accumulate merit. Accumulating merit during life means creating positive karma and purifying negative karma—but at death it is too late for that. The main thing at the time of death is to cut attachment, clinging, so we must give away our things, either mentally or actually. It is extremely urgent to let go of your material possessions, especially those that you are most strongly attached to. I discuss this in practice 9 as well.

The great enlightened being Phabongkha Dechen Nyingpo said that if you give away what you are attached to, nothing will be more helpful to you after your death—not even another person's creating root merits on your behalf.

You can do this by writing it down in a will—but in your heart you can offer everything to the Guru, Buddha, Dharma, and Sangha. Even if there is nobody around to hear you, from your heart think, "I am offering these things to the Guru Three Rare Sublime Ones." Having offered them, think it belongs to them; then there will be no more clinging. By making offerings like this, you not only let go, you also create inconceivable merit. Why? Because of the power of these four objects of offering: Guru, Buddha, Dharma, Sangha. Make the dedication in your heart right now, because death can come any day, any moment.

Even though material possessions, the samsaric perfections, are without essence, you can still make them worthwhile. You can dedicate them toward preserving and spreading the teachings of the Buddha, or you can dedicate your possessions to holy objects. (See practices 85–87.) It all depends on how open your heart is and on how well you understand the law of cause and effect. Having faith in karma opens up skies of opportunity to be most beneficial. Most beneficial for whom? For other sentient beings. And if something is most beneficial for others, it will just naturally be most beneficial for you.

Of the things that terrify us at death, the loss of what we are attached to—our body, possessions, and loved ones—is the most frightening, as we discussed above. Clinging even to our altar, our buddha statues, and our Dharma books is still attachment.

Having given away everything, we will have no regrets and no worries caused by attachment.

Die with the Six Perfections

Another approach, as explained in the teachings, is to die with the six perfections: charity, or generosity, morality, patience, perseverance, concentration, and wisdom.

You could divide your belongings into three parts: offer the first part to the Guru Three Rare Sublime Ones to collect merit, use one part to make charity to sentient beings, and use one part to throw a party and so forth. To do any of these is *charity*.

For *morality*, confess and abstain from breaking the vows of individual liberation, generate bodhichitta, and engage in the bodhisattva vows.

Patience: If you have a grudge from the past, offer forgiveness. If the person is around you now, dedicate one part of your material possessions and tell the person, "I have just this much; please forgive me." If the other person is unable to accept, be patient and let there be no unhappiness in your mind.

Regarding *perseverance*, whatever you do, do it with joy.

The other two, *concentration* and *wisdom*, are contained in the first four practices when we do them with concentration and see them as empty of true existence.

2. The Power of Planning: Remember Bodhichitta

This can also be called the *power of intention*, or the *power of motivation*, or the *power of the attitude*. It is the same at death as it is when we practice the five powers in our lifetime, although the texts list it in a different order. During our lifetime we constantly check our motivation to ensure it is as vast and positive as possible. Every morning we would think, "The purpose of my life is to free every sentient being from suffering and its causes and bring them every happiness. Today, that is my job and I will do nothing but that."

The motivation is exactly the same here, but now we extend it to the intermediate-state period and into the next life and all future lives. With devotion, totally give yourself up to the Three Rare Sublime Ones, completely relying on Buddha, Dharma, and Sangha. Motivate very strongly again and again, thinking, "From now until I achieve enlightenment—before the time of death, while I am dying, in the intermediate state, and in all future lives—I will never allow myself to come under the control of self-cherishing, and I will never separate from bodhichitta."

Set the intention to be really careful during however many seconds there are from now until the time of death. Put all your effort into this, just as someone crossing a dangerous rope bridge pays full attention to making sure they do not fall off. To be able to recognize the signs at the time of death and immediately and easily think these thoughts depends on having practiced every day, and especially when you are sick. Even if you can explain these practices, there will be no benefit at all unless you have actually attempted to do them.

So think: "Whatever I experience as I face death and move through the death process and into the next rebirth, I will always only ever think of benefiting others." With such a pure, altruistic motivation, we can be assured of a wonderful death and a very positive rebirth.

Imagine how terrible it would be in the lower realms. Besides the intense and continuous suffering, sentient beings there have no possibility of creating positive actions and therefore virtually no possibility of escaping their suffering.

Think of what happens when occasionally they escape and are reborn in the human realm. It's like the briefest of holidays for a poor person who has won a luxury cruise but tomorrow must return to their life of poverty. Like everybody, they only want happiness and can't bear the thought of even the slightest suffering, and yet, weighed down by the delusions and negative karma that have plagued them for eons, they're incapable of doing anything other than create more negative karma. In their brief time in the human realm, they have the potential but not the means to create the causes for happiness, so they spend their life creating negative actions and guaranteeing more rebirths in the lower realms. It is so pitiful.

There is no way we can help our kind mother sentient beings while we ourselves are overwhelmed by suffering, so we must do everything we can to ensure a better future rebirth. That means destroying selfishness and embracing the mind of bodhichitta. This attitude is important in our daily life, and it is crucial as we face death.

This is the power of planning.

3. The Power of Blaming the Ego: Give Up Self-Cherishing at the Time of Death

The next power is called the *power of blaming the ego* or the *power of destruction*. It's the same power as during life, but here it comes third in the list. What we blame is the ego, and what we destroy is self-cherishing. When we examine where all our problems in this life have come from and the source of all the problems we will face during death and in our next life, we find that it all comes down to the self-cherishing attitude.

It might seem like our life would be perfect if we could stop all the external factors that keep interfering and bringing us suffering. But if we examine more deeply, it will become obvious that without the attitude of self-cherishing, we simply wouldn't suffer, no matter the situation.

This is what we need to destroy, not some external enemy. This is where the blame lies for every tiny bit of suffering we have ever had to experience. Without this inner enemy, there is no outer enemy. We need to place the blame on this real cause of all our misery, not the external condition that we currently blame, and give all our problems to this enemy. By doing that we will destroy self-cherishing completely and attain liberation from suffering.

This power, of blaming the ego, loads all the problems of our life onto this internal enemy. Everything that has ever gone wrong, we heap onto this troublemaker. Every undesirable thing, in both our worldly and spiritual life, every obstacle to our worldly happiness and our spiritual progress, we lay on top of the self-cherishing attitude, smothering it as you would pile ashes on a fire to kill it. Every undesirable thing has come from the self-cherishing attitude: relationship problems, illnesses, disharmony, losing our job, feeling people don't love us, having things stolen, and so forth and so on. We would run out of paper if we tried to write down all the suffering, petty and major, that the self-cherishing mind has brought us.

We are mistaken to blame the mugger who takes our wallet or the person who steals our partner, but we are totally justified and right in blaming and begrudging this sneakiest of thieves, the self-cherishing mind that promises happiness but steals all our merit and delivers only suffering.

Kick Out Self-Cherishing!
It is the self-cherishing thought that brings every difficulty to everyone on this Earth—from the beggar up to the king, prime minister, or billionaire. Therefore you should resolve to not come under the control of this attitude but to kick it out immediately. Cast it off, renounce from the heart the great demon of self-cherishing.

As Nagarjuna says, when a fire spark jumps on your head or clothing, you immediately shake it off, not allowing it to remain there for even a second. Like that, engage in the practice of immediately abandoning self-cherishing the moment it arises.

4. The Power of Prayer: Die with Bodhichitta
During our life the power of prayer is the last, but at the time of death it comes fourth. Phabongkha Rinpoche explained that it doesn't mean praying to be born in a pure land; it means praying to take upon yourself all the sufferings, defilements, and negative karmas of all sentient beings and to generate bodhichitta.

So, pray strongly: "May I never be separated from bodhichitta, the supreme altruistic mind, now as I am dying, when I enter the intermediate state, and when I finally take rebirth."

Pray also: "May I be able to practice in order to meet again the guru who reveals the teachings on mind training and bodhichitta."

5. The Power of Training: Die Like the Buddha, in the Lion Position, and Transfer Your Consciousness to a Pure Land
This can also be referred to as the *power of acquaintance* or the *power of habituation*. Khunu Lama Rinpoche mentions that in the teachings it says, "With familiarity, there is nothing that doesn't get easier." In life this power means mainly training in bodhichitta, but at the time of death it refers to the way we die.

When your mind is thoroughly familiar with bodhichitta and your mind training has become powerful, you can meditate on bodhichitta at the time of death while trying to transfer your consciousness. Phabongkha Rinpoche explains that this is the power of training. There is nothing more than this, nothing extra.

At the time of death it's good to follow the example of our kind compassionate Buddha when he passed away into the sorrowless state and lie in the lion position. Lie on the right side, your head toward the north—which means you're facing west, where Amitabha's pure land is. Your legs are stretched out, the right hand is under the right cheek with the ring finger blocking the right nostril, and the left arm is stretched out along your left side. The breath coming through the right nostril is the breath of attachment, so stopping it helps the mind to not be controlled by attachment, so you do not die with attachment but with virtuous thoughts instead.

Dying like this is referred to as *conduct of transference*: this "conduct," this position, helps transfer the consciousness to a pure land. Remembering the Buddha plants the seed of enlightenment and immediately protects you from being born in the lower realms. Recollecting the Buddha also makes it easy to not be controlled by delusions and easy to give rise to bodhichitta.

I discuss this more in practice 55.

Integrate Life and Death with the Five Powers

Practicing the five powers is the best way to lead our life and the best preparation for making the end of our life happy, so we must integrate our entire life with this practice. To grow crops you need a field, to build a house you need land; this practice is the foundation of all our practices—sadhanas, mantras, prostrations, and so forth. And it prevents us from creating obstacles on the path.

Practicing the five powers destroys self-cherishing and stabilizes our guru devotion, supporting us during our life and preparing us for death. When death comes, we will practice it easily because we have practiced it during our lifetime. We will have a happy death.

The five powers is the best psychology of all and the best, deepest meditation.

6
Pray to Be Reborn in Amitabha Buddha's Pure Land

We Need the Strong Desire to Be Reborn in the Blissful Realm of Amitabha

IN ORDER to achieve enlightenment quickly for sentient beings—not for yourself, for sentient beings—we need to make sure we go to a pure land after we die. Guru Rinpoche Padmasambhava mentions this. And in many of his teachings Lama Tsongkhapa says we should pray to be born especially in Amitabha's pure land, the Blissful Realm (Tibetan: Dewachen; Sanskrit: Sukhavati), because it is easy for us ordinary people, those with delusions, to be born there. I was surprised by that. In his text *Benefits of the Blissful Realm*, for example, Lama Tsongkhapa says, "When reciting prayers to be reborn in the pure lands of the buddhas, one should mainly focus on rebirth in Sukhavati." (See practice 11.)

In fact, one of the eight prayers to benefit the dead that are traditionally recited in the Geluk Tibetan monasteries is Lama Tsongkhapa's "Prayer to Be Reborn in the Blissful Realm of Amitabha Buddha" (practice 66). And it's said that if you recite daily another of the eight, the "King of Prayers" (practice 64), you will definitely be born there. Of course, even though these prayers are traditionally recited after death doesn't mean we can't recite them before death; these prayers can be recited any time.

It Is Not Easy to Be Reborn in Most Pure Lands

There are numberless pure lands where you can practice tantra and achieve enlightenment. There are Vajrayogini's and Heruka's pure lands, where you can definitely become enlightened. And there is

AMITABHA BUDDHA

"It is easy for us ordinary people, those with delusions, to be born in Amitabha Buddha's pure land."

Tushita, Maitreya Buddha's pure land. And, of course, you can pray to be born in Shambhala, which is a place related to Kalachakra.

However, to be born in many of these pure lands is difficult. For some you need to have achieved the eighth bodhisattva level of the Mahayana path. To be reborn in some of the lower pure lands you need to have cut the ego, the ignorance holding the I as truly existent—that is, you need to have actualized the happiness, the bliss, of the ultimate reality of no self. And to be born in Tushita you need to have very pure morality. So it's very difficult.

If you don't have these realizations, if you still have delusions, your prayer to go to these pure lands won't succeed. In other words, ordinary beings cannot be reborn in many of the pure lands.

Ordinary People Can Be Reborn in Amitabha's Pure Land, and We Can Achieve Enlightenment There

However, as I mentioned, ordinary beings, those who have delusions and for whom it is difficult to be born in most pure lands, can easily take rebirth in Amitabha's pure land—unless, of course, you have committed any of the five heavy negative actions.

And not only that. According to my root guru, Trijang Rinpoche, you can practice tantra and become enlightened in Amitabha's pure land. It's also said that you can get enlightened more quickly there than in other pure lands. And once you are there, whatever you wish will be achieved, and from there you can go to any other pure land. So it is much more special than other pure lands.

Some lamas, however, say that you can't get enlightened in Sukhavati. Kirti Tsenshab Rinpoche, for example, says that having been there, you first have to take rebirth back in our world, this southern continent, as a human being in order to practice tantra and achieve enlightenment. Some other lamas say that after being there, you will at least never again take rebirth in the lower realms.

Amitabha Buddha's Prayer

It is because of Amitabha Buddha's prayer that it is easy for those who have delusions to take rebirth in his pure land. Savior Amitabha himself accepted that we ordinary beings can be born there. In the *Amitabha Sutra* it says, "Whoever hears the name of Amitabha and dedicates the merits to be born there will be born there." This is Amitabha's prayer. There is no pure land easier for us ordinary beings to go to than Amitabha Buddha's pure land, so we should make effort to be born there.

Everything Exists on the Tip of the Wish
There are several causes of birth in Amitabha's pure land.

First, always pray to be born there: this is a main cause. Without praying to be born there, it's not definite that you will be. There's a saying, "Everything exists on the tip of the wish." Whatever happens depends upon your intention. Whatever prayer, whatever wish, you make from the heart will be successful.

Second, think about the beauty of Amitabha's pure land, how fantastic it is there, how much better than the ordinary world: this makes you desire to be born there. There you will hear teachings directly from Amitabha Buddha, who is surrounded by Chenrezik, Vajrapani, and innumerable buddhas and bodhisattvas. It is incredibly joyful there, and there are unlimited qualities.

Third, practice bodhichitta, so then you will be born there as a Mahayana practitioner.

Shakyamuni Buddha's holy mouth mentioned that if, upon hearing Amitabha Buddha's name, you put your palms together and generate devotion for him and his pure land for just one second, you create much, much more merit than making charity to sentient beings of a great thousand of three thousand world systems filled with jewels.

Fly Like an Eagle to Amitabha's Pure Land
Before you die you can practice Amitabha phowa, which prepares you to transfer your consciousness to the Blissful Realm at the time of death (practices 48 and 81). Padmasambhava mentions that during their training before death, the best practitioners see signs of realizations within a day; the less capable ones can see signs of success within two days, and the least capable, three days.

Milarepa's disciple Rechungpa said that if you have done the phowa retreat, as soon as your consciousness leaves the body at the time of death, "you will fly like an eagle" straight to Amitabha's pure land.

A phowa practice can also be done on your behalf. A lama can do it as soon as your breath stops (practice 62), or it can be done during the forty-nine days after your death (practice 81).

Help Others Be Born There
One of the practices you can do to help your loved one who is dying, even if they're not Buddhist, is to talk about Amitabha's pure land. Tell them how beautiful it is there, that the enjoyments there are much better than here, as Lama Tsongkhapa describes in his *Benefits of the Blissful Realm* (practice 11).

And you need to say the name, the Blissful Realm, or Sukhavati, or Dewachen, because that is what their mind holds on to. It's like a rope that they can hold on to while they're climbing a mountain, pulling them up when they're in danger of falling. It saves them. Hearing the name of Amitabha's pure land helps their consciousness let go of this world: their body, their family, their possessions. It helps them to not be attached.

Part Two

How We Go from One Life to the Next

7

What Happens at Death?

When Does Death Occur?

DEATH OCCURS when the consciousness, the mind, separates from the body. Even when the breath has stopped—this is what is called the "outer breath"—or the brain doesn't function, or the heart doesn't beat, the person is not necessarily dead yet. There is still the "inner breath," and for this to stop and the consciousness to leave the body can take anywhere from a few seconds to three days after the outer breath has ceased—or even longer for experienced meditators; see chapters 10 and 24.

Dr. Adrian Feldmann, an Australian medical doctor who's one of the most senior FPMT monks, explained how he saw a person whose heart had stopped, who was clinically dead, but whose body started to function again. And I read a story in a newspaper about a man in Kalampur, India, who had been declared dead, who'd been put into a coffin and taken to the graveyard to be buried, but who then came back to life. In fact, this had happened to him many times. I heard another story about the father of a family in Nepal who was taken to the temple by the river for burning. They washed his feet, to purify negative karma I think, ceremoniously carried the body around the funeral pyre three times, then lit the fire—and then he came back to life.

There are many stories like this. These things happen because it's hard to tell when a person has died. You can't go by just the heart or the breath or brain activity.

THE COMPONENTS OF A PERSON

In order to better understand the process of death, which I describe below in chapter 9, it's helpful to understand what makes up a person, the one who dies.

Five Aggregates
Buddha explained that a person is made up of five "aggregates": form, feeling, discrimination, the aggregate of compounding aggregates, and consciousness.

Form refers to our body. *Feeling* and *discrimination* are two of the mental factors that we experience every moment. All the remaining mental states—jealousy, patience, love, and so on—are included in *the aggregate of compounding aggregates*. *Consciousness* refers to the six consciousnesses: the five senses and mental consciousness.

Four Elements
Our body is made up of the four elements of earth, water, fire, and air, or wind.

Gross, Subtle, and Extremely Subtle Body and Consciousness
According to the explanations in highest tantra, there is a gross body, a subtle body, and an extremely subtle, or very subtle, body conjoined, respectively, with gross consciousness, subtle consciousness, and extremely subtle, or very subtle, consciousness.

The gross body is this one that we can see; the subtle one is made up of the channels, winds, and drops described below; the extremely subtle body is subtle wind.

The sense consciousnesses are gross consciousness. Subtle consciousness includes the various conceptual states of mind called the eighty superstitions, as well as the minds of white appearance, red appearance or increase, and black, or dark, appearance. Finally, there is extremely subtle consciousness, or the mind of clear light.

Channels, Winds, and Chakras
The wind energies of the subtle body—more subtle than the air we breathe—carry our mind through a system of 72,000 channels throughout the body. It is said that our consciousness, our mind, "rides" on these winds.

The main channels are the central channel and the right and left channels. They are in the center of the body, measuring between the two breasts, and a little closer to the back.

At various points along these channels there are chakras, the main ones being at the crown, the throat, the heart, the navel, and the tip of the sex organ. The two side channels do not run straight down either side of the central channel but wrap around it at the chakras, forming "knots."

Red and White Drops

At the moment of conception, our consciousness mixes with the red drop, or *bodhichitta*, from the mother and the white drop from the father. The essence of the white and red bodhichitta—known as the indestructible drop, with its red and white halves, the size of a tiny bean—abides in the very center of our heart chakra. Part of the white bodhichitta also abides at the crown chakra and part of the red at the navel chakra. Our conjoined extremely subtle wind and extremely subtle consciousness resides in the indestructible drop.

The Clear Light Mind of Death

While we are alive the knots at the chakras prevent the winds from entering into and flowing in the central channel. Otherwise these various winds and the states of mind associated with them would all dissolve into the indestructible drop at the heart chakra, at which point our extremely subtle consciousness, the mind of clear light, would manifest, and with it we could meditate on emptiness and thus free ourselves from all delusions, eventually becoming enlightened.

Throughout their lives the great meditators train their minds to do this. Lama Yeshe, for example, in his daily tantric practice was able to experience the various visions of the dissolution process that occur naturally at death; in other words, he didn't need to wait until death to experience them. Lama was able to open the chakras, causing the winds to enter into and flow in the central channel and dissolve at the heart chakra, and thus could meditate in the clear light. Therefore, at the time of death, great yogis can remain in meditation in the clear light for as long as they like, which is what happened with Lama. I discuss this in chapters 10 and 24.

Death, Intermediate State, and Rebirth

The process of death occurs in eight stages, which I explain in chapter 9, and is experienced by those who have bodies constituted from the sperm of the father and the egg of the mother: human beings and some animals.

During the first four stages we experience the gradual dissolution of twenty-two of twenty-five components: four of the five aggregates, four of the five types of wisdom—the base-time wisdoms, not the result-time ones—the four elements, five of the six sense bases, and the five inner sense objects.

The breath has stopped by the end of the fourth stage, and by then gross consciousness—the five sense consciousnesses—has ceased.

During the fifth, sixth, and seventh stages, subtle consciousness gradually dissolves, which includes the eighty superstitions: the various delusions, the dualistic, wrong conceptions.

During the final four stages, the remaining three of the twenty-five components gradually cease: the fifth aggregate, the fifth wisdom, and the sixth sense base.

By the eighth stage, all that is left is the extremely subtle wind conjoined with the extremely subtle consciousness, the mind of clear light, at the indestructible drop at the heart. Death occurs when the indestructible drop splits open and the conjoined extremely subtle wind and mind leaves the body.

However, for ordinary people, the mind can stay in the body for up to three days after the breath stops, although they are not aware. The great yogis, as I mentioned, can meditate in the clear light for as long as they like.

As soon as the mind leaves the body, we take a "life" between this life and the next called the intermediate state (Tibetan: *bardo*), and up to forty-nine days later, we will take a new rebirth.

8
The Twelve Links of Dependent Arising at the Time of Death

CYCLIC EXISTENCE operates through the twelve links of dependent arising. From (1) the *ignorance* that believes in inherent existence, we create (2) *compounded action*, or karma, the imprints of which are left on our (3) *consciousness*. Some authors of the scriptures also count the result consciousness that enters the fertilized egg. Next is (4) *name and form*, "name" referring to the four mental aggregates and "form" to the physical, the egg and sperm, when the five come together in the womb. When they begin to develop as the fetus, they are known as (5) the *six sense bases*. Then comes (6) *contact*, when the consciousness connects with external objects through the sense bases of the eyes, ears, and so forth, followed by (7) *feeling* in relation to those objects, either pleasant, unpleasant, or neutral, which gives rise to (8) *craving* and (9) *grasping*, then (10) *becoming*. Next is (11) *birth*, and finally there is (12) *old age and death*.

The Twelve Links of This Perfect Human Rebirth
Let us discuss the twelve links in relation to this human body that we have now. What caused our consciousness to join the egg and sperm in our mother's body?

In past lives, because of *ignorance* we created both nonvirtuous and virtuous *karma*, which planted seeds, left potentials, in the field of our *consciousness*. At the time of death of our life before this one, whether we were a human or an elephant or a kangaroo, *craving* arose—craving to not separate from that body. Then fear arose, because of the attachment to not wanting to leave the body: that's what causes fear at the time of death. After that, *grasping* arose, a stronger form of attachment, this time—in our case—attachment to receiving a human body.

Now, in the case of someone who is going to be reborn in the hot hells, the craving is the same—not wanting to separate from their body—but the grasping is to heat, because they feel very cold. Many times dying people say they feel cold and beg for blankets, but even if you give them two or three, it won't be enough: their grasping at heat is so strong. This could also happen because the fire element is dissolving at that point; see chapter 9. The grasping at heat activates a negative karmic seed, the second link, which causes their mind to migrate to a hell being's body right after death. The grasping is the very close condition; there were, of course, the previously created causes: the first link, ignorance, and the second, karma.

Grasping at a Human Rebirth at the Time of Death Is a Cause for Achieving One

In our case, as humans, the very close condition at the time of our past death, just before the gross consciousness ceased, was the grasping at, the wish to receive, a human body. In other words, in order to receive this perfect human rebirth that we have now, we must have had not only the karma of perfect morality and great generosity but also the strong desire—grasping, the ninth link—to have a human body.

When we understand that attachment to this life is never virtuous but attachment at the time of death to either a human life or rebirth in a pure land is virtuous, then we can understand the function of this link of grasping at the time of death.

In other words, whereas craving and grasping certainly operate in our daily life in the form of attachment, in the context of the twelve links, they are more to do with the connection of one life to the next. The karmic seed that gives rise to the new rebirth is there on our mind, the second link, but it is grasping at the time of death that activates its ripening.

Five Causes from Past Lives, Seven Results in This Life

To summarize, five of the links are causes from past lives. Three are delusions—the links of ignorance, craving, and grasping—and two are karmas—the links of *compounded action* and *becoming*.

First there was the delusion *ignorance*, the first link, then the delusions arising at the time of death, the eighth link, *craving*, and ninth, *grasping*. Then there were the two karmas—the second link, in our case a virtuous *karma* (which could have been created thousands, even millions, of lives ago), and the second karma, *becoming*, the tenth link. The previously created karmic seed made ready by craving and grasping at death: that is what is called *becoming*.

It is these five that formed these aggregates, this body and mind, this samsara.

Of the seven results that manifest in this life, the eleventh link, *birth*, started at the moment our consciousness joined the fertilized egg. *Old age*, the beginning of the twelfth, *old age and death*, started the very next moment—"old age" is not just what is known in the world: the wrinkles, the white hair, and so forth.

Now, all there is left is *death*.

No Delusions and Karma, No Rebirth

From this evolution we can understand that if we had freed ourselves of delusions and karma in the past, there is no way we could have come into existence. There'd be no reason at all to have taken this human body: to have to experience the suffering of rebirth, the suffering of sickness, the suffering of old age, and the suffering of death—not to mention all the other problems that we experience in daily life not included in these four.

These delusions and karma formed, put together, these aggregates, this body and mind, and because we didn't cease delusions and karma in our past life by following the path, this self, this person, is still caught up in samsara. Wherever our consciousness goes, this self goes with it, because consciousness is the main base for the existence of self; the gross body exists for a short time and then disintegrates.

As long as this self is bound by delusions and karma, there is no choice, we will be burdened by these aggregates. Delusions and karma have bound this self to samsara, and no matter how much we do not want this suffering, as long as we are caught up in samsara, there is no freedom.

BUDDHA VAJRASATTVA

"In order to help our loved ones not be afraid of death, we need to help them purify their negative karma. The practice of Vajrasattva and the four opponent powers is an incredibly powerful method."

9

The Stages of Death, Intermediate State, and Rebirth

EVEN THOUGH we all go through the eight stages at the time of death, what I describe here is a gradual death. As for how long the process takes, it's hard to say. In general, as I mention below, from the time that the first of the eight stages has occurred, it can be a couple of hours before the breathing stops. However, those who die violently or suddenly go through the stages very quickly. And sometimes in a violent death, the mind could leave the body immediately and go straight to the intermediate state.

As I mentioned, and as we will see below in chapters 10 and 24, the great meditators, those who have deeply familiarized themselves with these stages in meditation during their lives, can recognize the stages of death as they occur and can meditate on emptiness throughout.

But ordinary people don't recognize them. (We go through these stages every time we sleep too, but we don't recognize them then, either.) It's like when you're looking at a person, let's say, but your mind is concentrating on another object, a sound for example, or you're thinking of something else, and even though the person is in front of you, you simply don't see them.

It's the same at death. We don't recognize the visions that occur at each stage of this evolution—first this, then that, then that; now the clear light, now the intermediate state, and so on—because of the pollution of our ignorance and our uncontrolled mind. Even though we might know these stages intellectually, not having trained our minds in the meditation techniques during our lifetime and not having created enough virtuous karma or purified our minds, we can't recognize these experiences as they occur.

But it's possible. I discuss this in chapter 10.

It's good to help your loved one meditate on these stages during the months and weeks before death (practice 39). They can also become familiar with these stages as they go to sleep (practice 41). And if they have a highest tantra practice, you can guide them through the stages of meditation when you help them with their daily practices (practice 47).

Apparently at the time of death of my past life (as the Lawudo Lama)—I don't remember this—a disciple was there to receive initiation, and they were discussing the death evolution. It seems that the death process started while they were having this discussion.

As I mentioned in chapter 7, twenty-five components dissolve during these eight stages: the five aggregates, the four wisdoms, the four elements, the six sense bases, and the five inner sense objects.

GROSS CONSCIOUSNESS

1. The Vision of a Mirage

As the *aggregate of form* dissolves, your body becomes thinner and your limbs become loose and unmanageable.

As the *mirror-like wisdom* dissolves—these and the four other wisdoms are labeled according to the function of the senses—your ability to see many objects at the same time, as a mirror reflects many objects together, ceases, and you cannot see the forms of people and objects clearly.

As the *earth element* dissolves, you feel as if you are sinking; you might even reach up as if to hold on to something.

As the *eye sense base* dissolves, you can no longer open or close your eyes. If your eyes are open, they will remain like that without blinking: this is a sign that you will die within one or two hours. In fact, this is the nearest sign of death.

This is what happened with Lama Yeshe during the last couple of hours before he passed away: he was unable to close his eyes; I talk about this in chapter 24. And I've seen it in other dying people.

As the *inner form* dissolves, your body loses its strength completely, and it loses its radiance.

You will have a *vision of a mirage*, an inner vision, like water shimmering in the heat. Your vision blurs; everything seems watery and wavy, like a mirage in the distance.

2. The Vision of Smoke

As the *aggregate of feeling* dissolves, you can no longer experience the three kinds of feelings: pleasure, pain, and indifference; you're indifferent to suffering and happiness.

The *wisdom of equanimity*, which sees these three together as having the same nature, dissolves.

As the *water element* dissolves, the liquids of your body dry up. Your mouth feels very dry; this too is a sign that death could be within one or two hours.

As the *ear sense base* dissolves, you can no longer distinguish sounds.

As the *inner sound* dissolves, you can no longer even hear the buzzing in your ears.

You will have a *vision of smoke*, like a room filled with incense or smoke from burning green wood swirling about.

Your Dying Thoughts Activate the Karmic Seed that Determines Your Next Rebirth

As Phabongkha Rinpoche says in *Liberation In the Palm of Your Hand*, your dying thoughts activate the karma that will be the cause of your next rebirth, and the activators of this "throwing karma" are the eighth and ninth links, craving and grasping, discussed in the previous chapter. Rinpoche says that this takes place while the mind is still active and you can still recall virtue or be reminded of it by other people.

At this point it is so important to be able to control the arising of the disturbing thoughts by remembering the guru, the teachings—renunciation of samsara, karma, emptiness, loving kindness, great compassion, and the rest—which gives us the chance to be born in a buddha's pure land or to take a perfect human rebirth.

If our last gross thoughts are virtuous, the throwing karma will be virtuous; if the last gross thoughts are nonvirtuous, the throwing karma will be nonvirtuous. The karmic seed that ripens is whichever is heavier, more strongly habitual—which, as I mentioned, could have been planted hundreds, even millions, of lifetimes ago. If they're equal, the seed that was planted first will be the one that ripens.

If we die with anger, say, or strong attachment to our life, our loved ones, and so on, our birth will be only in the lower realms, nowhere else. Generally, attachment causes rebirth as a hungry ghost, ignorance causes rebirth as an animal, and anger as a hell being. In these lower realms, we will experience unimaginable suffering for an incredibly long time. Compared to this, the suffering in the human realm is nothing—in fact, it's like great pleasure in comparison.

At this point, five things can occur if we're dying with nonvirtuous thoughts, though not all five will necessarily happen: soiling ourselves; our arms and legs thrashing about; screaming; blood coming from the ears, nose, and mouth; and our eyes rolling up. If we have created very heavy negative karma, all five will happen, and as we are dying, we will have terrible visions of our future life. We will feel that we are moving from light into darkness.

On the other hand, dying with a virtuous state of mind causes us to have a peaceful and happy death. In fact, if we're like the best spiritual practitioners, we will be joyful at the time of death and will have a sense of passing from darkness into light.

Nevertheless, it is possible that someone who has terrible experiences before they stop breathing can be peaceful at the actual time of death, which would cause karma to be activated for them to go to a pure land. In other words, these experiences can be a good sign: the finishing of some heavy negative karma.

This happened to one old lama from Ganden Monastery, a very good lama, who was very sick. As he was passing away, his body became very hot, unbelievably hot. But then he died very peacefully and, apparently, went to a pure land.

3. The Vision of Fire Sparks

As the *aggregate of discrimination* dissolves, you can no longer recognize your friends and relatives.

As the *wisdom of discriminating awareness* or *discernment* dissolves, you cannot remember anyone's names; the people around you become blurs.

As the *fire element* dissolves, the body's heat gradually ceases; the capacity to digest food ceases.

As the *nose sense base* dissolves, breathing in becomes difficult and weaker, and breathing out becomes stronger and longer.

As the *inner smell* dissolves, you can no longer smell anything.

You will have a *vision of fire sparks*, like the sparks that come when you burn dry grass, or like starlight, or a sky filled with fireflies.

THE STAGES OF DEATH, INTERMEDIATE STATE, AND REBIRTH 51

How the Heat Leaves the Body
You can judge the type of rebirth you will take by where the heat in your body begins to dissolve. If you are dying with a positive attitude, with virtuous thoughts, which causes a happy rebirth, your feet will get cold first, and the heat will eventually only be at the heart.

If you are dying with nonvirtuous thoughts, such as fear or anger or attachment, which causes a suffering rebirth, the head will get cold first, and again, the heat will eventually only be at the heart.

4. The Vision of a Flame
As the aggregate of *compounding aggregates* dissolves, you can no longer move your body, and your awareness of worldly activities and worldly success and their necessity cease.

As your *all-accomplishing*, or *completion*, *wisdom* dissolves, even if you could hear a name, you would not remember its meaning. In our daily life we normally remember the meaning of something and then act on it; now you can't think of the meaning of anything.

As your *wind element* dissolves, your breathing stops.

As your *tongue sense base* dissolves, your tongue becomes short and thick and turns blue at the root: this, too, is a sign of imminent death. If you try to talk—to discuss leaving your things to your family, for example—it will be hard to understand you.

As your *body sense base* dissolves, you can no longer experience soft or rough sensations.

As your *inner taste* dissolves, you can no longer taste anything.

As your *inner touch* dissolves, you can no longer experience tangible objects.

You will see a *vision of a flame*. Actually, according to Song Rinpoche, it is more like the light around the flame, a dim red-blue light.

The Outer Breath and the Five Senses Have Now Stopped
The outer breath and the gross consciousness have now ceased. As I mentioned in chapter 7, so far, twenty-two of the twenty-five components have ceased: four of the five aggregates, four of the five types of wisdom, the four elements, five of the six sense bases, and the five inner sense objects.

During the fifth, sixth, and seventh stages, subtle consciousness—

various mental states known as the eighty superstitions—gradually dissolves. And during the final four of the eight stages, the remaining three of the twenty-five components gradually dissolve—the aggregate of consciousness, the wisdom of the sphere of phenomena, and the mental sense base.

SUBTLE CONSCIOUSNESS

5. The White Vision
The first thirty-three of the eighty superstitions cease.

The winds in the right and left channels move up and open the head chakra, loosening the knots there, and enter the central channel.

This causes the *white bodhichitta* at the crown to melt and flow down the central channel to the heart, touching the central channel as it goes.

Now you experience the *white vision*, the *mind of white appearance*, like very bright moonlight in autumn, or like the almost-white sky caused by the light of the rising moon when everything is covered with snow. Whereas the previous inner visions had some movement to them, this and the following ones are perfectly still.

6. The Red Vision
The next forty of the eighty superstitions dissolve.

The winds in the right and left channels move down and open the sex and navel chakras, loosening the knots there, and enter the central channel.

This causes the *red bodhichitta* at the navel to shoot up the central channel to the heart chakra, touching the central channel as it goes. Now you experience the *red vision*, the *mind of red increase*. It's like the clear red sky just before the dawn breaks, or like a copper-red reflection in the sky, and it's perfectly still.

7. The Dark Vision
The final seven of the eighty superstitions dissolve.

The red and white bodhichitta meet at the heart chakra, in the indestructible drop in the central channel, with its red and white halves.

Now you experience the *dark vision*, the *mind of dark appearance*. It's as if you've fallen into darkness, or it's like a dark and empty sky or being in a dark room. At the beginning of this vision, you have some awareness and recognize an appearance of darkness, but then you become unconscious.

EXTREMELY SUBTLE CONSCIOUSNESS

8. *The Clear-Light Vision*
Now the *clear-light vision* appears. This is the subtlest level of mind, occurring only after all the grosser consciousnesses have ceased. It's like an autumn dawn, when the sky is so clear, no clouds, no dust. It is not bright like at noon, not red, and not dark. Nothing else appears.

The yogis continue to meditate at this point and can stay as long as they like, as I mentioned in chapter 7 and will discuss further in chapters 10 and 24. And again, for ordinary people, who have no awareness of what is happening, it could be three days before the mind leaves the body.

How the Mind Leaves the Body at the Time of Death
Death occurs when the indestructible drop splits open and the extremely subtle mind and wind leave your heart chakra in the central channel and, depending on which rebirth you will take, exit the gross body at one point or another.

If you will be reborn in a pure land of a buddha (or the formless realm), your mind leaves from the crown; if you will be reborn as a human being, your mind leaves from the eyes; as a hell being, from the anus; as an animal, from the sex organ; as a hungry ghost, from the mouth.

The consciousness can also leave from the navel, ears, or nose. It can also leave from midway between the eyebrows—perhaps this would be the case for someone who will be reborn in the form realm.

Signs of Death
When the mind leaves the body of a man, the white bodhichitta continues down the central channel and leaves through the sex organ and the red continues up and leaves through the nostrils; in a woman the white bodhichitta goes up and leaves through the nostrils and the red bodhichitta goes down and leaves through the organ. This is a sign

that the mind has left the body, the actual death. There are other signs, which I discuss in chapter 25.

The Intermediate State

The moment the indestructible drop splits open, your very subtle consciousness leaves from the heart chakra and becomes the intermediate-state being's mind, even before it leaves the gross body. The extremely subtle wind that is the vehicle of the extremely subtle consciousness becomes the condition for the intermediate-state being's mind, and the extremely subtle consciousness becomes the condition for the intermediate-state being's body.

You can see the world you just left, your relatives, and your dead body, but the karma is finished, so you do not recognize any of it and have no desire to go back.

You then go through the eight stages in reverse order: the dark vision, the red vision, the white vision, the eighty superstitions, and so on, then take the body of the intermediate-state being. This body, which is subtle and has no resistance to matter, is similar in appearance to the body of the next life.

The longest time spent in the intermediate state is forty-nine days, but if rebirth hasn't happened after seven days, you will experience what is called a small death, again taking a body in the intermediate state for a further seven days until another small death occurs or a new rebirth is found.

If your mind is not clouded by delusions, the intermediate state is a wonderful experience. It is even possible to attain enlightenment in the intermediate state, like Lama Tsongkhapa did.

For a mind clouded by negativity, the intermediate state is terrible. There is much fear as you experience karmically created visions, such as feeling pressed down by the earth, stuck in big cracks, tossed by a sea wave, or consumed in a whirlpool or in a great fire. You suffer because of not recognizing these as visions, as the projections of your deluded mind. If you could recognize this, the fear would be less. You believe them to be true, so the suffering is severe.

THE STAGES OF DEATH, INTERMEDIATE STATE, AND REBIRTH   55

Even If You're Destined for the Lower Realms, Things Can Change
However, even if you have created much negative karma and are destined for the lower realms, special practices that can be performed by lamas can influence you in the intermediate state and cause you to take a favorable rebirth, such as transference of consciousness or *phowa* (practice 62) and a practice known simply as *jangwa*, or "purification" (practice 78). Of course, success very much depends on your connection with the lama doing the practice, on their skill, and on the weight or intensity of your obscurations.

Rebirth as a Human
As I mentioned, the experience of being reborn is similar to the experience of waking up—but whether we wake up to a pleasant day or a violent storm is another matter! If we are reborn in the lower realms, the awakening will be a terrible one.

If from the intermediate state you will take rebirth as a human, you will see your future parents in sexual union. If you are to be born as a male you will be attracted to the mother and will have aversion for the father, and if as a female you will be attracted to the father and have aversion for the mother. Because of the habit, the karmic imprint, of attachment to sexual union, the intermediate-state being will want to embrace, have sexual intercourse with, the one it's attracted to. But as it approaches, it doesn't see the body of the parent, only the sexual organs, which causes anger to arise. This anger becomes the condition for the intermediate-state being to die and its mind to enter the mother's body.

It is easy to see how ordinary birth is caused by delusions and karma.

10
Death Is What the Yogis Have Been Waiting For

It's Possible to Get Enlightened at the Time of Death

GENERALLY it is not permitted to openly give details of the methods that the great yogis use, however I feel it would be useful to talk briefly about them here.

Death is the moment they have been waiting for. At the point in the death process when all the grosser consciousnesses have ceased and only the extremely subtle consciousness is left, as discussed in last chapter, the yogis—those who have observed karma well, kept their precepts purely, spent their lives training their minds in the clear light meditation and have been able to recognize the base-time clear light, the imagined, visualized one—are now able to recognize the clear light of death. They can remain in meditation in the clear light conjoined with emptiness for as long as they wish—one hour, three days, many months; some meditators stay in the clear light meditation in their hermitage for years. His Holiness the Dalai Lama's root guru Ling Rinpoche, for example, stayed in meditation for thirteen days. Lama Yeshe, too, remained in meditation after passing away. (See chapter 24.)

There are many examples like this. Apparently one of the previous Ganden Throneholders spent some twenty-one days in meditation. And I remember at Buxa, when we escaped from Tibet, there was a Sera Monastery monk in the same house that I lived in, a very simple monk, who spent many days in meditation after passing away. It seems that the great eighth-century bodhisattva Shantideva spent something like thirty years in meditation after he passed away. At Kopan Monastery I found among Lama's things a note that referred to a text in which this is written. I don't remember the details now.

By concentrating in this subtlest state without distraction, some practitioners achieve enlightenment at this time. They actually realize the three bodies, or *kayas*, of a buddha: they transform ordinary death into the wisdom body, *dharmakaya*, ordinary intermediate state into the enjoyment body, *sambhogakaya*, and ordinary rebirth into the emanation body, *nirmanakaya*. Some practitioners, like Lama Tsongkhapa, achieve enlightenment in the intermediate state.

Many Tibetan lamas have passed away in meditation since Tibetans first came to India as exiles in 1959. For those whose lives ended in Indian hospitals, it was difficult to receive permission to leave the body alone for a while. Ordinary Indians never believed that such a thing as meditating while passing away was possible because they had never seen it happen. Their usual concept was that the moment a person died, the body should be taken out and burned before it began to smell.

Thinking that a person was dead as soon as the breath stops, the doctors were amazed that these lamas could stay in meditation for long, long periods without the body decaying. Far from there being a bad smell, the room had a fantastic sweet smell due to the power of their realizations.

You Too Can Transform Death, Intermediate State, and Rebirth

The practices these yogis do are available to those who have taken a highest tantra initiation. They are the quickest methods for achieving enlightenment in one brief lifetime of this degenerate time. By doing these practices you can collect in just a few years the merit that would otherwise take you three countless great eons to collect on the Mahayana Perfection Vehicle path.

These practices have a very special arrangement, and doing the sadhana every day—the complete sadhana, not just simply generating yourself as the deity and reciting the mantra, without the mandala; not like that—is a very important preparation for death. You will understand this when you have received the commentaries on the generation stage and the completion stage practices.

Whether you do the long version of the sadhana of the deity you are committed to do or the middle-length version, they both contain the essence of the generation stage practice: transforming the three experiences of death, intermediate state, and rebirth into the three bodies. Even the short Yamantaka sadhana, for example, has these three important points.

By meditating in this way, you prepare your mental continuum by purifying ordinary death, ordinary intermediate state, and ordinary rebirth, enabling you to actualize the path-time dharmakaya, the path-time sambhogakaya, and the path-time nirmanakaya, thus planting the seeds to achieve the result-time three bodies.

When you just recite the words, there is of course a positive imprint left on your mind, but you are not strongly preparing your mind as you would if you were to actually meditate.

Serkong Tsenshab Rinpoche used to emphasize very much that if you are busy and can't do much meditation in the deity sadhanas, when it comes to your daily commitments, you should do more elaborate meditations for your main deity; you can do your other sadhanas quickly.

However, in all your sadhanas you must do the three kayas meditation. Even if it's not elaborate, even if you don't follow the extensive procedures, you should at least meditate on the last point, the four qualities of the foundation: having the divine pride, thinking, "This is the result-time dharmakaya; this is me," and so on.

And then on the day you die, because you have trained your mind by doing your sadhanas every day, you are able to recognize what's happening: the twenty-five stages of dissolution, without missing any, just as you had meditated. Because your mind is well trained, you are able to recognize the clear light, and during the intermediate state, and at the time of birth as well, you will be able to meditate on, visualize, the deity.

Practicing the highest tantra path like this—using death as a quick path to enlightenment—is incredible. It is the quickest way to purify the defilements, the dualistic view.

In other words, having prepared during the generation stage, on the basis of that realization you then actualize the path-time dharmakaya, sambhogakaya, and nirmanakaya on the completion stage, actually ceasing the intellectually acquired defilements and the simultaneously born defilements. Eventually you cut even the subtle defilements, the dualistic view, and in that moment achieve the result-time three bodies, enlightenment.

This is how you can enjoy death by using the tantric path, the quickest way to achieve enlightenment.

With Practice, We Can at Least Face Death with a Happy Mind

Right now, our mind is full of distractions. To try to stay on an object in meditation in ideal circumstances for even a few minutes is extremely difficult; while we are going through the process of dying, it will be even more so. This is why it is so important to train as well and as often as possible, practicing the sadhanas, as well as the purification practices—and of course destroying self-cherishing and developing bodhichitta. The weaker our self-cherishing is at death, the easier it will be to go through the death process with a focused mind.

As we get more control, as we familiarize our minds with these meditations, it's definite that we will be able to control our mind at the time of death. Even though we might not be able to realize this practice—actually get enlightened—we will at least face death with a happy mind.

Part Three

Practices to Do in the Months and Weeks before Death

Lotus Pinnacle of Amoghapasha
OM PADMO USHNISHA VIMALE HUM PHAT

Just by seeing purifies 100,000 eons of negative karma
OM HANU PHASHA BHARA HE YE SVAHA

Just by seeing you become enlightened
AH AAH SHA SA MA HA

The great increasing jewel fathomless celestial mansion extremely well-abiding secret holy mantra (root, heart, and near heart mantra)
OM BIBULA GARBHE / MANI PRABHE / TATHAGATA NI RADESHA NE / MANI MANI / SU PRAPHE / BIMALE / SAGARA GAMBHIRE / HUM HUM / JVALA JVALA / BUDDHA VILOKITE / GUHYA ADHIKRISHTHITE / GARBHE SVAHA / OM MANI VAJRE HUM / OM MANI DHIRI HUM PHAT

Mitrugpa Mantra
NAMORATNA TRAYAYA OM KAMKANI KAMKANI ROCHANI ROCHANI TROTANI TROTANI TRASANI TRASANI PRATIHANA PRATIHANA
SARVA KARMA PARAM PARA NI ME SARVA SATTVA NANCHA SVAHA

Buddha's Name Mantra
By hearing this mantra one will never be reborn in the lower realms and one will be liberated and will be able to enlighten all sentient beings from the ocean of samsara
CHOM DÄN DÄ DE ZHIN SHEG PA DRA CHOM PA YANG DAG PAR DZOG PAI SANG GYÄ RIN CHHEN TSUG TOR CHÄN LA CHHAG TSHÄL LO

Medicine Buddha Mantra
TA YA TA / OM BEKANDZAY MAHA BEKANDZAY [BEKANDZAY] / RADZA SAMUGATAY SOHA

Namgyalma Mantra
OM BHRUM SVAHA OM AMRITA AYUR DA DÄI SVAHA

Chenrezig Mantra
OM MANI PADME HUM

Amitabha Mantra
OM AMITABHA HRIH

My most dear kindest brother and sister,

Please look at these mantras quite often; especially, look at these mantras when you are leaving from this old body. Dear one, please don't cling to anything and let yourself become completely free. In this most important moment of life, you don't need to be afraid at all of being born in the lower realms and so forth. I give all my merits of the past, present, and future to you, to have a happy journey and a happy, wonderful, sunshining future. I give my big love to you. All the buddhas and bodhisattvas love you, and you are in their care. May anyone who sees these mantras be immediately reborn in the pure land where one can become enlightened or receive a perfect human body by quickly actualizing the causal vehicle, the three principals of the path, and the result vehicle, the secret mantra Vajrayana, based on correctly devoting and only pleasing one's own holy guru.
You can also pray in this way: "May I take rebirth in whatever place is most beneficial for sentient beings, no matter where it is."
To think this thought again and again is extremely good.
The other choice is to think; "May I be born in Amitabha's blissful field to quickly benefit all sentient beings."

Thank you.
With much love and prayers,
Lama Zopa

A CARD DESIGNED BY LAMA ZOPA RINPOCHE

*"You can make something like I made for a dying person.
It should be put where they can see it."*

11
Helping Others at the Time of Death Is a Big Responsibility

As we've discussed, a good rebirth—a perfect human rebirth or birth in a buddha's pure land such as Amitabha's Blissful Realm, where there's no suffering and where we can achieve enlightenment quickly—depends upon dying peacefully, with virtuous thoughts. If we die with anger or strong attachment or fear, our birth will be only in the lower realms.

Therefore the people surrounding the person who is dying—friends, family, professional caregivers—have a big responsibility. I will put it this way: Whatever arises in your loved one's mind, whether their thoughts are virtuous or nonvirtuous, very much depends upon you and other helpers, how you behave toward them. It is a great responsibility. If you are not careful, if you do not have this education—that the way you behave affects the mind of the person and therefore their future life—you will only harm them, not help them.

Chöden Rinpoche says that even if you cannot help the person become virtuous, at least help them become neutral—neither nonvirtuous nor virtuous. But best, of course, is to help them become virtuous.

Helpers Should Be Close to the Dying Person
Rinpoche says that the people who help, who give advice and support, and especially the one who speaks the name of the person's guru in their ear when their breath stops (see practice 60), shouldn't be someone they dislike; in fact, there should be pure *samaya* between them, a pure spiritual relationship.

Also, in order to ensure that attachment doesn't arise in your loved one's mind—especially when the time of death is close—Rinpoche advises that it's best not to allow anyone for whom they have strong attachment to be in their presence; ideally, you shouldn't even mention their name. Of course, if that person can help your loved one, help them solve their problems or alleviate their fears, then that's okay. But if their presence simply increases their attachment, their fears of separation, then it's very harmful, making it difficult for your loved one to let go.

An Aspiration for Helpers

> May whoever
> sees me,
> touches me,
> remembers me,
> thinks about me,
> talks about me,
> praises me,
> even criticizes me—
> may they immediately be free from all spirit harms
> and negative karma,
> and may they complete the path
> and achieve full enlightenment as soon as possible.

By thinking this way you become wish-fulfilling for your loved ones—for all sentient beings. As soon as they see you, hear your voice, touch you, or even remember you, they will immediately be free of the fear of death, and their mind will be filled with great joy. Then they will be able to go to a pure land, where they can get enlightened.

Use Your Wisdom

And remember, your ability to help your loved one depends on what you have practiced throughout your life. The more you understand what you are supposed to do for your own death, the more you will know how to help your loved one. The less you know, the less wisdom you will have. When you know how to die with a peaceful mind, then you can confidently help your loved one. You will be able to create the right conditions so that it's easy for their minds to be transformed into virtue.

You need to be skillful in advising your loved one according to their state of mind, their background, their life—whether they are a nonbeliever or have a religion, and if they have a religion what their level of understanding is.

Most of us are not clairvoyant, so we won't know exactly what fits the mind of the person or when the right time to explain it to them is, or even whether they have the karma to listen to the advice or to understand it. Check, analyze how to present the advice—the right time, the right mood—and then educate them however you can, with as much compassion as possible and as much wisdom, with skillful means.

Merely Hearing Some of the Practices Can Help
But remember, as I mentioned and as Chöden Rinpoche has advised, even if the dying person doesn't have faith in Buddha's teachings, it's still good for them to hear the practices. Receiving the benefits of reciting or hearing them doesn't require devotion.

12
Create a Conducive Environment for a Peaceful Death

Make the Place Beautiful

YOU SHOULD make the room as beautiful as possible: a calm, peaceful, serene, holy environment is so important. There should be beautiful views, beautiful art, flowers—flowers give a very special spiritual feeling. The point is to help put positive imprints on your loved one's mind. If their mind is elevated, they will not be afraid of dying.

Display Holy Objects Such as Statues, Images, Stupas, Texts, and Prayer Wheels

Display images of the buddhas and your loved one's gurus. If they're not Buddhist, you could have images from their own religion, such as Mary or Jesus or Shiva. Also display stupas, prayers wheels, texts, and so on, ready to use for blessings. Put things around nicely.

The Position of the Bed

If possible, your loved one should be lying with their head pointing toward the north, which means they are facing the west, which is where Amitabha Buddha's pure land is.

This prepares them for the practice of going to sleep in the lion posture (practice 40), which in turn prepares them for dying in this position (practice 55), which is how Buddha himself passed away. Lying like this reminds them of the Buddha, that they're following in his footsteps.

No Tobacco

Do not allow anyone to smoke anywhere near the dying person. Besides causing physical problems, without question smoking is harmful spiritually. It pollutes the subtle nervous system, the channels, and so on.

When someone asked the great lama Panchen Lama Chökyi Gyaltsen—who composed the incredible teaching *Guru Puja* as well as many other teachings, including the root text of Geluk *mahamudra*—to perform phowa at the time of death, the first thing he would ask is whether the person smoked, and if they did, he wouldn't do the practice. It seems that smoking makes it difficult to transfer the consciousness to a pure land.

No Pets or Animal Skins

There should be no cats and dogs in the room with your loved one, especially cats—it's said that their hair is polluted.

In *Tibetan Ceremonies of the Dead* the author, Thupten Sangay, says that if the person who is dying is lying on an animal skin, you should remove it before they die; the same if they're wearing an animal skin or are covered by one. It says that being around animal skins at the time of death makes transference of consciousness to a pure land more difficult, even if it's a lama who is performing phowa. I haven't heard this said in other teachings, but it says it here. Also, it is said that the skins make the body smelly.

A Calm and Peaceful Environment

You must not create a situation that disturbs your loved one's mind, makes them angry or upset. Don't have anyone emotional in the room, especially when death is close. It is best that people don't cry within hearing distance of your loved one, as this creates clinging in their mind. And you should not hold on to them. Crying and pleading with them not to die won't keep them alive and will only agitate them and make their death more difficult.

In other words, create an environment that is calm and peaceful—this cannot be stressed enough.

13

The Practices: What to See and Touch

> **WHAT YOU NEED**
>
> - Pictures and statues of gurus and buddhas
> - Written mantras to see
> - A text to touch
> - A stupa to touch
> - A prayer wheel to touch
> - A blessed cord to wear

You may not be able to take all the advice here if your loved one is not at home or in a private room in a hospital or hospice. Just understand the essential points and do the best you can.

SEE HOLY IMAGES

Show Statues or Pictures of Gurus, Buddhas [1]

Make sure the various images of your loved one's guru, the buddhas, and so on are close to their bed where they can see them easily—the picture of the guru should show them with a very happy, joyful, blissful expression. Merely looking at this photo helps your loved one purify negative karma and sows the seeds of enlightenment.

You can make something like I made for a dying person. I framed various pictures: the person's root guru, Amitabha, the Compassion Buddha, Medicine Buddha, Mitrukpa, and so on, as well as the mantras. It should be put where your loved one can see it.

It's also good to write a message, some Dharma advice, and have that put in the frame as well. Seeing that, too, purifies their mind and helps them collect skies of merit.

Show the Mitrukpa Mantra [2]

I have written out the mantra of Mitrukpa (Sanskrit: Akshobhya); it can be put next to the dying person's pillow or where they can see it easily. It doesn't matter whether they're Buddhist or non-Buddhist: as I mentioned, receiving benefit doesn't depend upon faith.

According to *Giving Breath to the Wretched* by Kusali Dharmavajra, simply seeing this mantra, one of the ten powerful mantras and the five great mantras (see practices 21–31), purifies even the heaviest of the very heavy negative karmas—avoiding the holy Dharma, which is heavier than destroying all the monasteries, all the statues, stupas, scriptures, every single holy object that exists in this world. Also purified is the negative karma of having taken things from the Sangha without permission or having deprived them of receiving things. If it can purify karmas like that, then no question it can for all other negative karmas.

Show the Name Mantra of the Buddha Who Protects from the Lower Realms [3]

Have your loved one look at this mantra quite often: have it close by. It's the name mantra of Buddha Rinchen Tsuktorchen (Sanskrit: Ratna Shikhin), the buddha who protects from the lower realms. (See also practice 19.)

Show the Mantra Called "Just by Seeing" [4]

This mantra is so powerful that just seeing it purifies a hundred thousand eons of negative karma and causes you to become enlightened.

TOUCH WITH HOLY OBJECTS

Bless the Body with a Text [5]

Chöden Rinpoche advises that it is good to put a text near the head of the dying person—you could put it on their pillow—first touching the crown with it. Use either of the below texts, or any text you like.

By Wearing, Liberates

There is a very powerful text, the benefits of which are unbelievable, called *By Wearing, Liberates* (*Takdröl*, or *Shitro* "peaceful and wrathful").

There are several texts with this title. The one I use is related to peaceful and wrathful concentration and is used by Trulshik Rinpoche.

I have made a very small version of it—there is good technology these days—so it's easy to carry with me wherever I go and to put on the heads of people or animals when they die. Again, whether your loved one is a believer or nonbeliever, the benefits are the same. There is a copy of it in the Liberation Box, a collection of things to facilitate a good rebirth.

I'd heard about this text, but I wasn't sure where it came from, its lineage. Years ago, in Bodhgaya, Trulshik Rinpoche told me a story that gave me faith that it must be authentic. In the Solo Khumbu region of Nepal, there is a very precious, holy place of Padmasambhava called Maratika. Rinpoche would always go to this incredible place to do long-life retreat for His Holiness the Dalai Lama. Apparently there's a long-life vase there as well as a special stone. It is said that whatever you pray for in front of the long-life vase will be achieved, all your wishes will be fulfilled. And I've heard that people who can't have a child pray to the stone for a child, and then they have a child—and the next year they come back and give thanks. Apparently this is very common.

Anyway, Rinpoche told me that Ngawang Chöphel, the main disciple of the Lawudo Lama—the lamas say that it was my past life, but as I said earlier, I don't remember—built a monastery in Maratika in 1980. He's known as the Maratika Lama. He wrote the life story of the Lawudo Lama after his guru passed away in 1946.

Trulshik Rinpoche told me that whenever the monks at Maratika Monastery would do pujas in the evening, blowing the *gyaling* and other instruments, all the clouds would disappear from the sky. This would happen so often that the villagers would attack the monastery—they tried to burn it down—since they needed the clouds for rain! So Ngawang Chöphel decided to take the villagers to court. I think he must have had to decide between allowing the villagers to attack the monastery and holding a court case, and he chose the court case because to destroy a monastery creates negative karma. Trulshik Rinpoche said to me, "He was a very special person, very religious, but he also held court cases."

When Ngawang Chöphel passed away in 1997, he stayed in a meditation state for seven days. Rinpoche went there with this text and put it on his head. When I heard that, then I had faith in it. I thought, "Oh, Rinpoche uses this to help people, to save them from the lower realms. It must be an authentic method."

The Lamrim Chenmo

Chöden Rinpoche advises using Lama Tsongkhapa's *Great Treatise on the Stages of the Path*, the *Lamrim Chenmo*. Rinpoche explains that this text is the essence of Manjushri's wisdom, that Manjushri's knowledge manifests in the form of letters. The 84,000 teachings of Buddha are included in it: the Lesser Vehicle teachings, the Mahayana Perfection Vehicle teachings, the Mahayana Tantra Vehicle teachings—all are embodied in this text.

It's usually mentioned during commentaries on Lama Tsongkhapa's texts that when he wrote this text he consulted Manjushri and received clarifications on the subtler meaning of all the important points directly from him. Therefore, the teachings in this text are the same as Manjushri's teachings. It's also said that Lama Tsongkhapa is the embodiment of Manjushri.

Chöden Rinpoche says that in your daily life, it's good to have the text on your altar as an object of prostration and to make offerings to it. And then when death comes, it will be nearby. Rinpoche says that if you have this text near your loved one when they are dying, there's no need to perform phowa.

Or you could use any Dharma text you like.

Bless the Body with a Stupa [6]

You can use a stupa to bless a dying person, in particular a stupa that contains the four dharmakaya relic mantras: Ornament of Enlightenment, Secret Relic, Beam of Completely Pure Stainless Light, and Stainless Pinnacle. These mantras—which are usually written in gold on the "life tree," the wooden central pole inside the stupa—are what make the stupa powerful.

From time to time place the stupa on your loved one's chest or let them hold it. Every time the stupa touches them, their negative karma is purified.

This is also good to do with babies or with people who don't understand. To a non-Buddhist you can say that the stupa is for peace or healing or purification.

You can lead your loved one in a meditation involving visualizing light rays coming from the stupa, blessing them (practice 37).

There is a stupa in the Liberation Box.

Bless the Body with or Turn a Prayer Wheel [7]
Having a prayer wheel near your loved one is another powerful way of ensuring a good death and a better rebirth. Touching a prayer wheel purifies negative karma and obscurations, so encourage them to turn it or touch them with it.

In fact, if there is a prayer wheel in the room, you don't need to do phowa: at the time of death, the person's simply thinking of a prayer wheel helps shoot their consciousness through the central channel and out the crown to reincarnate in the pure land of Amitabha.

Bless the Body with a Blessed Cord [8]
A blessed cord (usually a piece of thin red dressmaker's cord) has been blessed with many thousands of mantras such as the Compassion Buddha, or Namgyalma (Sanskrit: Ushnishavijaya), or one of the other five great mantras (practices 21, 25, and 31). Tie it around the neck of your loved one or around their wrist or upper arm.

Don't see these cords as merely a custom, or as something to be put on the altar or put away somewhere in a container. They should be worn: the idea is for them to touch the body. The mantras used for the blessing have so many benefits and can purify so much negative karma.

You can carry blessed cords with you, and when a person or animal dies, you can put one on the body. Even if they died a long time ago, and no matter where their consciousness is now, this can still help purify their negative karma, the blessings will still have an effect.

There is a blessed cord in the Liberation Box.

14

The Practices: What to Think About

> **What You Need**
> - Pictures or statues of gurus, buddhas

Perhaps you can't take all the advice here if your loved one is not at home or in a private room in a hospital or hospice. But understand the essential points and do the best you can.

Make Sure Your Loved One Has Given Away Their Possessions [9]
The author of *Tibetan Ceremonies of the Dead* says that it's important, before the person who is dying is unable to speak, to make sure that they have made a will or to remind them to make one. (See also the first of the five powers in chapter 5.)

You don't need to wait until just before they die to do this, and often people in the West do this earlier anyway. The point here is to understand how it helps your loved one psychologically to have decided whom they want to dedicate their possessions to. Because then, at the time of death, there is nothing to cling to, and they won't die with attachment—they've already dedicated their possessions to the Guru, Dharma, or Sangha or to sentient beings, or for projects that will benefit sentient beings.

Writing a will also prevents the family from fighting over what's left: the house, the possessions, the money. Sometimes there is so much fighting, even court cases, and people holding grudges, often for years.

In Sydney, one student of the FPMT center there, Vajrayana Institute, left his house to the center. I think he had no family or children, so he offered everything to the center. I suggested some pujas that the center should do for him.

If, when you leave something like this to a Dharma center, you don't specify what should be done with it, the organization has to decide what is the most beneficial way to use the gift.

There is a Tibetan saying—it's in *Tibetan Ceremonies of the Dead*:

> Your last speech is the will,
> your last food is the relics,
> and your last drink is the blessed pills.

In the tantric teachings it is revealed that just before the person stops breathing, you can give them blessed pills or relics, which you can obtain from lamas; I discuss this in practices 56 and 57. This is a common tradition among Tibetans.

Talk about Your Loved One's Guru, or Buddha, or God [10]

The role of the guru in our life is vital, and certainly at the time of death. If your loved one has received teachings from a lama in their lifetime and if they feel strong devotion, it is important to remind them of their guru now. This helps them to let go of attachment, to remember the teachings, especially bodhichitta; and then at the time of death it's easy to remain virtuous. Also, talking to them about their guru can reconnect them with their personal deity (see practice 47).

It is advised in the lamrim that when we are in a critical situation, experiencing heavy obstacles, including at the time of death, making requests to the guru is the best thing to do. When all other methods have failed, remembering the lama is the best solution.

Even if your loved one doesn't have a strong practice, if their connection with their guru is strong, the guru can help them go to a pure land: merely hearing the name of their guru is considered an effective method of transference of consciousness. Chöden Rinpoche refers to a quotation from the *Kalachakra Tantra*: "Even for one second to recall the name of your guru is the best phowa."

If they don't have a guru but have faith in the Buddha, talk about the qualities of any of the enlightened beings: Shakyamuni Buddha, the Compassion Buddha, Amitabha, or whomever they feel close to.

If your loved one has another religion, not Buddhism, an important way to help them generate virtuous thoughts is to talk about God. Describe God as being totally pure, having perfect wisdom or omniscience, loving kindness and compassion for them and all living beings, and the power to help liberate them and others from suffering and lead them to temporary and ultimate happiness. This becomes an excellent refuge for the dying person.

You are describing the meaning of a buddha, actually—infinite wisdom, compassion, and power—but you're not using the Sanskrit word. You could mention just one quality and then let the person think about that, or you could mention all three qualities.

Explain that the nature of their own mind, their heart, is completely pure; that God has compassion for everyone, including them. Help them think that their loving heart is oneness with God, that the kingdom of God is within. This frees them from guilt and anger, allowing them to die with faith and a peaceful mind.

Talk about Amitabha's Pure Land, or Heaven [11]

Another approach is to talk about the pure lands of the buddhas, such as Amitabha's pure land. You can read the *Benefits of the Blissful Realm* by Lama Tsongkhapa to them. As I said in chapter 6, for ordinary people, those who have delusions and for whom it is difficult to take rebirth in most pure lands, it is easy to be born in Amitabha's pure land.

Saying the name of the pure land is important. It's like a rope that the person can hold on to while they're climbing a mountain that pulls them up when they're in danger of falling: it saves them. It's a method to help their consciousness let go of this world: their body, their family, their possessions; to not be attached.

Tell your loved one how beautiful it is there—as described in Lama Tsongkhapa's words. You can tell them how whatever they're attached to is better there, that there are better enjoyments there. This means you need to know what they normally enjoy—like the monk in the story I told above who was told that the butter tea was better in Tushita (see page 24). Tell them that there are many wonderful friends in Amitabha's pure land or someone in particular who loves them. Wishing to be there causes them to be reborn there; it directs their consciousness to it. Amitabha Buddha becomes their main refuge.

You could also read Lama Tsongkhapa's prayer to be reborn in Amitabha's pure land (practice 66).

For somebody who doesn't understand "pure land," saying "Heaven" makes it easier; that's a very common word. "Heaven" has the meaning of eternal; something very beautiful, with great enjoyments. Hearing about it makes it easier for the person's consciousness to leave, for them to die easily, without mental suffering. Knowing that there's some place that's better makes it very easy for them to let go of attachment for this world. This is very skillful psychology.

Talk about Your Loved One's Good Qualities [12]

It is important to emphasize all the good, positive things the person has done during their life and not dwell on what they consider to be failures or weaknesses. Tell them: "You have lived a good life, sincere, and you have done many good things."

Use whatever compassion your loved one has expressed during their life to show how important compassion is, and encourage them to feel compassion and loving kindness even as they are dying.

Talk about Compassion, Bodhichitta [13]

His Holiness the Dalai Lama says that the best way to die is to die with the thought of benefiting others—a "self-supporting death," His Holiness calls it.

It is your responsibility to help your loved one develop compassion. Thinking of the happiness of others as they die rather than their own terrible circumstances is amazing! Compassion is the ultimate attitude to bring to the next life. If the person could remember this, they will without one single doubt be saved from the lower realms.

You can tell them that with this attitude of bodhichitta, they use their death to achieve enlightenment for others. Their bodhichitta brings all the happiness—this life's happiness, future lives' happiness, liberation from samsara, enlightenment—to numberless sentient beings. How? Because their bodhichitta causes them to achieve enlightenment, and when they achieve enlightenment, they can work perfectly for all sentient beings.

On the basis of realizing that sentient beings have so much suffering, and on the basis of realizing that sentient beings are so precious, so kind, that they are the ones from whom the dying person has received all their own past, present, and future happiness—on the basis of this, great loving kindness and great compassion arise: the wish that other sentient beings have happiness and that they, the dying person, will give it to them, and the wish that others be free of suffering and that they, the dying person, will free them. On the basis of this understanding, your loved one will be able to enjoy the experience of death for others, for all sentient beings. Psychologically that is how it works.

Even if your loved one doesn't have a religion, you can explain that so many others are dying right now, that everyone has to go through this experience. Help them think in a broad way instead of thinking only of themselves.

You could also lead your loved one in the *tonglen* meditation (practice 38).

THE SEVEN MEDICINE BUDDHAS

"The main practice to do before, during, and after death is Medicine Buddha."

15

The Practices: What to Hear

> **WHAT YOU NEED**
> - NAMES OF BUDDHAS, WRITTEN OR RECORDED
> - MANTRAS, WRITTEN OR RECORDED
> - SUTRAS AND TEACHINGS, WRITTEN OR RECORDED

PERHAPS YOU CAN'T take all the advice here if your loved one is not at home or in a private room in a hospital or hospice. Just understand the essential points and do the best you can.

HEAR NAMES OF BUDDHAS

Recite or play the names of the buddhas. As discussed, this is something that can be done for someone who is not a Buddhist as well; for animals too. You don't need to have faith in Buddha's teachings to receive benefit. The names themselves have the power to save beings who are dying from the lower realms.

Any buddha the person feels close to is good, but any of the following names could be recited over and over again.

Recite the Names of the Seven Medicine Buddhas [14]
There is a practice in which you visualize the main Medicine Buddha and six others, recite the prayer of the seven limbs, offer a mandala, and so on; see practice 36. Here, however, the practice is to simply recite their names.

There is an entire sutra—the *Medicine Buddha Sutra*—that describes the unbelievable benefits of the Medicine Buddha practices. I think they read it frequently in Chinese temples.

The Medicine Buddha promised that whoever chants his name or mantra will have all their prayers and wishes fulfilled. In the past, when the Medicine Buddha was a bodhisattva, with unbearable compassion that encompasses all us sentient beings, he made countless prayers that we pacify our many problems and achieve all temporary and ultimate happiness, especially during the time of the five degenerations. That time has come; this is our time. Therefore all the prayers that the Medicine Buddha made in the past will now be fulfilled.

The power and blessings of the Medicine Buddhas are greater and swifter in degenerate times. The power of prayer has been accomplished by the Medicine Buddha, so this practice is very effective in making your prayers succeed. One of the ten powers is the power of prayer, so pray as if you are the Medicine Buddha's agent on behalf of your loved one.

I heard a story about someone who was very sick and could not move his body. He was alone in the house, his medicine was in the bathroom, and he was unable to get up off his bed to fetch it. Lying there thinking about how to get his medicine, he turned his head toward the Medicine Buddha statue on his bedside table—and there was his medicine, in the hand of the Medicine Buddha.

Recite the Names of the Thirty-Five Buddhas of Confession [15]

Merely hearing the names of the Thirty-Five Buddhas of Confession purifies many thousands of eons of negative karma and makes it impossible to be reborn in the lower realms. (See also practice 49, the full practice of prostrations to the Thirty-Five Buddhas of Confession.)

HEAR MANTRAS

It is good to chant or play mantras so the dying person can hear them: this can lift them from sadness or depression. In general, all mantras are very powerful: simply hearing them can purify negative karma and protect from the lower realms.

Chant nicely, in an uplifting way, as the Chinese do: the person feels that nothing is more important than Amitabha Buddha, for example. They feel protected, supported, and guided.

Even if a person has no interest in listening to mantras, hearing them leaves a positive imprint on the mind, so that sooner or later they will meet the path and have the ability to practice the teachings, clear obscurations, and attain enlightenment.

Even if someone gets upset when they hear mantras and dies with an angry mind, it's still better than not hearing mantras and merely being peaceful. The power of Buddha's words can change their rebirth; because the mantras purify negative karma, they might even be reborn in a pure land. Or even if they are reborn in the lower realms, because of the imprint left on their mind from hearing the mantras, they will later achieve enlightenment. On the other hand, a person who doesn't hear any mantras might die peacefully, but then negative karma ripens after death.

There are many, many mantras; here are some that I recommend.

Recite the Mantra of Beam of Completely Pure Stainless Light and the Mantra Taught by Buddha Droden Gyalwa Chö [16]

It is extremely beneficial for you and other helpers to recite these two mantras a few times every day in the months and weeks before death. As a result, anyone who hears, sees, or touches you has all their negative karma purified. In addition, whatever you touch becomes a holy object.

It is not necessary to recite them at the time of death.

Recite the Mantra for Alleviating Fear or Pain [17]

This mantra, which includes the name of one of the eight bodhisattvas, can alleviate pain and calm fears. You can recite the mantra and help your loved one learn it. If they recite the mantra at least seven times every day, they won't have a difficult death, they won't experience frightening karmic appearances. Their death will be very easy, without fear. Then it's very easy for the people taking care of them. If the person is fearful, you will also be scared or worried, and then you can't help them; you won't know what to do.

Recite the Name Mantra of His Holiness the Dalai Lama or of Your Loved One's Own Guru [18]

You could have your loved one recite His Holiness the Dalai Lama's name mantra or their own root guru's mantra. While they recite it, they could visualize His Holiness or their guru and imagine purifying all their negative karma and defilements.

You can also recite it for them.

Recite the Name Mantra of the Buddha Who Protects from the Lower Realms [19]

Khunu Lama Rinpoche would tell people to recite the name mantra of this buddha, Rinchen Tsuktorchen, who dedicated especially for the sake of sentient beings who hear his name that they won't be reborn in the lower realms. (See also practice 3.)

Having heard this mantra, it is impossible for any animal or person to be reborn in the lower realms. So don't just recite it to yourself, and don't mumble it: say it loudly so that your loved one can hear it.

If you come across an animal who is dying, this is the first thing you would recite in their ear.

Recite Other Mantras, Such as Amitabha Buddha's [20]

There are many mantras of the various buddhas, such as Amitabha. Or you could recite a very special mantra that fulfills all wishes: The Great Increasing Jewel Fathomless Celestial Mansion Extremely Well-Abiding Secret Holy Mantra.

THE TEN POWERFUL MANTRAS

It is good to chant any of the ten powerful mantras mentioned in *Giving Breath to the Wretched* that liberate not only those who are dying but also those already dead, and even those in the lower realms.

The various explanations below of the benefits of reciting mantras (and holy names) are not metaphorical. We do not need to interpret the meaning—the meaning is exactly as stated. Therefore do not have doubt, for the holy gurus have emphasized the benefits received from devotion and belief.

1. Recite the Compassion Buddha Mantra [21]

The benefits of reciting the mantra of the Compassion Buddha (Tibetan: Chenrezik; Sanskrit: Avalokiteshvara) are infinite, like the limitless sky. If your loved one doesn't have much intellectual understanding of Dharma and the only thing they know is this mantra and, free of attachment to this life, they have spent their life chanting it, that is enough.

This is how it was with my mother, who passed away in 1991. She had no education at all and had very little Dharma knowledge; she didn't even know the alphabet. But she had the biggest heart, filled with loving kindness and compassion for her family, her friends, the people she knew, the animals she tended. Despite her extreme poverty, she was incredibly generous. Whatever food she had she would offer with such a warm heart to whoever was hungry.

And what she did, all day long and at night, was recite the mantra of the Compassion Buddha. This was her main practice.

When she was quite sick, I asked His Holiness the Dalai Lama about her death, as I thought it would be better to do something before her death rather than after it. Apart from all her kindness, since I am her son, I felt responsibility for her life. His Holiness said, "She won't have a problem when she dies, and it is sufficient for her to recite the Compassion Buddha mantra; she doesn't have to do anything else." At the time of death she was so peaceful.

2. Recite the Medicine Buddha Mantra [22]

As I mentioned in practice 14 in this chapter, the Medicine Buddha promised that whoever chants his name or mantra will have all their prayers and wishes fulfilled.

Reciting the Medicine Buddha mantra every day will purify negative karma and prevent rebirth in the lower realms. The Medicine Buddha said that even an animal who hears his mantra would never be reborn in the lower realms.

Reciting it and hearing it ceases the gross and subtle defilements and causes enlightenment. So have the dying person recite the mantra with full trust in Medicine Buddha, or you recite it so they can hear it.

Explain that Medicine Buddha is always with them—in their heart, on their crown, in front of them. Tell them that there is not one second Medicine Buddha does not see them or have compassion for them.

3. Recite the Lotus Pinnacle of Amoghapasha Mantra [23]

Reciting this mantra of Buddha Pema Tsuktor seven times every day with the thought to benefit others creates the cause to be reborn in the pure lands.

4. Recite the Mitrukpa Mantra [24]

The mantra of Mitrukpa (Sanskrit: Akshobhya) is for purifying karmic obscurations.

As I mentioned in practice 2, merely seeing it purifies the heaviest of the very heavy negative karmas, avoiding the holy Dharma, which is heavier than destroying all the monasteries, all the statues, stupas, scriptures, every single holy object that exists in this world.

Reciting or seeing it also purifies the negative karma of having taken things from the Sangha without permission or having deprived them of receiving things—karmas like that. No question then about all other negative karmas.

5. Recite the Namgyalma Mantra [25]

Namgyalma (Sanskrit: Ushnishavijaya) is a deity for long life and purification. The mantra has infinite benefits. It is said to be so powerful that for anyone who hears it, this life will be their last birth from a womb. And if animals hear it, they will not be born in the lower realms.

6. Recite Guru Rinpoche Padmasambhava's Mantra [26]

According to Guru Rinpoche himself, whoever recites his mantra "will meet with me again and again in this life, in future lives, and in the intermediate state between death and rebirth."

7. Recite the Kunrik Mantra [27]

Kunrik (Sanskrit: Vairochana), who is white, has three faces, and holds a Dharma wheel, is known as "the king of deities for purifying the lower realms." It is said that Kunrik practice can even liberate someone who is already in the lower realms.

Kirti Tsenshab Rinpoche has explained that laypeople in Amdo prepare for their death by taking an initiation of Kunrik. Because the Amdo people have faith that they have purified everything, they are not worried when death comes; they are relaxed, comfortable.

8. Recite the Milarepa Mantra [28]

Milarepa himself said that merely remembering his name and thinking about him will cause us to be born in a pure land, where we will meet him and receive teachings. He generated this very special bodhichitta in order to offer extensive benefit to sentient beings.

Depending on the level of our devotion, we can even receive instructions from Milarepa in our dreams.

9. Recite the Mantra of Beam of Completely Pure Stainless Light [29]

As I mentioned in practice 16 above, whoever hears, sees, or touches a person who has recited this mantra will have their negative karma purified.

10. Recite the Maitreya Buddha Mantra [30]

Reading and reciting the mantra of Maitreya Buddha's promise, contemplating the meaning, or merely hearing it—this includes animals—causes one not to be reborn in the lower realms. One will follow the path of the ten virtuous actions and receive all the enjoyments one seeks. And when Maitreya Buddha shows the twelve deeds of a Buddha, he will lead this sentient being from poverty.

Maitreya will definitely find even the sentient beings in a hell and give them the prediction of the time of their enlightenment.

Recite the Five Great Mantras [31]

Four of the five great mantras are among the ten powerful mantras; the fifth is the mantra of Buddha Stainless Pinnacle (Tibetan: Drimé Tsuktor; Sanskrit: Ushnishavimala).

Kunrik [27]
Mitrukpa [24]
Namgyalma [25]
Stainless Pinnacle
Lotus Pinnacle of Amoghapasha [23]

These five are mentioned in *Giving Breath to the Wretched*, and reciting them, as I mentioned, liberates not only those who are dying but also those already dead, and even those in the lower realms.

The mantra of Buddha Stainless Pinnacle has many benefits. You can attach it above a doorway, and every time anyone passes beneath it—

whether human or animal, even insects—one thousand eons of their negative karma will be purified. It is also one of the four dharmakaya mantras in stupas (see practices 37 and 87).

HEAR SUTRAS

Recite the Sutra for Alleviating Pain [32]
It is said that listening to the *Great Noble Sutra on Entering the City of Vaishali* can help alleviate the pain of those who are sick or dying.

Recite the Heart Sutra [33] or the Vajra Cutter Sutra [34]
It is mentioned in a sutra called *Roar of the Lion* that the merit of merely listening to teachings on emptiness, the perfection of wisdom—the topic of these two sutras—is far greater than practicing the other five perfections for ten thousand eons. Even having faith in emptiness can purify the heaviest of negative karmas.

The minute you have even the mere idea of the understanding of dependent arising—that's the reason things are empty—you begin to liberate yourself from all the sufferings of samsara.

HEAR TEACHINGS

Play Recordings or Videos of Teachings [35]
It is good for your loved one to receive the blessings of His Holiness the Dalai Lama's holy speech, so play recordings or watch videos of his teachings. Of course, you can play recordings of the teachings of other lamas as well, especially the person's own lama.

Hearing the subject matter, especially bodhichitta, reminds them to practice, inspires their mind, arouses devotion, and of course helps them avoid being born in the lower realms.

16
The Practices: What to Meditate On

> **WHAT YOU NEED**
> - Pictures and statues of gurus and buddhas
> - The Medicine Buddha practice, written or recorded
> - A stupa for meditating
> - Your loved one's daily practices, written or recorded
> - Other meditations that suit your loved one

Perhaps you can't take all the advice here if your loved one is not at home or in a private room in a hospital or hospice. Simply understand the essential points and do the best you can.

PRAY AND MEDITATE

Recite the Medicine Buddha Practice [36]
The main practice to do before, during, and after death is Medicine Buddha. As I mentioned in practice 14, there is an entire sutra—the *Medicine Buddha Sutra*—that describes the unbelievable benefits of this practice and how the Medicine Buddha himself made a promise that whoever chants his name or mantra will have all their prayers and wishes fulfilled.

I translated a short version of the practice many years ago in which you visualize the seven Medicine Buddhas—the main Medicine Buddha and six others—above your head. It's very powerful, and unique, with the prayer of the seven limbs, a mandala offering, and so on, then a strong requesting prayer to each buddha, recited seven times.

A simpler alternative is to visualize just the main Medicine Buddha above your head, and as you recite the mantra, you imagine nectar flowing from the Medicine Buddha, purifying you.

Meditate Using Stupas [37]

Stupas and other holy objects can be used for purifying or healing meditation. Lead your loved one in the meditation.

As I mentioned in practice 6, what makes a stupa powerful is the presence in them of the four dharmakaya relic mantras (see also practice 87)—the Ornament of Enlightenment, Secret Relic, Beam of Completely Pure Stainless Light, and Stainless Pinnacle—usually written in gold on the "life tree," the central wooden pole within the stupa.

Meditate on Tonglen, Giving and Taking [38]

If your loved one has a compassionate nature, a brave mind, they will be able to do tonglen: giving and taking. It is a profound and powerful practice in which they can use their own suffering, in particular their death, to develop compassion for others. Rather than rejecting death as something to fear, they can use it to develop the ultimate good heart of bodhichitta.

First your loved one generates great compassion by visualizing *taking* upon themselves the suffering and causes of suffering of the numberless other living beings, imagining that this destroys their own self-cherishing, the source of all problems.

Then they generate great loving kindness by imagining *giving* others everything they have: their body, their relatives and friends, their possessions, their merit, and their happiness.

Encourage them to think, "Even as I am dying, I will try to make my death beneficial for all other living beings. I prayed in the past to take upon myself the suffering of others. I am now experiencing my death on behalf of everyone who is dying now and who will have to die in the future. How wonderful it would be for all of them to be free from the suffering of death and for me alone to experience it! May they have this ultimate happiness!"

If they have faith in Jesus Christ, you can suggest that they think like this, like some saints do. In this way, as they have to experience death anyway, they make it most meaningful.

Meditate on the Death Process [39]

Help your loved one become familiar with the death process (as described in chapter 9) by leading them through a meditation on the various stages: the dissolution of the elements, the senses, all the way to the extremely subtle consciousness. Help them learn to recognize the visions, and at each stage get them to think, with strong determination: "I must recognize the clear light and definitely meditate on bliss and voidness."

As I discussed in chapter 10, the death-process meditation is an important aspect of a highest-tantra deity practice, where the meditator visualizes going through the death process, then the intermediate state, and then being reborn as the deity. This is called taking death, intermediate state, and rebirth into the path as the three bodies of the buddha.

Your loved one can also practice this as they go to sleep; see practice 41.

SLEEP MEDITATIONS

We need sleep because we don't have realizations, but we can use it to prepare for death. You can explain to your loved one that they should think of sleep as sustenance for the body, just like food. There are various ways they can use sleep to create virtue.

Sleep in the Lion Position [40]

You could have the person go to sleep in the lion position, the position that our compassionate Buddha lay in when he passed away. This position is recommended also for the time of death, as discussed in chapter 5 and in practice 55. Sleeping in this position makes it easier to adopt it at the time of death. It is better to do this than to lie in the position of a frog, with legs splayed!

Each time your loved one goes to sleep like this, they can think about the Buddha, how he passed into the sorrowless state and how they're following in his footsteps. Recollecting the Buddha before they become absorbed in sleep leaves a profoundly positive imprint on their mind. As many thoughts of the Buddha they have is as many seeds they plant to achieve enlightenment.

Then at the time of death, the thought of the Buddha will arise in their mind easily. There'll be no worries, and they'll be saved by this final thought.

Also, going to sleep like this protects us from nightmares. And it prevents spirits from harming us while we're asleep: say that we go to sleep one night not coughing, but we have a cough when we wake up in the morning. It can happen like this.

Your loved one need not spend the night in this position, just when they first go to sleep.

Meditate on the Process of Going to Sleep [41]

As I mentioned in chapter 9, the stages of dissolution that occur at death also occur when we go to sleep, but because it all happens very quickly and because we lack control, we don't recognize them.

If your loved can go through the stages while going to sleep, as they did while awake in practice 39, they will find it much easier to recognize the stages at the time of death. As they lie there, they can imagine the whole process: the mirage-like vision, the smoke-like vision, and so forth, ending with the clear light, each stage taking them into a state of increasing subtlety. When they visualize the clear light, they can try to see their "I" as empty of inherent existence. If they can get some feeling for this, their entire night will be profoundly transformed. This, in turn, will be enormously helpful at the time of death.

Holding for even a few seconds the feeling of the oneness of the clear-light vision and the emptiness of the self is a profound mind and a wonderful one to fall asleep with.

They could learn to extend the awareness to the whole duration of sleep, including dreaming.

Remember, passing from sleep into a dream is similar to passing from this life to the intermediate state. Now while we are dreaming, we rarely recognize dreams as dreams, but it is possible to train our mind to do this.

Sleep with Bodhichitta [42]

Encourage your loved one to go to sleep with the thought of bodhichitta. Think: "The purpose of my life is to free the numberless sentient beings from the oceans of samsaric suffering and bring them to enlightenment: the numberless hell beings, the numberless hungry ghosts, the numberless animals, the numberless human beings, the numberless gods and demigods, the numberless intermediate-state beings. Therefore I must achieve enlightenment. Therefore I am going to go to sleep."

Sleep in the Guru's Lap [43]
Your loved one could go to sleep with guru devotion. With the virtuous thought of compassion, they imagine that their head is in the lap of their guru, visualized as the buddha they feel closest to. They should strongly take refuge. Visualize radiant white light coming from the guru buddha's holy body and pouring into theirs. All their negativities are purified, and they become oneness with the guru's holy qualities.

This protects them, and it makes it easier to remember the guru at the time of death.

Sleep with Emptiness [44]
If your loved one has studied emptiness, you can talk to them about how all the fears and problems that everybody faces come from the wrong view of seeing everything, even life, as existing from its own side.

They could go to sleep while thinking about emptiness and dependent arising. Or they could sleep with the thought that everything is a dream, is a mirage, is an illusion—actually, not *is* an illusion but *like* an illusion. Seeing everything *as if* it is an illusion cuts the grasping at the appearance of it as existing inherently, from its own side. In their heart they can understand that the I is empty, everything is empty.

Sleeping Yoga. If they have received a highest tantra initiation, they could practice sleeping yoga, either with creativity or without creativity. "Without creativity" refers to basically meditating on emptiness while falling asleep; see practice 41.

As discussed in chapters 10 and 24, the great tantric practitioners who can recognize the clear light at sleep are able to recognize the clear light of death, no question.

"With creativity" refers to going to sleep while meditating on the deity's mandala. When they wake up, they would arise from the clear light according to whichever deity they practice.

If your loved one practices a deity within the lower tantras, such as the Compassion Buddha as explained in the *nyungné* fasting practice, they would visualize themselves as the Compassion Buddha dissolving into the syllable HRIH, and then the HRIH gradually dissolving into emptiness or into the mandala.

Meditate on the Emptiness of Death [45]
Remind your loved one that death is natural, that the mind that clings is what makes death terrifying. Death is merely the mind separating from the body, and this is labeled "death."

You can tell them that in emptiness, there is no such thing as birth and death. They can think: "Death appears to be real and existing from its own side, and I believe it to exist in this way, but actually this is a hallucination. There is no such thing. It is totally empty." Encourage them to keep their mind in that state.

You can remind them that they are striving to attain enlightenment for all sentient beings, and that even before then, when they reach the state of the arya-bodhisattva and perceive emptiness directly, they will have transcended disease, old age, and death. This is what awaits them, so there is no reason to fear death.

Meditate on the Emptiness of the Mind [46]
You can help your loved one think about how their mind is empty because it is a dependent arising, to meditate on the emptiness of the mind that appears to be not merely labeled by thought. Tell them that the base of the label "mind" is that which is formless, that which is not obstructed, not obscured by substantial phenomena, and therefore is clear. This means that phenomena can appear to it, that it can perceive phenomena—just like a mirror, which, because it is not obscured by the substantial phenomenon of dust, is clear. Objects can be reflected in it; it can reflect objects.

That is the base. And "mind" is the label that is simply imputed by their own thought on the base. Mind is merely imputed by thought *because* there is this phenomenon that is formless, not obstructed by phenomena, clear, and that perceives objects.

So what is their mind? It is nothing *except* what is merely imputed by a thought. They can see now that there is no such thing as mind existing from its own side. There is a mind that exists in mere name, merely imputed by thought, but it is empty of existing from its own side. And while the mind is empty, it is existing. How is it existing? It exists in mere name, merely imputed by thought. It is unified with emptiness and dependent arising.

This is how all phenomena exist.

Recite Your Loved One's Daily Practices [47]

It is very good to recite your loved one's daily practices to them, especially their main sadhana if they have received initiations—the visualizations, prayers, and mantras. They can meditate as you recite. Helping them strengthen the connection with their particular deity, and with the guru, is a precious gift.

They should meditate on and strongly wish to be reborn into the pure land of that buddha.

Help Your Loved One Practice Phowa [48]

As I mentioned in chapter 6 and elsewhere, it is possible to be reborn in a pure land by practicing phowa, the transference of consciousness. This practice is one of the six yogas of Naropa. In fact, it is said that even someone who has led a very negative life, if they're careful at death and with the help of this practice, can be born in a pure land.

The practice can be done either by the dying person—they forcefully push their own consciousness from their body just before death and send it to a pure land—or by their guru or another lama, or even a close friend.

If your loved one has their own practice of phowa, the right time to practice it is now, the months and weeks before death. Lama Tsongkhapa said that you can practice phowa up to six months before you die.

Why so long in advance? Why not wait until death is close? Because when the actual death comes, the person may be very sick and in much pain and their mind not clear, or other problems could occur. So to be safe, rather than waiting until the time of death, phowa should be practiced in advance, when the mind is clear.

If it is to be performed by a lama, it should happen as soon as the person's breath stops (practice 62), not before.

It can also be done by a lama during the forty-nine days after the mind has left the body (practice 81).

If it is to be performed by you and your Dharma friends, you can recite the Amitabha phowa practice written by Lama Yeshe (practice 81) during the forty-nine days after the mind has left the body.

17
The Practices: What to Do to Purify Negative Karma

> **WHAT YOU NEED**
> - PICTURES AND STATUES OF GURUS AND BUDDHAS
> - PRACTICE OF PROSTRATIONS TO THE THIRTY-FIVE BUDDHAS OF CONFESSION
> - PRACTICE OF VAJRASATTVA AND THE FOUR OPPONENT POWERS
> - PRACTICE OF SAMAYAVAJRA
> - PRACTICE OF *TSOK*
> - PRACTICE OF SELF-INITIATION

Purification Helps Alleviate Fear

THE NEGATIVE KARMA that we have already created is what causes fear, so in order to help our loved one not be afraid of death, for it not to be frightening, we need to help them purify their negative karma. Purification practices are the solution. Then they can have a happy death, and it will be much easier to attain liberation and actualize the path to enlightenment.

You can lead your loved one in various purification practices, depending on their level of practice: prostrations to the Thirty-Five Buddhas of Confession, for example, and the practice of Vajrasattva and the four opponent powers.

If they have taken a highest tantra initiation, you could help them with other practices, such as Samayavajra and the offering of tsok. And if they have completed the deity's retreat and the fire puja, the burning offering, one of the most powerful ways for them to purify is to take a self-initiation. It purifies everything: negative karma in general and

THE THIRTY-FIVE BUDDHAS OF CONFESSION

"Merely hearing the names of the Thirty-Five Buddhas of Confession makes it impossible to be reborn in the lower realms."

particular negative actions, as well as broken vows of individual liberation, bodhisattva vows, and tantric vows and commitments, even root downfalls.

When you lead your loved one in these practices, it is essential to remind them to generate strong faith that they have purified the various negative karmas, broken vows, and obscurations collected during beginningless rebirths. How much we purify depends on how much faith we have that we have purified, in just the same way that how much blessing we receive from the buddhas depends on how strong our devotion is.

This is the way our own mind creates enlightenment. Enlightenment is the creation of our own pure mind, our positive thoughts. Hell is created by our own mind as well: the impure mind, the negative thoughts. All happiness and all suffering of all sentient beings are the products, the creations, of our own minds, depending on whether we are peaceful or unpeaceful, virtuous or nonvirtuous, good-hearted or self-centered.

With these purification practices you can help your loved one make their life most fruitful and most satisfying. They are prepared for death at any moment.

Purify with the Practice of Prostrations to the Thirty-Five Buddhas of Confession [49]

This practice contains the four opponent powers: reliance, regret, the remedy, and restraint. Merely hearing the names of these thirty-five buddhas purifies many thousands of eons of negative karma and makes it impossible to be reborn in the lower realms. See also practice 15: reciting the names of these thirty-five buddhas.

Purify with the Practice of Vajrasattva and the Four Opponent Powers [50]

The Vajrasattva recitation meditation, which also includes the four opponent powers, is an incredibly powerful method. Practicing it at the end of every day prevents negative karma from multiplying. It also helps purify that day's negative karma, as well as the negative karma created since the time we were born and the karma from all our previous lives.

Purify with the Practice of Samayavajra [51]

The practice of Samayavajra (Tibetan: Damtsik Dorje) is a powerful practice that purifies in particular the negative karmas accumulated in the relationship with the guru. Those of us who have taken all three levels of vows have continually broken and degenerated our commitments—our pledges to our gurus—especially the tantric commitments. Because of their compassion, all our gurus have manifested as Samayavajra so that we can purify all these negative karmas.

Purify with an Abbreviated Offering of Tsok [52]

Another very powerful way to help your loved one purify broken vows of individual liberation, bodhisattva vows, and tantric vows and commitments, as well as to collect merits, is to offer tsok. It is one of the main causes to achieve the Heruka and Vajrayogini pure lands, to be born there.

Purify with an Offering of Tsok to Vajrasattva by Lama Yeshe [53]

When Lama Yeshe wrote the Vajrasattva tsok offering in 1982, he said he composed it "in case students were getting bored with the older pujas. It's shorter, too, and therefore suits our busy lifestyles!"

This tsok offering can be made to other highest-tantra deities by substituting that deity's name for Vajrasattva's and by blessing the offerings in accordance with the yoga method of that deity and reciting that deity's mantra.

Purify with the Self-Initiation of Your Loved One's Main Deity [54]

Chöden Rinpoche says that if the person who is passing away is qualified to take the self-initiation—that is, they have received a highest tantra initiation and have completed the retreat and fire puja, the burning offering puja—and cannot themselves do it, they can invite someone else to recite the prayers for them while they meditate on the meaning.

Of course, if there is a lama nearby, according to Rinpoche, it is good to take the initiation again.

As mentioned above, performing a self-initiation purifies not only degenerations of tantric vows, such as root downfalls, but also broken bodhisattva and individual-liberation root and secondary vows. All these negative karmas get completely purified, making it impossible to be born in the lower realms.

With this practice you plant the seeds to achieve the bodies of a buddha (as discussed in chapter 10). This leaves such strong imprints of the tantric path on your mind, which causes you to quickly gain realizations of the path to enlightenment.

Rinpoche explained that one of his gurus, also my guru—a former abbot of Sera Je Monastery, Khensur Rinpoche Losang Wangchuk, who was one of the top, most famous learned ones from Tibet—knew that he was not going to live long so started taking the self-initiation in the Tibetan fifth month and did it every day until he passed away in the seventh month. He prepared for death like this.

While I was with Lama Yeshe a couple of months before he passed away—we were at a farmhouse near Delhi, in India—I would read the Heruka self-initiation to Lama, the middle-length version, every day. Before that we'd been at Kopan Monastery, where I'd given the November course. Lama was not planning to go, but I insisted. At the end of the course, Lama gave the bodhisattva vows. It was Lama's last teaching.

Anyway, while I recited, Lama would meditate. In Lama's case, of course, as somebody who had achieved the clear light and the illusory body, who had already overcome death, there was no need for these practices.

18

Finally, What to Do in the Hours before Death

> **WHAT YOU NEED**
>
> - Blessed pills and relics for the tongue
> - Pictures and statues of gurus and buddhas
> - Mantras to see
> - A text to touch
> - A stupa to touch
> - A prayer wheel to touch
> - A blessed cord to wear
> - Written mantras for the body
> - Medicine Buddha practice for reciting
> - Other practices, mantras, and so on, for reciting

PERHAPS YOU CAN'T take all the advice here if your loved one is not at home or in a private room in a hospital or hospice. Simply understand the essential points and do the best you can.

Be Quiet

Now that death is close, it is extremely important—essential—that your loved one is not disturbed. This is the main point. As I mentioned in chapter 12, do not create any situation that upsets them. People should not cry within hearing distance of your loved one. Helping them avoid strong attachment and the other delusions during this time gives them a chance to have virtuous thoughts. If they have a peaceful, happy mind, they will have a peaceful, happy death.

Only the sounds of prayers and mantras should be heard.

Recognize the Stages of Death

If you have studied the death process described in chapter 9, you will be able to recognize the stages the person's consciousness goes through as they gradually die—the twenty-five stages of dissolution, the various signs, and so on—and thus be more skillful in helping them.

Have Your Loved One Lie in the Lion Position [55]

As discussed in chapter 5, it's good to have your loved one follow the example of our kind, compassionate Buddha when he passed away into the sorrowless state and have them lie in the lion position. Of course, if they are a practitioner, they can sit in the meditation posture; it's up to the individual.

If they've practiced sleeping in this position (practice 40), it will be easier now. Lying in this position naturally makes it easy to transfer the consciousness from the crown to a pure land—especially, remember, as we discussed in chapter 12, if your loved one is facing west, which is where Amitabha Buddha's pure land is.

Lying in this position also helps virtuous thoughts arise in the person's mind at the time of death; it makes it easy for this to happen. And it reminds them of the Buddha, that they're following in his footsteps. At the time of death, there will be no worries, they'll be saved by this last thought of reflecting on the Buddha.

If they are a practitioner, they may choose to die sitting in the meditation posture; it's up to the individual.

TASTE BLESSED SUBSTANCES

Offer a Mani Pill from His Holiness the Dalai Lama [56]

As advised in *Tibetan Ceremonies of the Dead*, it is good to give the person who is dying a mani pill. This blesses and purifies your loved one's mind, helping them generate virtuous thoughts.

Crush the pill, mix it with water, and put a little into your loved one's mouth, making sure they swallow it. Chöden Rinpoche says it's important to do this before the outer breath has stopped, because after that you should not touch the body, as discussed in the next chapter.

These pills contain many blessed substances and relics of enlightened beings, bodhisattvas, and great yogis. They have been blessed with the prayers of His Holiness the Dalai Lama, the actual Compassion Buddha, for the benefit of sentient beings; and many great lamas, meditators, and sangha have also prayed day and night for many days, continuously blessing them.

You can give the pills to children and people who don't have the ability to understand, as well as to animals.

Offer a Relic of the Buddha [57]
Another method to help the dying person avoid being reborn in the lower realms is to give them a relic of a buddha; you put it into their mouth.

Again, the relic must be put in the mouth before the breath has stopped, otherwise, as it says in *Tibetan Ceremonies of the Dead*, it will just sit there and not go down the throat. Also, offering the relic after the breath has stopped could delay the death.

As with the blessed pills, the relic can be given to children and animals.

THINK ABOUT THE BUDDHA, ETC.

Talk about the Guru, the Buddha, Amitabha Buddha's Pure Land, Your Loved One's Good Qualities, Compassion [10–13]
If your loved one has a relationship with a guru it is good to remind them now to talk about the guru, to say their name. As I discussed in chapter 14, practice 10, merely hearing the name of the guru is one of the best methods for transferring the consciousness to a pure land.

And it's good to mention the buddhas, such as Amitabha and his pure land, the Blissful Realm. As I mentioned in chapter 6, this is a cause for being reborn there.

SEE HOLY IMAGES, MANTRAS

Show Holy Images, Mantras [1–4]
Especially now, at the time of death, have the dying person look at the images of the gurus or buddhas, or the mantras, as discussed in chapter 13. It's one hundred percent certain that they won't be reborn in the lower realms.

TOUCH WITH HOLY OBJECTS

Bless the Body with a Text [5]
Touch the crown of your loved one's head with texts such as Lama Tsongkhapa's *Lamrim Chenmo*, or *By Wearing, Liberates*, as discussed in chapter 13, or any text you like. You could leave it there, touching the body.

Bless the Body with a Stupa, Prayer Wheel, or Blessed Cord [6-8]
Now that the time of death is close, it is good to touch the body with a stupa or a prayer wheel, as well as put a blessed cord around their neck or wrist, as discussed in chapter 13. Place the stupa so that it is touching your loved one's crown.

Merely being touched by holy objects purifies so much negative karma and helps the person receive a higher rebirth. You can leave the objects there, touching the body.

Bless the Body with Written Mantras [58]
Place a sheet of paper or card with mantras written on it face down on the person's body so that the words touch the skin; any part of the body will do.

I have written out eleven mantras, a small version of which is in the Liberation Box; included are some of the five great mantras (practice 31) and the ten powerful mantras (practices 21–30), as well as the mantra of Vajra Armor. Or you could use any of the five great mantras or the ten powerful mantras.

Namgyalma (practice 25), which is included in both groups (and is also in the Liberation Box), is one of the best for the dying; or Kunrik (practice 27), Mitrukpa (practice 24), Stainless Pinnacle (practice 31)—any mantras you like can be used.

PRAY AND MEDITATE

You could have a group of monks and nuns or friends join you to do practices such as Medicine Buddha, mantra recitation, or any of the practices below, making sure that your loved one can hear the recitations.

It is very powerful for people who care about the dying person to practice together. The lojong teachings mention that doing prayers in a group is far more beneficial than doing them alone. Not only does it benefit the person you're praying for, it also inspires you and the others. You are supporting each other in purifying negative karma and collecting merit to achieve enlightenment quickly.

And remember to dedicate for your loved one's future rebirth. Now is the time to dedicate strongly for their future life to be a most precious one: either that they take a perfect human rebirth, meet the Dharma and a perfectly qualified Mahayana teacher, practice, and become enlightened as quickly as possible, or that they take rebirth in a pure land.

Recite the Medicine Buddha Practice [36]

As I mentioned, the main practice to do before, during, and after death is Medicine Buddha. The benefits are incredible—both for your loved one and for you.

Recite Your Loved One's Daily Practices [47]

It is very good to recite the person's daily practices, especially their main sadhana if they have received initiations—the visualizations, prayers, and mantras. This helps them strengthen their connection with their particular deity and their guru.

They can meditate as you recite.

Recite Purification Practices [49–54]

Recite any of the purification practices, especially if they have taken a highest tantra initiation. But even if they haven't, as I mentioned, practices such as prostrations to the Thirty-Five Buddhas of Confession and Vajrasattva and the four opponent powers can calm their fears and help them have a happy death by purifying their negative karma.

HEAR

Recite or Play the Names of the Buddhas [14–15]

Especially now, when death is close, it is good to recite or play the names of the buddhas. Even if your loved one doesn't have faith in Buddha's teachings, this can help.

Recite or Play Mantras [16–31]

Recite the name mantra of His Holiness the Dalai Lama or of your loved one's own guru, or the mantras of the buddhas they feel close to.

As I mentioned, chant nicely, in an uplifting way, especially now.

Recite or Play Sutras [32–34]

You could recite either the sutra to alleviate pain and fear or the sutras relating to emptiness.

ORGANIZE

Sponsor Monasteries, Dharma Centers, or Friends to Perform Practices Such as Medicine Buddha [59]

It is excellent to make offerings to other people—monks and nuns in monasteries or Dharma centers, or friends—and request them to perform Medicine Buddha or other practices for your loved one.

Part Four

Practices to Do in the Hours and Days after the Breath Has Stopped

SHAKYAMUNI BUDDHA

"Have your loved one lie in the lion position, like our compassionate Buddha did when he passed away."

19

The Practices: What to Do as Soon as the Breath Stops

WHAT YOU NEED

· BLESSED SUBSTANCES FOR THE CROWN

PERHAPS YOU CAN'T take all the advice here if your loved one is not at home or in a private room in a hospital or hospice. Simply understand the essential points and do the best you can.

Do Not Touch the Body
Now that your loved one's breath has stopped, apart from putting the blessed substances on the crown (practice 61 in this chapter) you should not touch the body. Touching the wrong part of the body before the mind leaves can potentially disturb the person, causing their consciousness to leave at that point and take a lower rebirth. If the consciousness leaves through the mouth, for example, they will be reborn as a hungry ghost.

HEAR

Shout in Your Loved One's Ear the Name of Their Guru or the Buddha [60]
The very first thing you should do as soon as the person's breath stops is shout loudly close to their ear the name of their lama, or of His Holiness the Dalai Lama, or the name of the buddha they usually pray to, or any buddha, and remind them to take refuge.

As I mentioned in practice 10, hearing the name of their guru is considered a very effective kind of transference of consciousness. Chöden Rinpoche refers to a quotation from the *Kalachakra Tantra*: "To recall the name of your guru for even one second is the best phowa."

This is true even for someone who has created the five heavy negative actions: if they have devotion in their guru, merely hearing the name of their lama can help their consciousness take a good rebirth.

TOUCH WITH BLESSED SUBSTANCES

Put Blessed Substances on Your Loved One's Crown [61]
Once your loved one has stopped breathing and you have shouted the name of their guru or any buddha in their ear, you can now put one of the following blessed substances on their crown, at the chakra, which is toward the back of the head. Doing this can help your loved one's consciousness go to the crown chakra so that it leaves from there and goes to a pure land.

- A phowa pill
- An inner-offering pill
- A mani pill
- Sand from a Kalachakra mandala

You can use butter and honey to help them stick. Be sure not to touch any other part of the body, as discussed in chapter 19.

The phowa pills consist of the ashes of the great yogis and bodhisattvas, also relics of buddhas—I made some using Phabongkha Dechen Nyingpo's ashes. Some lamas also use these while they're doing phowa. If hearing, taking a blessing from, touching, seeing, or even remembering great Heruka practitioners like Phabongkha Rinpoche and Lama Yeshe can liberate us from all our negative karmas, then there's no question that it's the same when we have contact with their ashes.

If you don't have phowa pills you can use an inner-offering pill made by high lamas. The mani pills are from His Holiness the Dalai Lama. The sand is from a Kalachakra mandala, also blessed by His Holiness.

When the body is taken out, you can keep the pill or sand and use it for others who die.

ORGANIZE

Request a Lama to Perform Phowa [62]

Assuming that your loved one has requested this, now is the time to invite a lama to perform phowa. You should request this immediately after the breath has stopped and, except for putting the blessed substances on the crown (practice 61), before you touch the body.

The lama can either come to where the body is or, as advised in *Tibetan Ceremonies of the Dead*, "Do the practice from a distance." If the latter, it's important you tell him in what direction your loved one's head is pointing; this helps the phowa be more precise.

It is said that phowa can be done only after the breath has stopped, not before (except if the dying person is doing it themselves, as discussed in practice 48). Because phowa has the power to transfer the consciousness from the body, if it's done before death, there is a risk the mind could leave before it's ready.

There was a lama in Tibet who heard that some people were going to be executed by the Chinese. He somehow managed to get the execution delayed and then sat in meditation and did the practice—and the people waiting to be executed simply collapsed in a heap, their consciousnesses having left their bodies, presumably for a pure land. They didn't need the bullets of the Chinese soldiers! The lama not only saved the people from whatever rebirth was awaiting them, he also saved the soldiers from the negative karma of killing.

When there is a very strong connection between a dying person and their guru, it is possible in some circumstances that the guru can help the dying person's mind move away from negativity and toward virtue—even if the person's mind is already in the intermediate state—so that they take a good rebirth, perhaps even in a pure land.

When a high lama transfers somebody's consciousness to a pure land, many special signs happen, such as rainbows in the sky or white light emitting from the person's body. However, if your loved one is an accomplished meditator actually in meditation, there is no need to do phowa; they can take care of themselves.

Phowa can also be practiced during the forty-nine days after death, as discussed in practice 81.

Now Follow the Instructions in the Appropriate Chapter

Chapter 20: If Your Loved One Is at Home when They Die
Chapter 21: If Your Loved One Is in the Hospital when They Die
Chapter 22: If Your Loved One Has Offered Their Organs
Chapter 23: If Your Loved One Dies Suddenly
Chapter 24: If Your Loved One Has High Realizations and Is Meditating at the Time of Death

20

The Practices: If Your Loved One Is at Home When They Die

What You Need

- Lights for offering
- A text for the body
- A stupa for the body
- A prayer wheel for the body
- A blessed cord for the body
- Written mantras for the body
- Medicine Buddha practice, written or recorded
- The eight prayers to benefit the dead, written or recorded, or the "King of Prayers"
- Any other practices you would like to do

Because it can take up to three days for the mind to leave the body—in other words, for death to occur—it is ideal to leave the body undisturbed for that long.

After following the instructions in chapter 19 as soon as the breath stops, do any of the following practices. You may not be able to follow all the advice here, but understand the essential points and do the best you can.

Remember: No Pets

Especially now that the breath has stopped, you should not allow cats or dogs in the room, especially cats. As discussed in chapter 12, cat hair is said to be polluted. Also, if a cat sits on the dead body, it's possible a spirit could follow it and enter the body.

Remember: Be Quiet
Continue to keep the environment peaceful and quiet. Only the sounds of prayers and mantras should be heard.

OFFER

Offer Lights in Front of the Body [63]
Chöden Rinpoche said that as long as the body is in the house, you must always offer a light nearby. In Tibet, of course, they would offer a butter lamp; you can use any kind of lights: electric, candles, and so on.

This is not an offering to the body but to the Three Rare Sublime Ones. It is mentioned in the root tantra of Heruka Chakrasamvara that one will achieve realizations if one offers lights—hundreds, thousands of lights. There are many statements like this in the teachings.

Another reason to have lights on—you could keep the room lights on—is that it helps prevent a spirit from entering the body, which is a danger. You should have the lights on all the time, day and night.

By the way, Rinpoche explained that the wick of a butter lamp in front of the body is heavy and dark, which means the light is unclear. The pollution from the body affects the light, Rinpoche said, and it's always like this.

TOUCH WITH HOLY OBJECTS

Bless the Body with a Text, Stupa, Prayer Wheel, or Blessed Cord [5–8]; or Written Mantras [58]
As discussed in chapters 13 and 18, if you haven't already put a text, a stupa, a prayer wheel, a blessed cord, or written mantras on your loved one's body, it is beneficial to do so now. Be very careful not to disturb the body.

PRAY AND MEDITATE

If there is a monastery or Dharma center nearby you can invite the monks or nuns to come to the house and perform prayers and pujas near the body continuously until it is taken out. However, in the West it is rare for this to happen because the opportunity is not there.

Or you could invite friends to come and do the practices mentioned below at different times throughout the three days, or groups of you can take turns. As I mentioned, doing prayers and practices in groups has more benefit than doing them alone.

Recite the Medicine Buddha Names [14] or Mantra [22], or Perform the Practice [36]

The main practice to do before, during, and after death is Medicine Buddha—meditating, reciting the names, or saying the mantra. As I mentioned in practice 14, the Medicine Buddha made a promise that all your prayers and wishes will succeed if you chant his name and mantra.

Sponsor Monasteries, Dharma Centers, or Friends to Perform Practices Such as Medicine Buddha [59]

You can make offerings to other people who are not there—monks and nuns in monasteries or Dharma centers, or friends—and request them to perform Medicine Buddha or other practices for your loved one.

Recite the Eight Prayers to Benefit the Dead [64–71]

These prayers are traditionally recited in the Geluk Tibetan monasteries when someone dies. Recite as many times as you like.

1. The "King of Prayers"
2. The "Dedication" chapter from Shantideva's *Guide to the Bodhisattva Way of Life*
3. "The Prayer to Be Reborn in the Blissful Realm of Amitabha Buddha" by Lama Tsongkhapa
4. "The Prayer for the Beginning, Middle, and End of Practice" by Lama Tsongkhapa
5. "Until Buddhahood"
6. The daily prayer to Bodhisattva Maitreya taught by Buddha Shakyamuni
7. "A Prayer for the Statue of Maitreya" by the First Dalai Lama Gendun Drup
8. "The Prayer for Spontaneous Bliss" by the Second Dalai Lama Gendun Gyatso

Recite the "King of Prayers" [64]

If you can't recite all eight, recite at least the "King of Prayers." In commentaries it is said that this prayer contains "ten numberless times one hundred thousand prayers of the bodhisattvas." It is said to be very, very powerful for purification and collecting extensive merit.

And, as I mentioned in chapter 6, if you recite it daily, you will definitely be reborn in Amitabha's pure land.

Recite the Guru Puja [72]

The *Guru Puja* is an incredible practice to do. It's got everything in it, including phowa.

If you like, you can recite just the refuge section. Whatever practices you do—jangwa, phowa, self-initiation—the foundation is refuge, relying on Buddha, Dharma, Sangha. So take strong refuge in the guru buddha, whom you visualize above the head of your loved one, or you could visualize the entire merit field or just Shakyamuni Buddha.

Then, as you recite a few hundred of each of the refuge mantras, pray that they purify all your loved one's negative karma immediately and they are born in the pure lands of the buddhas or receive a perfect human rebirth.

Do a Nyungné Fasting Retreat [73]

It is excellent to do a two-day nyungné fasting retreat. It is an unbelievable way to create merit, skies of merit.

On the first day you take only lunch, and on the second day you fast completely, including no drinks. You can think that you are fasting for the sake of your loved one and all sentient beings.

The practice combines many powerful practices, such as reciting mantras, the Eight Mahayana Precepts, meditation on the Compassion Buddha, and bodhichitta. When you meditate, you can either visualize yourself as the Compassion Buddha or see him in front of you, and as you recite his mantra, the long one or short one (practice 21), imagine nectar flowing from his heart, purifying your loved one.

The practice also includes a lot of prostrations, which you perform while you recite a praise to the Compassion Buddha as well as the names of the Thirty-Five Buddhas (practice 15).

Alternatively, you could do a retreat related to the person's main deity, Vajrasattva, Medicine Buddha, or any other retreat you like.

There are many other practices you could do during the three days, depending on the time and your preference.

Recite the Names of the Buddhas [14–15]
Recite the Name Mantra of Gurus [18]
Recite Other Mantras [16–31]
Recite Sutras [32–34]
Recite Your Loved One's Daily Practices [47]
Recite Purification Practices [49–54]

WHEN THE TIME HAS COME TO MOVE THE BODY

Check That the Mind Has Left the Body [74]
After three days have passed, before you move the body, make sure that the mind has left. There are various signs, described in chapter 25, that indicate that the mind is no longer there.

Tug at the Hair at the Crown Chakra [75]
As discussed in chapter 25, if the indication is that the mind has not yet left the body, tug the hair at the crown chakra a few times—toward the back of the head—or firmly tap on the crown there. Anyway, the first time you touch the body, it is auspicious to do this.

If the consciousness is still there, doing this can encourage it to go to the crown chakra and leave from there, which means your loved one will go to a pure land, as I discuss in chapter 9.

Consult a Tibetan Astrologer [76]
Typically, a Tibetan would consult an astrologer immediately after the mind of their loved one has left the body. Astrology can indicate what practices should be done to prevent your loved one from being born in the lower realms or to help them to take a good rebirth. For instance, it can indicate which statue or thangka painting should be made on their behalf or whether, if you do this or that practice, they will have a good rebirth or be reborn as a monk or a nun or even as a great lama.

It can even predict where the good rebirth will be taken. However, it is said that this usually only works for ordinary people; astrology cannot predict the future of either great holy beings or very evil people.

You need to tell the astrologer which of the twelve animal signs your loved one was born under as well as the date and time they passed away, even perhaps the hour or whether it was in the morning, the afternoon, and so on. It's important to be accurate.

There is astrology in the West, of course, but I'm not sure if it predicts future lives and so forth.

Prepare Your Loved One's Body
Now you can prepare the body for cremation or burial according to the instructions in chapter 26.

21

The Practices: If Your Loved One Is in the Hospital when They Die

What You Need

- A text for the body
- A stupa for the body
- A prayer wheel for the body
- A blessed cord for the body
- Written mantras for the body
- Medicine Buddha practice, written or recorded
- The eight prayers to benefit the dead, written or recorded, or the "King of Prayers"
- Any other practices you would like to do

Stay with the Body, Even for an Hour

Ask the hospital to allow you as much time as possible with the body of your loved one, even an hour. When Lama Yeshe passed away at about five o'clock in the morning of March 4, 1984, Tibetan New Year, at the Cedars-Sinai Medical Center in Los Angeles, the staff gave us a room to put Lama in while he was in meditation. Lama was there the whole day. I discuss this more in chapter 24.

After following the instructions in chapter 19 as soon as the breath stops, do any of the following practices. You may not be able to take all the advice here, but simply understand the essential points and do the best you can.

You Could Have the Body Moved to the Hospital Morgue

After you've done some of the practices and when it's time to move the body (see page 123), you could arrange to have it moved to the hospital morgue and kept there for three days. This would be okay, as long as there is not much disturbance to the body of your loved one, not much movement. Then you could do more prayers and practices during the three days at home.

Remember: Be Quiet
Do your best to keep the environment peaceful and quiet. Only the sounds of prayers and mantras should be heard.

TOUCH WITH HOLY OBJECTS

Bless the Body with a Text, Stupa, Prayer Wheel, or Blessed Cord [5–8]; or Written Mantras [58]
As discussed in chapters 13 and 18, if you haven't already put a text, a stupa, a prayer wheel, a blessed cord, or written mantras on your loved one's body, it is beneficial to do so now. But be very careful not to disturb the body.

PRAY AND MEDITATE

At the Very Least, Recite the Medicine Buddha Names [14], Mantra [22], or Practice [36]
The main practice to do before, during, and after death is Medicine Buddha—meditating, reciting the names, saying the mantra.

As I mentioned in practice 14, Medicine Buddha made a promise that all your prayers and wishes will succeed if you chant his name and mantra.

Sponsor Monasteries, Dharma Centers, or Friends to Perform Practices Such as Medicine Buddha [59]
You can make offerings to other people who are not there—monks and nuns in monasteries or Dharma centers, or friends—and request them to perform Medicine Buddha or other practices for your loved one.

Recite the Eight Prayers to Benefit the Dead [64–71]
These prayers are traditionally recited in the Geluk Tibetan monasteries when someone dies.

Recite the "King of Prayers" [64]
If you can't recite all eight, recite at least the "King of Prayers." As I mentioned, in commentaries it is said that this prayer contains "ten numberless times one hundred thousand prayers of the bodhisattvas," and if you recite it daily you will definitely be reborn in Amitabha's pure land.

There are many other practices you could do, depending on the time and your preference.

Recite the Names of the Buddhas [14–15]
Recite the Name Mantra of Gurus [18]
Recite Other Mantras [16–31]
Recite Sutras [32–34]
Recite Your Loved One's Daily Practices [47]
Recite Purification Practices [49–54]
Recite the Guru Puja *[72]*

WHEN THE TIME HAS COME TO MOVE THE BODY

Check That the Mind Has Left the Body [74]
Before you move the body—whether after a short time in the hospital bed or after three days in the hospital morgue—make sure that the mind has left. There are various signs that indicate that the mind is no longer there, described in chapter 25.

Help the Mind Leave the Body: Tug at the Hair at the Crown Chakra [75]
As discussed in chapter 25, if the indication is that the mind has not yet left the body, tug the hair at the crown chakra a few times—toward the back of the head—or firmly tap on the crown there. Anyway, the first time you touch the body, it is auspicious to do this.

If the consciousness is still there, doing this can encourage it to go to the crown chakra and leave from there, which means your loved one would go to a pure land, as described in chapter 9.

Consult a Tibetan Astrologer [76]

Once you are confident the mind has left the body, you could consult an astrologer to determine what practices are best to ensure a positive rebirth.

Prepare Your Loved One's Body

Now you can prepare the body for cremation or burial according to the instructions in chapter 26.

22

The Practices: If Your Loved One Has Offered Their Organs

> ### What You Need
>
> - A text for the body
> - A stupa for the body
> - A prayer wheel for the body
> - A blessed cord for the body
> - Written mantras for the body
> - Medicine Buddha practice, written or recorded
> - The eight prayers to benefit the dead, written or recorded, or the "King of Prayers"
> - Any other practices you would like to do

Does Cutting Out the Organs Disturb the Mind?

SOME PEOPLE DECIDE to offer their organs to others after they have died. Does this disturb the mind?

It seems that when the person is considered brain-dead, the doctors keep the body breathing artificially, and they continue to keep the body breathing when they actually cut out the organs.

I question this. The brain may no longer be functioning, but if the person has the karma to breathe, even if artificially, this means they have the karma to be alive, which means the mind—the subtle consciousness—is still there.

Also, as we discussed in chapter 7, even when the breath has stopped and someone has been declared brain-dead, people have been known to come back to life. This means that the usual definition of death is wrong. This is a big question that needs to be discussed with learned great meditators. The hospital needs to be careful.

BUDDHA AMITAYUS

"Pray that throughout all future lives your loved one attains whatever length of life they wish for, becoming just like Buddha Amitayus."

However, if the person is brain-dead—which means the gross consciousness has ceased—they may not feel anything when the organs are cut out. If the person is not in meditation when this happens, then I think it may not matter.

Also, because your loved one, as an organ donor, died with the thought of benefiting others, I think they won't be disturbed when the body is cut and therefore won't be reborn in the lower realms. The subtle consciousness is still there, but because earlier, with their gross mind, they dedicated their body, they made charity of their body, which is a virtue, they acquired merit.

Your Loved One Has Created So Much Merit

Making charity of their body before they passed away, dedicating for others, is the same as if they were alive and made charity of their body. It's as if they had chosen to offer their life or their limbs to others when they are alive—many great masters actually did this.

Of course, I can't say one hundred percent that there's no worldly concern for everyone who offers their organs, but generally speaking, I think you can say that because there are no expectations, no worldly mind involved, they are really making charity. As there is no concern about reputation, no thought of power, no thought of getting something, this would be sincere giving, which means the mind is virtuous.

Still, it is good to make sure that the practice of jangwa is done for your loved one after the cremation or burial; see practice 78.

BEFORE THE ORGANS ARE REMOVED

Ask the hospital to allow you as much time as possible with the body of your loved one before they take it to cut out the organs. Perhaps you can't take all the advice here, but understand the essential points and do the best you can.

Remember: Be Quiet

Do your best to keep the environment peaceful and quiet. Only the sounds of prayers and mantras should be heard.

TOUCH WITH HOLY OBJECTS

Bless the Body with a Text, Stupa, Prayer Wheel, or Blessed Cord [5–8]; or Written Mantras [58]
As discussed in chapters 13 and 18, if you haven't already put a text, a stupa, a prayer wheel, a blessed cord, or written mantras on your loved one's body, it is beneficial to do so now. But be very careful not to disturb the body.

PRAY AND MEDITATE

At the Very Least, Recite the Medicine Buddha Names [14], Mantra [22], or Practice [36]
The main practice to do before, during, and after death is Medicine Buddha—meditating, reciting the names, saying the mantra.

As I mentioned in practice 14, the Medicine Buddha made a promise that all your prayers and wishes will succeed if you chant his name and mantra.

Sponsor Monasteries, Dharma Centers, or Friends to Perform Practices Such as Medicine Buddha [59]
You can make offerings to other people who are not there—monks and nuns in monasteries or Dharma centers, or friends—and request them to perform Medicine Buddha or other practices for your loved one.

Recite the Eight Prayers to Benefit the Dead [64–71]
These prayers are usually recited in the Geluk Tibetan monasteries when someone dies.

Recite the "King of Prayers" [64]
If you can't recite all eight, recite at least the "King of Prayers." As I mentioned, in commentaries it is said that this prayer contains "ten numberless times one hundred thousand prayers of the bodhisattvas," and if you recite it daily you will definitely be reborn in Amitabha's pure land.

There are many other practices you could do, depending on the time and your preference. Once the body has been taken away for the removal of the organs, you can continue to do the practices at home.

Recite the Names of the Buddhas [14–15]
Recite the Name Mantra of Gurus [18]
Recite Other Mantras [16–31]
Recite Sutras [32–34]
Recite Your Loved One's Daily Practices [47]
Recite Purification Practices [49–54]
Recite the Guru Puja *[72]*

WHEN THE TIME HAS COME TO RECEIVE THE BODY FROM THE HOSPITAL

Check That the Mind Has Left the Body [74]
Just because the organs have been cut out doesn't mean the subtle mind has left the body. However, I can't say yes and I can't say no; it depends on the individual. For some people, depending on which organs have been taken, the subtle consciousness could still be there. So it's good to check if the consciousness is still there; see chapter 25.

Help the Mind Leave the Body: Tug at the Hair at the Crown Chakra [75]
As discussed in chapter 25, if the indication is that the mind has not yet left the body, tug the hair at the crown chakra a few times—toward the back of the head—or firmly tap on the crown there.

Doing this can encourage the consciousness to go to the crown chakra and leave from there, which means your loved one would go to a pure land, as described in chapter 9.

Consult a Tibetan Astrologer [76]
Once you are confident the mind has left the body, you could consult an astrologer to determine what practices are best to ensure a positive rebirth.

Prepare Your Loved One's Body

Now you can prepare the body for cremation or burial according to the instructions in chapter 26.

23

The Practices: If Your Loved One Dies Suddenly

> **WHAT YOU NEED**
>
> - A text for the body
> - A stupa for the body
> - A prayer wheel for the body
> - A blessed cord for the body
> - Written mantras for the body
> - Medicine Buddha practice, written or recorded
> - The eight prayers to benefit the dead, written or recorded, or the "King of Prayers"
> - Any other practices you would like to do

If your loved one dies suddenly at home or where they can be undisturbed, there are various practices you can do before you call emergency services. Even if they die in a public place, you can still do something before the body is taken away.

After following the instructions in chapter 19 as soon as the breath stops—or when you first discover the body of your loved one—you can do any of the following practices. You may be unable to take all the advice, but simply understand the essential points and do the best you can.

Remember: Be Quiet

Do your best to keep the environment peaceful and quiet. Only the sounds of prayers and mantras should be heard.

TOUCH WITH HOLY OBJECTS

Bless the Body with a Text, Stupa, Prayer Wheel, or Blessed Cord [5–8]; or Written Mantras [58]
As discussed in chapters 13 and 18, put a holy object or written mantras on the body of your loved one. But be very careful not to disturb the body.

PRAY AND MEDITATE

At the Very Least, Recite the Medicine Buddha Names [14], Mantra [22], or Perform the Practice [36]
The main practice to do before, during, and after death is Medicine Buddha—meditating, reciting the names, saying the mantra.

As I mentioned in practice 14, the Medicine Buddha made a promise that all your prayers and wishes will succeed if you chant his name and mantra.

Sponsor Monasteries, Dharma Centers, or Friends to Perform Practices Such as Medicine Buddha [59]
You can make offerings to other people who are not there—monks and nuns in monasteries or Dharma centers, or friends—and request them to perform Medicine Buddha or other practices for your loved one.

Recite the Eight Prayers to Benefit the Dead [64–71]
These prayers are usually recited in the Geluk Tibetan monasteries when someone dies.

Recite the "King of Prayers" [64]
If you can't recite all eight, recite at least the "King of Prayers." In commentaries it is said that this prayer contains "ten numberless times one hundred thousand prayers of the bodhisattvas." It is said to be very, very powerful for purification and collecting extensive merit.

There are many other practices you could do, depending on the time and your preference.

Recite the Names of the Buddhas [14–15]
Recite the Name Mantra of Gurus [18]
Recite Other Mantras [16–31]
Recite Sutras [32–34]
Recite Your Loved One's Daily Practices [47]
Recite Purification Practices [49–54]
Recite the Guru Puja *[72]*

WHEN THE TIME HAS COME TO MOVE THE BODY

Check That the Mind Has Left the Body [74]
Before you move the body, make sure that the mind has left. There are various signs that indicate that the mind is no longer there, described in chapter 25.

Help the Mind Leave the Body: Tug at the Hair at the Crown Chakra [75]
As discussed in chapter 25, if the indication is that the mind has not yet left the body, tug the hair at the crown chakra a few times—toward the back of the head—or firmly tap on the crown there. Anyway, the first time you touch the body it is auspicious to do this.

If the consciousness is still there, doing this can encourage it to go to the crown chakra and leave from there, which means your loved one would go to a pure land, as described in chapter 9.

Consult a Tibetan Astrologer [76]
Once you are confident the mind has left the body, you could consult an astrologer to determine what practices are best to ensure a positive rebirth.

Prepare Your Loved One's Body
Now you can prepare the body for cremation or burial according to the instructions in chapter 26.

LAMA THUBTEN YESHE IN MUSSOORIE, INDIA, IN 1973

*"Lama passed away in March 1984 and remained
in meditation for many days."*

24
If Your Loved One Has High Realizations and Is Meditating at the Time of Death

Don't Disturb the Meditator

As I DISCUSSED in chapter 10, people with high tantric realizations can remain in meditation in the clear light conjoined with emptiness for as long as they wish—one hour, three days, many months. Some meditators stay in the clear-light meditation in their hermitage for years.

If your loved one is in meditation, you must not disturb them.

The face of the meditator is very radiant, peaceful, even blissful; they look magnificent, totally different from an ordinary dying person. Sometimes there even seems to be a light at the tip of their nose. While they're in meditation, even though the breath has stopped, there will be no smell of decay. They smell the same as when they were alive. Or, as I mentioned above, there could even be a sweet smell.

Here the author of *Tibetan Ceremonies of the Dead* advises that for somebody who is in meditation, you should not consult an astrologer about when to move the body until their meditation is over. There's a risk the astrologer might recommend moving the body while the mind is still there.

If Circumstances Demand That You Move the Body

However, if the meditation is not over, but for various reasons, such as the country's laws, you have no choice but to move the body, you need to request the meditator to end their meditation. While you are requesting them, you can offer music with cymbals, bell, *damaru* drum, and so forth, as Song Rinpoche advised me when Lama Yeshe was in meditation. Or you could recite the *Guhyasamaja Root Tantra*. More simply, you could put incense very close to the nose of the meditator. And it's very auspicious to recite prayers that they be reborn in a pure land.

In the case of some holy beings, such as Ling Rinpoche and Lama Yeshe, even though their bodies were moved several times, their meditation did not cease, and they were not disturbed. As I mentioned above, Ling Rinpoche meditated for thirteen days after the breath had stopped.

Lama Yeshe Remained in Meditation for Many Days

As I mentioned in chapter 21, Lama Yeshe passed away at Cedars-Sinai Medical Center in Los Angeles, a wonderful hospital. Before Lama passed away, the nurses were watching intently throughout the night. The moment Lama's heart stopped, people rushed in with a defibrillator and wanted to try to get it started again. It was all very hectic in the room. I had checked with Song Rinpoche, who earlier had come to be with Lama but now was back in Switzerland, and he said to do everything possible to save Lama. The defibrillator is very strong: it pulls the body up violently. Lama opened his eyes for a moment, then his body fell back down. The doctor then said there was no hope. It was about five o'clock in the morning.

This was my first time dealing with someone passing away in the West; I had had no experience. Apparently they usually take the body to the mortuary, where they prepare it. But I didn't think we needed to do that; that's for ordinary people, not for those who are in the meditation state, like Lama.

Anyway, Lama remained in meditation in a private room throughout the day. By the late afternoon, we couldn't stay there any longer, so I asked Song Rinpoche what should be done to release Lama from his meditation. As I mentioned, Rinpoche advised me to play instruments, so I made three prostrations, rang a bell, and requested Lama to stop. I also recited the prayer to be born in a pure land from the Vajrayogini practice, and I touched Lama's crown (practice 75).

Of course, Lama didn't need all this, as he had already achieved the clear light and the illusory body, all the high realizations. Apparently there was a candle, and one of the students present in the room said that he saw a second flame leap up from the flame nearby—I didn't see it.

They put Lama's holy body in a box, packed it in ice, and took it to a mortuary. The box looked very dirty, and the body was covered by what looked to me like an animal skin, like the Tibetan nomads would use. The next day one of the students very slowly drove it the 350 miles north to Lama's center near Boulder Creek, Vajrapani Institute. It was kept in the gompa.

When they were preparing Lama's body for the burning offering puja (see chapter 27), Losang, who had been one of the monks from the first Geluk monastery at Boudhanath Stupa in Nepal and who was familiar with the rituals, reported to Song Rinpoche that even though the body had been lying in the coffin for many days, Lama's limbs were still flexible. It was he who prepared the holy body in the Tibetan way, putting on the self-initiation costume, with the crown, bell, and vajra, and putting the legs and hands in the right position. He explained to Song Rinpoche that it was only when he moved Lama's legs that the white bodhichitta came out.

In other words, it seems that Lama had been in the meditation state for at least five days, even though the body had been moved many times—from the hospital to the mortuary, the long drive from Los Angeles to Boulder Creek, and then preparing it for the burning offering puja. Song Rinpoche was very surprised.

Lama Yeshe Wanted to Stay in Meditation for a Year

Actually, Lama had told some students at Tushita Meditation Centre in Dharamsala, India—he didn't tell me—that after he passed away, he would stay in meditation for one year, and that he wanted the students to come and do Vajrasattva retreat for that year. He had checked in his collection of teachings about what lamas do when they pass away; he checked a lot. He had already planned to do this.

When I asked Song Rinpoche about keeping Lama's body for one year, Rinpoche said that in Tibet only the holy bodies of a few high lamas would be kept like this. If I were to do this, Rinpoche said, people might complain. You see, in the common view, Lama was not known as a great meditator; he did not have that title. Perhaps I was not strong enough in making it clear. So in the end, we did not keep Lama's body for a year and do the retreat.

However, a Vajrasattva retreat was done in many places: Kopan

Monastery, for example, held a retreat, day and night, continuously for one year. Perhaps the Osel Ling center in Spain held a retreat, and other centers as well. I'm sure these retreats created so much benefit, pacifying the karmic obstacles of the students, enabling us to receive a very beneficial incarnation, Lama Tenzin Osel Rinpoche, who was born to Spanish parents in 1984.

When the Meditator's Mind Leaves the Body

The body of a meditator will start to smell when the meditation is finished—in other words, when the mind leaves—just like the bodies of ordinary people. On the other hand, no matter how long the meditator's mind remains in the body—days, months, or even years—there may be no smell at all.

As with ordinary people, the red and white drops coming out of the body is a sign that the meditator's mind has left the body. But both drops don't necessarily come out, such as with Lama himself, as well as in the case of Gen Jampa Wangdu, a friend of Lama's who passed away in Dharamsala shortly after Lama.

Gen Jampa Wangdu was one of my teachers. I had received from him the oral transmission of the practice called *chulen*, or "taking the essence." Yogis in isolated places make pills from the essence of flowers, minerals, and so on, and can live on just these for long periods of time; they don't need any food, which means they have more time for meditation.

Anyway, after bringing Lama's relics to Switzerland for blessing by Song Rinpoche—although, of course, Lama didn't need that—I went to Dharamsala for teachings from His Holiness the Dalai Lama. The day after the teachings had finished, there was a long-life puja for His Holiness, but I couldn't attend because Gen Jampa Wangdu passed away early that morning after being in meditation for three days.

One of the tantric monks and I checked to see if the bodhichitta had come out. It seemed that the white bodhichitta had but not the red. Not only had he had great, great success in achieving the three principal aspects of the path, guru devotion, and so on, but also the six yogas of Naropa and the clear light and the illusory body, and he had experienced the transcendental nondual great bliss-voidness.

Another sign that the mind has left the body of a meditator, whether they're sitting up or lying down, is that the head shifts. Also, the color of their face usually changes, becoming dark, but Gen Jampa Wangdu's face still looked very bright, exactly the same as when he was alive—no change. When his body was taken to the place behind Tushita Retreat Centre to be offered to the fire, one of his disciples was very worried that Geshe-la was still alive. He requested Kirti Tsenshab Rinpoche to come and say prayers and to check. Rinpoche simply looked at Geshe-la's face and could tell immediately that his meditation was over.

Also, it seems that Gen Jampa Wangdu had chosen to pass away on the very day of His Holiness the Dalai Lama's long-life puja so that His Holiness could live a long life. In other words, he sacrificed his own life for His Holiness.

Great Meditators Can Choose Where to Go after Death

Many great practitioners become enlightened in the intermediate state or go to a pure land. Many others reincarnate in human form again in order to help sentient beings, as Lama Yeshe did. For great practitioners such as Lama, they can choose their parents and the environment they will be reborn into, and the child they become is completely different from normal people.

25

Make Sure the Mind Has Left the Body Before You Move It

Check That the Mind Has Left the Body [74]
BEFORE YOU MOVE the body of your loved one it is important to check that the consciousness has already left. There are various signs that indicate that the mind is no longer there. These signs are visible in both ordinary people and meditators.

No Longer Warm at the Heart
The easiest, most common way to check that the mind has left the body is to put your hand just above the heart chakra, without touching the body. If you feel warmth there, even if the rest of the body is cold, your loved one's consciousness is still present.

The White and Red Drops Have Left the Body
As described in the presentation of the death process in chapter 9, the consciousness has left the body when, in the male, the white drop (a whitish liquid) leaves through the lower chakra and the red drop (a pinkish liquid) leaves through the nose; for the female it's the opposite. Both will not necessarily come out of the body; sometimes it may be just one. And sometimes, perhaps because of chronic disease or long-time illness, nothing comes out.

The Body Smells
If the body starts to smell like rotten meat, this is another indication that the consciousness has left. One lama with a lot of experience helping dying people says bodies take on a very particular smell once the consciousness leaves. Sick bodies may smell already, but when the

mind goes, he said, the smell is different: a very terrible smell, very deep somehow. Sometimes people call it the smell of death.

The Flesh Does Not Respond
Another indication that the mind has left the body is if when you press with your fingers on part of the body, the flesh doesn't respond; the impression of your fingers remains.

The Head Moves
For meditators, whether they're sitting up or lying down, another sign is that the head shifts when the consciousness leaves, as I mentioned in chapter 24.

Tug at the Hair at the Crown Chakra [75]
If the indication is that the mind has not yet left the body, tug the hair at the crown chakra a few times—toward the back of the head—or firmly tap on the crown there. Anyway, it is auspicious to do this when you first touch the body.

If the consciousness is still there, doing this can encourage it to go to the crown chakra and leave from there, which means your loved one would go to a pure land, as I discussed in chapter 9.

Rigor Mortis
It is possible that there could be signs of rigor mortis after the breath has stopped but before the mind leaves the body. If so, and after having checked using the above methods, you think the mind is still there, it's recommended to make the *sur* offering (practice 82) near the body, which can help the person come back to life again.

Part Five

Practices to Do after the Mind Has Left the Body

BUDDHA NAMGYALMA

"Whoever is touched by the wind that has blown on Namgyalma mantras written on cloth or paper will be purified of their negative karma."

26

How to Prepare Your Loved One's Body for Cremation or Burial

Sprinkle Blessed Seeds, Water, and So Forth on Your Loved One's Body [77]

GET SOME SESAME or mustard seeds, say, or talcum powder, water, perfume, or something you can easily sprinkle. Now recite the Namgyalma mantra twenty-one times (practice 25)—the long mantra is better, but the short mantra is okay—or any other mantras that you know, such as the Compassion Buddha mantra (practice 21).

Having blessed your breath with the recitation, now blow on the seeds or water or whatever, blessing them. Now sprinkle it over the body.

Usually I keep a big packet of mustard seeds or baby powder close by. Every day, after I have chanted thousands of various mantras, I blow on the powder or seeds to bless them. I use them whenever I see dead insects or animals, or for people who have died. You could also do this. And you could send the blessed seeds to other people, for them to use when people die.

The Namgyalma mantra is especially powerful for purification of negative karma. For example, whoever is touched by the wind that has blown on mantras written on cloth or paper and placed on a mountain top will be purified of their negative karma. Circumambulating a stupa that contains the mantra purifies the karma to be reborn in the hot hells.

Bless Your Loved One's Body with Written Mantras [58]

If you have not already put written mantras on the body of your loved one, it is especially good to do so now.

You could use the eleven mantras that I wrote out, as discussed in chapter 18, or the Namgyalma mantra (practice 25), one of the best to use. You can use the small protection mantra in the Liberation Box. If you like, you could use any of the five great mantras (practice 31) or the ten powerful mantras (practices 21–30).

You can put the sheets of mantras on any part of the body so that the words are touching the skin, or you can rub the body with them.

You can also put rolls of the mantras on the body—on the head, for example. Or you could wrap mantras around the body, the chest, for example, as Kirti Tsenshab Rinpoche explained that they do in Amdo in Tibet; they use Mitrukpa mantras.

You should leave the mantras there when the body is buried or cremated. This helps purify negative karma and cause a good rebirth. You can do this for animals as well.

Retain Ashes, Hair, or Nails to Be Blessed Later
Make sure you keep some hair or nails if the body will be buried, and ashes if it will be cremated, to be blessed later in a jangwa ceremony, practice 78, and included in holy objects, practice 79.

27

The Funeral Service

You could invite a lama, or a monk or nun, to lead the ceremony. Use any of the practices recommended to do during the forty-nine days after the death of your loved one (see chapter 29). Or you could select verses from these various practices.

You could start with a motivation and then talk about impermanence. You could also talk about your loved one's life and rejoice in all their good actions.

Use whatever structure for the ceremony suits your culture, including prayers and teachings.

Offer Lights, Flowers, and So Forth on Behalf of Your Loved One [84]

You could set up an altar with pictures of your loved one's guru and statues of the buddhas, and you could make extensive offerings. Everyone could participate. As I mention in chapter 29, you could use candles, butter lamps, or electric lights. And you could make other offerings, such as water bowls or flowers.

Recite Medicine Buddha's Names [14], Mantra [22], or Practice [36]

As always, the best practice for your loved one and yourself is Medicine Buddha. You could all recite together.

Dedicate with the "King of Prayers" [64]

At the end, everyone can dedicate for your loved one's precious human rebirth or rebirth in Amitabha's pure land by reciting the "King of Prayers," or even just a few verses.

Remember

As I said in chapter 26, if you will have your loved one's body cremated, don't forget to keep some ashes; or some hair or nails if the body will be buried. You can have them blessed with the jangwa practice, as I discuss in the next chapter.

Lama Yeshe's Funeral

This is what I did with all of Lama Yeshe's relics after the burning offering puja at Vajrapani Institute in California. I first took them to Switzerland and asked Song Rinpoche to bless them with jangwa ceremony—although of course, as I mentioned above, owing to his realizations, Lama did not need that.

The relics were divided up and given to the centers around the world. The ashes were offered to the students, and they made *tsa-tsas* with them and put them on their altars (see practice 79). They also received the ashes in little capsules—vitamins to strengthen the weak mind!

The ceremony we had for Lama was a Yamantaka fire offering. Students came from everywhere. Geshe Sopa came from Wisconsin, and Geshe Thinley, one of Lama Yeshe's brothers, came from Australia, where he was resident teacher at Chenrezig Institute.

I had invited Song Rinpoche to come again from Switzerland. Before the burning offering puja, we did many days of practices, including the Heruka Body Mandala self-initiation, Vajrayogini, a *Guru Puja*, and we all offered the Vajrasattva tsok written by Lama (practice 53) with prostrations to the Thirty-Five Buddhas of Confession (practice 49). We did these practices not for Lama's sake but for our own.

Finally, we were ready to offer Lama's holy body to the fire. A special cremation stupa was built according to Song Rinpoche's design. Lama was dressed in the costume of self-initiation, put upright on a chair, tied securely, then carried to the site and placed in the stupa. Rinpoche himself did a lot of work, with his own hands putting in the bricks, putting the firewood around Lama's holy body in the lower part of the stupa, then helping build up the top part and making the holes for offering the ingredients of the burning puja.

Everything went so well, the beginning, middle, and end; so neat and perfect.

28

How to Bless Your Loved One's Ashes and Include Them in Holy Objects

Bless the Ashes, Hair, Nails, and So Forth of Your Loved One with Jangwa [78]

As soon after the funeral service as possible, you should organize a jangwa practice, during which the buddhas' wisdom is invoked into the remains, thus purifying and blessing them. As I mentioned, you need only a small amount of the ashes or bones, hair, nails, or the like.

Keeping the ashes of your loved one that haven't been blessed has no benefit for the dead or the living. Whereas, as Kirti Tsenshab Rinpoche said, now that the ashes are purified and blessed with jangwa, they are actual relics or holy objects.

Even if the person died with nonvirtuous thoughts—which usually means it's definite to be born in the lower realms—and they are in the intermediate state, you can help them change direction and receive a human body instead, or even go to the pure lands, by relying on jangwa. They're on their way to the lower realms, but because of the power of the Vajrayana, the power of the Buddha's words, and the power of the meditation of the lama or the person who does the practice, suddenly the person changes their journey.

Then you can dedicate to your loved one all the merits created by doing the blessing, praying that their negative karma is purified and that they receive a perfect human rebirth or rebirth in a pure land, meet the perfectly qualified virtuous friend, hear the holy Dharma, and quickly achieve full enlightenment.

Who Can Do the Practice?

The practice of jangwa is usually performed by qualified lamas. You can ask the lama at your nearest Tibetan Buddhist center to perform the ceremony, or you can ask monks or nuns to do it. If you cannot get lamas or sangha members to do the practice, you and your Dharma friends can do the practice.

Originally jangwa was done in conjunction with Buddha Kunrik, who, as mentioned in practice 27, is known as the king of deities for purifying the lower realms. Eventually other buddhas were used as well, such as Medicine Buddha, Vajrayogini, and Maitreya. The practice I recommend is in association with the Medicine Buddha.

At the end of jangwa there is phowa, shooting the consciousness into a pure land.

Make Tsa-Tsas, Statues, or Stupas Using the Blessed Ashes [79]

Now you can do even more to benefit your loved one. Having blessed the ashes with jangwa, you can include them in holy objects such as tsa-tsas, statues, or stupas, which brings so much benefit, both to your loved one and to you. As I mention in practice 87, it is said that if a person is destined to be reborn in the lower realms, making a holy object—even simply on their behalf—can change the situation and help them get a good rebirth.

Some people say that you shouldn't put ordinary people's ashes in holy objects, but as I said, by doing the practice of jangwa, the wisdom of the buddhas has been invoked into them, thus purifying and blessing them. This is also stated in *Tibetan Ceremonies of the Dead*.

Including the blessed ashes in tsa-tsas or other holy objects creates inconceivable merit for your loved one and also for you. Typically people offer flowers or lights to a loved one at the cemetery, but this doesn't accumulate any merit; it's not even a virtuous action. But now because you are offering to a holy object, you create huge amounts of merit.

You can decide which buddha to use for the tsa-tsa or statue—Medicine Buddha, Amitabha, or the Compassion Buddha, for example—or you could ask a lama or a Tibetan astrologer which buddha would have the strongest effect in liberating your loved one. Or, as I mentioned, you could make a stupa.

You can make these holy objects yourself, or you can request Dharma centers to make them for you. There are FPMT centers set up for this purpose in Australia, New Zealand, and the United States, where stupas can be made and kept in memorial shrines, where you can visit and make offerings.

Throw Blessed Ashes into the Wind or Water [80]
If you like, you could also throw some of the blessed ashes into the wind from a high mountain or into the sea, a lake, a river, and so on. All the sentient beings touched by the ashes in the air or by the water are purified of their obscurations and negative karma.

BUDDHA MITRUKPA

"The mantra of Buddha Mitrukpa, who is powerful for purifying karmic obscurations, can be used for looking at, reciting, and blessing the body of your loved one."

29

Practices to Do During the Forty-Nine Days after the Mind Has Left the Body

It can take up to forty-nine days after the mind has left the body for your loved one to take a new rebirth. It is traditional to perform prayers, pujas, offerings, and so on during those seven weeks, dedicating the merits to the person who passed away.

As I mentioned in chapter 18, when people who care about a person do practices together, there is much more benefit.

The ideal, of course, would be to do prayers and practices for your loved one throughout the entire seven weeks, day and night. When Lama Pasang passed away at Kopan, Lama Lhundrup had three or four monks at any one time reciting the extensive Medicine Buddha practice, all day every day for the forty-nine days.

Some people do practices once a week for the seven weeks; others every day. Do what you can.

You can request monasteries to do any of these practices for your loved one.

Four Possibilities of What Can Happen after the Mind Leaves the Body

1. The karma that was activated at the time of death was virtuous, and the mind is still in the intermediate state. You can pray that your loved one is born in the pure lands, where they can achieve enlightenment, or receive a perfect human body, where they can meet a perfectly qualified Mahayana guru and the Mahayana teachings and then achieve enlightenment.

2. The karma that was activated at the time of death was virtuous, and the mind has already taken rebirth in the human realm or the pure lands. In this case it's still beneficial to do prayers and practices.

Dedicate all the merit from doing these practices for the person who has passed away.

3. The karma that was activated at the time of death was nonvirtuous and the mind is still in the intermediate state. This means the person will be born in the lower realms. It's possible that prayers and practices can help the mind change direction and instead receive a human body or even be reborn in a pure land, as I mentioned in chapter 9—practices such as jangwa (practice 78), phowa (practice 81, below), and making a stupa on behalf of your loved one (practice 87, below).

4. The karma that was activated at the time of death was nonvirtuous, and the mind has already taken birth in the lower realms. Again, in this case it's even possible to liberate a person from the lower realms, as I discuss in relation to Buddha Kunrik (practice 27) and jangwa (practice 78).

PRAY AND MEDITATE

Recite Medicine Buddha Practice [36]

As I mentioned, the main practice to do before, during, and after death is Medicine Buddha. The benefits are incredible, for your loved one and, of course, for you.

As discussed, it's best if family members and friends do it every day, throughout the entire seven weeks, day and night, with a more elaborate puja and more extensive offerings (see practice 84) at the end of each week. Or you could do the practice once a week for the seven weeks. The last puja should have even more extensive offerings, and you should recite the "King of Prayers" (practice 64) at the end.

Sponsor Monasteries, Dharma Centers, or Friends to Perform Practices Such as Medicine Buddha [59]

You can make offerings to other people who are not there—monks and nuns in monasteries or Dharma centers, or friends—and request them to perform Medicine Buddha or other practices for your loved one.

Recite the Eight Prayers to Benefit the Dead [64–71]

These prayers are usually recited in the Geluk Tibetan monasteries when someone dies.

Recite the "King of Prayers" [64]

If you can't recite all eight, recite at least the "King of Prayers." As I've mentioned, in commentaries it is said that this prayer contains "ten numberless times one hundred thousand prayers of the bodhisattvas." It is said to be very, very powerful for purification and for collecting extensive merit.

Request a Lama to Practice Phowa, or You and Your Dharma Friends Can Perform Lama Yeshe's Amitabha Phowa [81]

If a lama does the practice. If phowa has not been performed already—either by your loved one (practice 48) or by a lama as soon as the breath stopped (practice 62)—it can be performed by a lama now.

As I mentioned in practice 62, when there is a very strong connection between the dying person and their guru, it may be possible for the guru to help their mind move away from negativity and toward virtue—even if the person's mind is in the intermediate state—so that they take a good rebirth, even one in a pure land.

When a high lama transfers somebody's consciousness to a pure land, special signs appear, such as rainbows in the sky or a white light streaming from the person's body.

If you and your friends do the practice. If you cannot request a lama, you and your Dharma friends can do the Amitabha phowa composed by Lama Yeshe.

I once asked Kirti Tsenshab Rinpoche how to make a phowa practice effective. Rinpoche said that during our daily Vajrasattva practice we should visualize sentient beings at our heart on a moon disc and then, when we do the purifying meditation, we can imagine the nectar beams radiating from Vajrasattva and entering the hearts of the sentient beings, purifying them. By doing this we are better able to transfer someone's consciousness to a pure land, Rinpoche said.

Kirti Tsenshab Rinpoche said that the practice becomes more effective, more powerful, when you do Medicine Buddha meditation beforehand. You recite the names of the seven Medicine Buddhas and the mantra—both included in the practice here. Rinpoche himself does it that way. I remember years ago when one of the dogs at Tushita Retreat Centre in Dharamsala died—we had many dogs there—Rinpoche first did the Medicine Buddha practice. During it I recited each of the seven names seven times.

Normally it is necessary to have received an empowerment into this Amitabha phowa practice before practicing it, but if you have faith in the Dharma, you can practice it without the empowerment, especially with the motivation of helping your loved one.

These days there are many people interested in the hospice movement, especially in the West. Practicing phowa is an extraordinary service they can offer others.

Make the Offering of Sur [82]

After they die, all beings except those destined for the formless realm have to go through the intermediate state. Because the body of beings in the intermediate state is subtle, as discussed in chapter 9, their only food is smells—this is all they can consume. Thus they are sometimes called "smell eaters."

It is excellent to make the offering of the smell of food to them with the practice called *sur*. The Tibetan word *sur* refers to the smell of roasted barley flour. Chöden Rinpoche advised that the practice can be done three times each day: in the morning, in the afternoon, and in the evening.

This practice has many benefits. It pacifies obstacles. It's an offering to the Guru, Buddha, Dharma, and Sangha. It's a practice of charity to all beings of the six realms, in particular the intermediate-state beings, those who have passed away from the human and other realms and have not yet been reborn. You finish your karmic debts. It's a method for helping be reborn in the pure lands. It's a cause of success of whatever wishes you have.

By doing it you collect so much merit, purify obstacles, and all your wishes are achieved according to the holy Dharma; you complete the two types of merits and, ultimately, achieve enlightenment.

Ribur Rinpoche tells a story about someone imprisoned in Tibet for many years. They were given very small amounts of food: a dish called *tien momos*, but they didn't receive actual *momo* dumplings, only small pieces of flour in thin soup that was basically water. Because the prisoners were unbelievably hungry, when they went outside their rooms, they would search for bones in the fields, which they would chew. Even this gave them such strength and changed their bodies, Rinpoche said.

They would also poke around with a stick in the feces of the Chinese staff, looking for undigested beans, which they would eat.

The Chinese staff kitchen was nearby, so the starving Tibetan prisoners could smell the frying food. This Tibetan person said that the smell would help so much! It would sustain him. When he was freed, he decided that he would offer *sur* every day to the spirits, the smell eaters, because of his experience of hunger and how the smell of food helped him so much.

Practice Dorje Khadro Burning Offering or Other Fire Puja [83]

The practice of Dorje Khadro has many benefits. It is very powerful for purifying defilements and negative karma, it restores degenerated samaya and vows, and it dispels obstacles.

I received the lineage of this practice from Lama Yeshe at Kopan. It is highly admired and has great blessings as an instruction for success taught by Vajradhara.

OFFER

Offer Lights, Flowers, and So Forth on Behalf of Your Loved One [84]

It's good to make light offerings to the Three Rare Sublime Ones on behalf of the person who has passed away, especially at the end of each of the seven weeks; you could use candles, butter lamps, or electric lights. And you could make other offerings, such as water bowls or flowers.

It is very common for the Tibetans to offer hundreds, even thousands, of light offerings; for them this is a very important practice. They make offerings at home, where the person is, but they also go to the monasteries, where there are many precious holy objects.

They do this not only when a family member passes away but generally to collect merit. Sometimes if they cannot offer individual butter lamps, they bring a pot of liquefied butter and carry it around to all the butter lamps and add a little to each. In this way the lights are offered continuously, in every temple, in every shrine room. This collects so much merit.

In Tibet they go to the most precious historical statue of Shakyamuni Buddha in Lhasa, which was made during the Buddha's time. Every day there are people lined up there to make offerings or prayers. In India they go to the Great Stupa in Bodhgaya and make hundreds of thousands of butter lamp offerings. They go to wherever there are holy objects.

Offer Money on Behalf of Your Loved One [85]

Offering money to organizations that help, such as charities, collects inconceivable merit, which you can dedicate for your loved one. As well as making these offerings during the forty-nine days, you could also do so on the holy days in the Tibetan lunar calendar, such as the Buddha days when the merit is multiplied a hundred million times.

If, say, you offered one dollar, you would collect the merit of having offered one hundred million dollars. If you offer one cup of tea to a monk or nun in a monastery, it's as if you have offered one hundred million cups of tea.

Years ago I started putting aside money to fund pujas and the construction of stupas and prayer wheels. We now have the FPMT Puja Fund, the main purpose of which is to collect merit by making offerings to monasteries such as the three main Geluk monasteries in south India, Sera, Ganden, and Drepung, which altogether have six colleges. In particular, we offer tea and breakfast, as well as some rupees, to each one of the thousands of monks during pujas.

You could make offerings to:

- The FPMT Puja Fund
- Your loved one's gurus or your own guru
- The ordained sangha
- Students who have the same guru as the person who died
- A Dharma center—a place, in other words, where people can meditate on the path, learn Dharma, and purify their minds and collect merit
- The sick, the poor, or the homeless
- Places that take care of animals
- The activities in practice 86

Sponsor Dharma Activities with Your Loved One's Money [86]
There are many ways you can use your loved one's money to help them. For example:
- You could sponsor someone to do a retreat—a monk or nun or a layperson—who can't afford it themselves. You would request them to dedicate all the merits to the person who passed away, the sponsor.
- Use the money to make a contribution to a Dharma center, or in any of the ways suggested in practice 85.
- Publish or sponsor the publishing of Dharma books.

Make Holy Objects on Behalf of Your Loved One [87]
You could make, or have made, holy objects and dedicate them for your loved one. It is said that if a person is destined to be reborn in the lower realms, doing this can change the situation and help them get a good rebirth.

If you decide to make tsa-tsas, you yourself can choose which deity to make unless you have particular advice from a Tibetan astrologer or a lama. It's common to make Mitrukpa tsa-tsas, which is very powerful for purifying negative karma. Or you could choose Medicine Buddha, the Compassion Buddha, the Thirty-Five Buddhas—whichever buddha you like. You could make as many as you like—the more the better.

If you choose to make a stupa, as you insert the four dharmakaya relic mantras—Ornament of Enlightenment, Secret Relic, Beam of Completely Pure Stainless Light, and Stainless Pinnacle—you should say the name of your loved one and dedicate for their future rebirth. As I mentioned in practice 6, it's the presence of these mantras that give the stupa power.

You could also have statues made or thangkas painted.

There are many other practices you could do, depending on the time and your preference.

Recite the Heart Sutra *[33] or the* Vajra Cutter Sutra *[34]*
Meditate on Tonglen, Giving and Taking [38]
Recite Your Loved One's Daily Practices [47]
Purify with an Offering of Tsok to Vajrasattva by Lama Yeshe [53]
Recite the Self-Initiation of Your Loved One's Main Deity [54]
Recite the Guru Puja *[72]*

Do a Nyungné Fasting Retreat [73]
It is excellent to spend some time during the forty-nine days in a retreat dedicated to the person who has passed away, such as a nyungné retreat.

As I mentioned in chapter 20, you'd either visualize yourself as the Compassion Buddha or see him in front, and then as you recite the mantra, the long one or short one (practice 21), you would imagine strong beams of nectar flowing from the Compassion Buddha's heart, purifying your loved one and all sentient beings.

You could recite one hundred thousand mantras, or as many as you like.

Alternatively, you could do a retreat related to the person's main deity, Vajrasattva, Medicine Buddha, or any other retreat you like.

Part Six

The Practices in Numerical Order

BUDDHA SAMAYAVAJRA

"Because of their compassion all our gurus have manifested as Buddha Samayavajra so that we can purify our broken commitments."

SHOW STATUES OR PICTURES OF GURUS, BUDDHAS [1]

See chapters 13 and 18.
See also other practices related to the guru: 10, 18, 35, 43, 47, 60, 72, and 85.

Make sure the various images of your loved one's guru, the buddhas, and so on are close to their bed where they can see them easily—the picture of the guru should show them with a very happy, joyful, blissful expression. Merely looking at this photo helps your loved one purify negative karma and sows the seeds of enlightenment.

You can make something like I made for a dying person (see page 62). I framed various pictures: the person's root guru, Amitabha, the Compassion Buddha, Medicine Buddha, Mitrukpa, and so on, as well as the mantras. It should be put where your loved one can see it.

It's also good to write a message, some Dharma advice, and have that put in the frame as well. Seeing that, too, purifies their mind and helps them collect skies of merit.

SHOW THE MITRUKPA MANTRA [2]

See chapters 13 and 18.
See also practice 24.

The mantra of Mitrukpa (Sanskrit: Akshobhya) can be put next to the dying person's pillow or where they can see it easily. It doesn't matter whether they're Buddhist or non-Buddhist: as I mentioned, receiving benefit doesn't depend upon faith.

According to *Giving Breath to the Wretched* by Kusali Dharmavajra, simply seeing this mantra, one of the ten powerful mantras and the five great mantras (see practices 21–31), purifies even the heaviest of the very heavy negative karmas—avoiding the holy Dharma, which is heavier than destroying all the monasteries, all the statues, stupas, scriptures, every single holy object that exists in this world. Also purified is the negative karma of having taken things from the Sangha without permission or having deprived them of receiving things. If it can purify karmas like that, then no question it can for all other negative karmas.

NAMO RATNA TRAYAYA / OM KAMKANI KAMKANI / ROCHANI ROCHANI / TROTANI TROTANI / TRASANI TRASANI / PRATIHANA PRATIHANA / SARVA KARMA PARAM PARA NI ME SARVA SATTVA NANCHA SVAHA

SHOW THE NAME MANTRA OF THE BUDDHA WHO PROTECTS FROM THE LOWER REALMS [3]

See chapters 13 and 18.

Have your loved one look at this mantra quite often: have it close by. It's the name mantra of Buddha Rinchen Tsuktorchen (Sanskrit: Ratna Shikhin), the buddha who protects from the lower realms.

For the pronunciation and meaning of this mantra, see practice 19.

བཅོམ་ལྡན་འདས། དེ་བཞིན་གཤེགས་པ། དགྲ་བཅོམ་པ། ཡང་དག་པར་རྫོགས་པའི་སངས་རྒྱས་རིན་ཆེན་གཙུག་ཏོར་ཅན་ལ་ཕྱག་འཚལ་ལོ།།

SHOW THE MANTRA "JUST BY SEEING" [4]

See chapters 13 and 18.

This mantra is so powerful that just seeing it purifies a hundred thousand eons of negative karma and causes you to become enlightened.

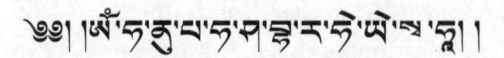

ཨོཾ་ཧ་ནུ་པ་ཧ་ཤ་བྷ་ར་ཧེ་ཡེ་སྭཱ་ཧཱ།

OM HANU PAHASHA BHARA HE YE SVAHA

BLESS THE BODY WITH A TEXT [5]

See chapters 13, 18, 20, 21, 22, and 23.

Chöden Rinpoche advises that it is good to put a text near the head of the dying person—you could put it on their pillow—first touching the crown with it. Use either of the below texts, or any text you like.

By Wearing, Liberates

There is a very powerful text, the benefits of which are unbelievable, called *By Wearing, Liberates* (*Takdröl*, or *Shertor* "peaceful and wrathful"). I have made a very small version of it—there is good technology these days—so it's easy to carry with me wherever I go and to put on the heads of people or animals when they die. Again, whether your loved one is a believer or nonbeliever, the benefits are the same. There is a copy of it in the Liberation Box, a collection of things to facilitate a good rebirth.

The Lamrim Chenmo

Chöden Rinpoche advises using Lama Tsongkhapa's *Great Treatise on the Stages of the Path*, the *Lamrim Chenmo*. Rinpoche explains that this text is the essence of Manjushri's wisdom, that Manjushri's knowledge manifests in the form of letters. The 84,000 teachings of Buddha are included in it: the Lesser Vehicle teachings, the Mahayana Perfection Vehicle teachings, the Mahayana Tantra Vehicle teachings—all are embodied in this text.

Rinpoche says that if you have *Lamrim Chenmo* near your loved one when they are dying, there's no need to perform phowa.

A Liberation Box Is Available From
Website fpmt.org/death/
Email shopfpmt@fpmt.org

BLESS THE BODY WITH A STUPA [6]

See chapters 13, 18, 20, 21, 22, and 23.
See also practices 37 and 87.

You can use a stupa to bless a dying person, in particular a stupa that contains the four dharmakaya relic mantras: Ornament of Enlightenment, Secret Relic, Beam of Completely Pure Stainless Light, and Stainless Pinnacle. These mantras—which are usually written in gold on the "life tree," the wooden central pole inside the stupa—are what make the stupa powerful.

From time to time, place the stupa on your loved one's chest or let them hold it. Every time the stupa touches them, their negative karma is purified.

This is also good to do with babies or with people who don't understand. To a non-Buddhist you can say that the stupa is for peace or healing or purification.

There is a stupa in the Liberation Box.

A Liberation Box Is Available From
Website fpmt.org/death/
Email shopfpmt@fpmt.org

BLESS THE BODY WITH OR TURN A PRAYER WHEEL [7]

See chapters 13, 18, 20, 21, 22, and 23.

Having a prayer wheel near your loved one is a powerful way of ensuring a good death and a better rebirth. Touching a prayer wheel purifies negative karma and obscurations, so encourage your loved one to turn it, or touch them with it.

In fact, if there is a prayer wheel in the room, you don't need to do phowa: at the time of death, the person's simply thinking of a prayer wheel helps shoot their consciousness through the central channel and out the crown to reincarnate in the pure land of Amitabha.

BLESS THE BODY WITH A BLESSED CORD [8]

See chapters 13, 18, 20, 21, 22, and 23.

A blessed cord (usually a piece of thin red dressmaker's cord) has been blessed with many thousands of mantras such as the Compassion Buddha, or Namgyalma (Sanskrit: Ushnishavijaya), or one of the other five great mantras (practices 21, 25, and 31). Tie it around the neck of your loved one or around their wrist or upper arm.

Don't see these cords as merely a custom, or as something to be put on the altar or put away somewhere in a container. They should be worn: the idea is for them to touch the body. The mantras used for the blessing have so many benefits and can purify so much negative karma.

You can carry blessed cords with you, and when a person or animal dies, you can put one on the body. Even if they died a long time ago, and no matter where their consciousness is now, this can still help purify their negative karma; the blessings will still have an effect.

There is a blessed cord in the Liberation Box.

A Liberation Box Is Available From
Website fpmt.org/death/
Email shopfpmt@fpmt.org

MAKE SURE YOUR LOVED ONE HAS GIVEN AWAY THEIR POSSESSIONS [9]

See chapter 14.
See also chapter 5.

Before the person who is dying is unable to speak, make sure that they have made a will or remind them to make one.

You don't need to wait until just before they die to do this, and often people in the West do this earlier anyway. The point here is to understand how it helps your loved one psychologically to have decided whom they want to dedicate their possessions to. Because then, at the time of death, there is nothing to cling to, and they won't die with attachment—they've already dedicated their possessions to the Guru, Dharma, or Sangha, or to sentient beings, or to projects that will benefit sentient beings.

TALK ABOUT YOUR LOVED ONE'S GURU, OR BUDDHA, OR GOD [10]

See chapters 14 and 18.
See also other practices related to the guru: 1, 18, 35, 43, 47, 60, 72, and 85.

The role of the guru in our life is vital, and certainly at the time of death. If your loved one has received teachings from a lama during their lifetime and if they feel strong devotion, it is important to remind them of their guru now. This helps them to let go of attachment, to remember the teachings, especially bodhichitta; and then at the time of death it's easy to remain virtuous. Also, talking to them about their guru can reconnect them with their personal deity (see practice 47).

Even if your loved one doesn't have a strong practice, merely hearing the name of their guru is considered a very effective kind of transference of consciousness.

If they don't have a guru but have faith in Buddha, talk about the qualities of any of the enlightened beings: Shakyamuni Buddha, Compassion Buddha, Amitabha, or whomever they feel close to.

If your loved one has another religion, not Buddhism, an important way to help them generate virtuous thoughts is to talk about God. Describe God as totally pure, having perfect wisdom or omniscience, loving kindness, and compassion for them and all living beings, and the power to help liberate them and others from suffering and lead them to temporary and ultimate happiness. This becomes an excellent refuge for the dying person.

You are describing the meaning of a buddha, actually—infinite wisdom, compassion, and power—but you're not using the Sanskrit word. You could mention just one quality and then let the person think about that, or you could mention all three qualities.

Explain that the nature of their own mind, their heart, is completely pure; that God has compassion for everyone, including them. Help them think that their loving heart is oneness with God, that the kingdom of God is within. This frees them from guilt and anger, allowing them to die with faith and a peaceful mind.

TALK ABOUT AMITABHA'S PURE LAND, OR HEAVEN [11]

See chapters 14 and 18.
See also chapter 6 and other practices related to Amitabha: 20, 64, 66, and 81.

Talk about the pure lands of the buddhas, such as Amitabha's pure land. You can read aloud *Benefits of the Blissful Realm* by Lama Tsongkhapa, which starts on the next page. As I said in chapter 6, for ordinary people, those who have delusions and for whom it is difficult to take rebirth in most pure lands, it is easy to be born in Amitabha's pure land.

Saying the name of the pure land is important. It's like a rope that the person can hold on to while they're climbing a mountain that pulls them up when they're in danger of falling: it saves them. It's a method to help their consciousness let go of this world: their body, their family, their possessions; to not be attached.

Tell your loved one how beautiful it is there—as described in Lama Tsongkhapa's words just below. Tell them how whatever they're attached to is better there, that there are better enjoyments there. Tell them that there are many wonderful friends in Amitabha's pure land, or someone in particular who loves them. This means you need to know what they normally enjoy—like the monk who was told that the butter tea was better in Tushita (see page 24). Wishing to be there causes them to be reborn there; it directs their consciousness to it. Amitabha Buddha becomes their main refuge.

You could also read Lama Tsongkhapa's prayer to be reborn in Amitabha's pure land (practice 66).

For somebody who doesn't understand "pure land," saying "heaven" makes it easier; that's a very common word. "Heaven" has the meaning of eternal; something very beautiful, with great enjoyments. Hearing about it makes it easier for the person's consciousness to leave, for them to die easily, without mental suffering. Knowing that there's some place that's better makes it very easy for them to let go of attachment for this world. This is very skillful psychology.

BENEFITS OF THE BLISSFUL REALM
BY LAMA TSONGKHAPA

Nama Shri Guru Manjughoshaya.

> I prostrate to Amitabha, leader of humans and gods.
> Through compassion you always see each migrator as your own child.
> Remembering you just once leaves fear of the Lord of Death far behind.
> May your eminent activities for migrators be glorious and without end.
>
> The Buddha praised the supreme buddhafield
> many times in an excellent manner.
> Moved by compassion, various prayers were composed
> mentioning the potential to be born in Sukhavati.

Many stainless scriptures explain that the lords of the victorious ones manifested pure lands from their completely established emanation bodies. These buddhafields came about in accordance with the exalted minds generated and prayers made at the time [the buddhas] were still bodhisattvas, practicing the vast deeds of bodhisattvas.

Due to the Buddha, who taught extensively about the qualities of the pure land of Sukhavati, and to the ones gone to bliss who often praised their own individual, immeasurable pure lands, it is said that immeasurable bodhisattvas take rebirth in Sukhavati. It is also said that one should make strong aspirations that persons of the present and future times can go to this pure land. Various chapters in sutras and dharani texts, while explaining the benefits, mention instructions for different methods to be reborn in Sukhavati.

It is not impossible for persons of the present time to take rebirth in this pure land. Some say that the saturation of the five degenerations has rapidly decreased the number of beings born in this pure land. Others say that [pure lands] are only filled with those who are in the retinue of bodhisattvas and that it is difficult to be reborn there because the enormous wealth of those beings and their environment [that is, it requires great merit].

Those who are born in Sukhavati have definitely accumulated some pure [merit]. In short, the greater the aspiration for a particular pure land is, the quicker one will be reborn in that pure land, and [in general], people are more inclined to being born in Sukhavati. When reciting prayers to be reborn in the pure lands of the buddhas, one should mainly focus on rebirth in Sukhavati.

[The Causes for Rebirth in Sukhavati]
Which causes should one create so as to be reborn in this pure land? It is said in the *Display of the Pure Land of Sukhavati Sutra*:

> Ananda, one should look at the sugata [Amitabha], take that buddha to heart again and again, create immeasurable amounts of virtue, generate bodhichitta, and with prayers dedicate this all completely to be reborn in that world.
>
> Then, at the time when death comes close, one will, in front of oneself, face the One Gone to Bliss, the Foe Destroyer, the Completely Fully Enlightened One Amitabha surrounded by a great assembly of fully ordained sangha. Seeing the Bhagavan Amitabha, one's mind will become clear, and when one's consciousness leaves [the body], one will take birth in the world of Sukhavati.
>
> Ananda, any son or daughter of the lineage should, during their life, perfectly generate the intention to be reborn in this buddhafield. They should generate the mind of the unsurpassed, complete enlightenment for this purpose while thinking how wonderful it will be if they could see Amitabha. They should dedicate their roots of virtue for this purpose.
>
> Ananda, they should take the sugata to mind again and again, generate immeasurable amounts of roots of virtue in their mental continuum, and perfectly direct their mind to be reborn in this buddhafield. When they are close to death they come into the presence of the One Gone to Bliss, the Foe Destroyer, the Completely Fully Enlightened One Amitabha

and see his color, shape, complexion, and his retinue of fully ordained sangha, being emanations of the Buddha. By seeing the sugata they will have stable, serene faith, have the mindfulness of never forgetting [Amitabha], and when they die they will be reborn in his buddhafield.

The first section of this sutra mentions four points that cause one to be reborn in the pure land [of Amitabha]:

1. Remembering the victorious one Amitabha again and again
2. Accumulating immeasurable amounts of roots of virtue
3. Generating the mind of enlightenment
4. Reciting prayers dedicating the accumulated virtue toward rebirth in this pure land

Although one can find persons of both Hinayana and Mahayana vehicles in this pure land, this first section [of this sutra] is related to those who have generated the lineage of the Mahayana. The last section is common [to both vehicles].

The third section explains—as mentioned before—that one should perfectly generate the intention to be reborn in the pure land. This means that one should, after reflecting on the pure land's qualities again and again, generate, from the depth of one's heart, the wish to be reborn there.

The middle section mentions that the cause to be reborn in this pure land when passing away is the generation of the wish to see Amitabha in this life. Having generated the mind of enlightenment and continuously accumulated various amounts of root virtues, take the victorious one Amitabha to mind again and again and pray from the depth of your heart that you may be reborn in the Mahayana lineage only, within the pure land of Sukhavati.

This is just a small explanation. An important point is to recollect the array of qualities of the beings in and the environment of this pure land as has been described in the sutras. In particular, when one initially makes prayers, one should remember the qualities of this pure land. While focusing on the victorious Amitabha together with his retinue, generate serene, stable faith and have a strong aspiration to be reborn there by reflecting on the marvelous array of qualities of this pure land.

[11] TALK ABOUT AMITABHA'S PURE LAND, OR HEAVEN 177

The final important point is the need to generate a strong intention that thinks, "How wonderful it will be if I can witness the object of my prayers easily, without obstacles." The main cause for rebirth in this pure land is a strong aspiration to be reborn in Sukhavati, which combines the wish to witness [this pure land] with the expressing of the qualities of this pure land.

It is important to praise this pure land at the outset because everything that is said [above] depends on a mind that knows the qualities of this pure land.

The Qualities of the Trees Beautifully Adorning the Fields

> On the western side of this world system
> are hundreds of thousands of buddhas,
> each with their own pure land.
> All are surpassed by marvelous Sukhavati.
> The grounds are adorned with precious jewels,
> smooth as the palm of one's hand and pleasant to the touch.
> All mountains and hills, made of precious jewels,
> are beautiful, clean, and free of dark colors,
> resplendent, pleasant, pure, and surrounded by a garland
> of celestial trees made of seven precious jewels
> and of precious palm trees,
> like the moon surrounded by a constellation of stars.

In this way the grounds are beautified with various celestial trees. Each of these trees has seven roots, seven trunks, seven branches, seven leaves, seven petals, seven flowers, and seven fruits. Some say that [the tree has] golden roots, silver trunks, lapis lazuli branches, crystal leaves, cat-eye stone petals, red pearl flowers, and diamond fruits. Some say that the seven parts [of the trees], like the roots and so forth, are each made of one of the seven precious jewels. Some say that each [of the seven parts of the tree] are made of two, three, four, five, or six different precious jewels, or each of the parts, like the roots and so forth, are made of the seven precious jewels.

These kinds of celestial trees have crown ornaments, earrings, necklaces, bracelets, armlets, rings, golden belts, golden dresses, dresses made out of pearl, and an arrangement of bells made out of precious jewels. In this way the buddhafield is totally filled with an embellishment of hundreds of thousands of precious jewels, as many as one would wish for.

In the morning a breeze from the four directions brings a variety of magnificently scented divine incense, redolent everywhere. This pleasant, fragrant breeze moves the colorful celestial trees, and by looking at [the trees] one sees a variety of beautiful flowers fall on the ground of precious jewels. These flowers pervade this buddhafield, [spreading around each tree for] seven human measures. These flowers are soft like *kantsalitha* silk cloth and generate bliss when touched. One's feet will sink in the flowers for about four fingers' width [when standing on them], and by raising one's feet [the flowers] will come up [again].

Directly after the morning passes, all of the old flowers disappear, and the ground of the buddhafield becomes a solitary, delightful, and pure place. Again, like before, a breeze arises from the four directions, spreading new and pure flowers. This process of [old flowers disappearing and the arising of fresh flowers] in the morning also happens in the afternoon, at twilight, at night, and at dawn.

The celestial trees, made of the seven precious jewels—gold, silver, lapis lazuli, crystal, cat-eye stone, red pearl, and diamond—have immeasurable attractive, beautiful ornaments hanging from them; they possess everything one wishes for.

The roots, trunks, and branches of the trees are smooth and soft, generate bliss upon touching, and possess a pleasant fragrance. One can never tire of hearing the explanations of the pleasant [qualities] of the fragrance circulating.

The Qualities of the Streams Beautifully Adorning the Fields

Further, different valleys in the fields are beautified with fragrant waters, measuring depths of around twelve leagues and widths of one, ten, twenty, thirty, forty, fifty, or even a hundred thousand leagues. Entering [these waters] is easy. [The banks], free of mud, are spread with golden sand and covered with aromatic flowers of the gods, like utpala flowers, red and white lotuses, and water lilies. When one moves the water, various birds, like swans, cranes, geese, ducks, parrots, egrets, cuckoos, kunalas, white garudas, and peacocks, fly up and make pleasant sounds. The two embankments [on both sides] of these waters are filled with precious celestial incense trees. These [fields], possessing sonorous water streams with lovely mangosteen trees, agarwood trees, incense, and the best of sandalwood trees, are the foundation for pure sentient beings' spiritual life.

The Qualities of the Lotuses Beautifully Adorning the Fields

Further, these fields are blanketed with a golden maze of lotus flowers resembling the seven precious jewels. Some lotuses are one, two, three, four, five, or even ten leagues tall. Each of these precious jewel-like lotuses emanates 360,000 million rays of light. At the end of all these light rays are 360,000 million bodies of buddhas, gold in color, possessing the thirty-two signs of a great being, going to countless, immeasurable world systems teaching the Dharma to sentient beings.

> Through the power of the highest prayers,
> precious jewel-like lotuses emanating light rays arise,
> at the ends of which are emanation bodies
> satisfying the [swarming] bees of trainees
> with the festival of the honey-like noble Dharma.

The Qualities of the Mansions and Enjoyments Beautifully Adorning the Fields

Further, these fields are beautified with wonderful mansions. There are numerous hundred-thousand-story celestial mansions made of various precious jewels, adorned with precious thrones with colorful divine cushions and spread with calicos. The fields are also totally filled with everything one wishes for: incense, garlands, ointments, [fragrant] powders, parasols, victory banners, pennants, musical instruments, and cloths of a hundred thousand colors.

In a similar way, nicely scented incense appears everywhere, and from time to time there arise clouds of the incense of the gods, bringing scented rains. Likewise, divine flowers, the seven precious jewels, sandalwood powders, parasols, victory banners, and pennants fall like rain. Divine canopies, parasols [made] of the seven precious jewels, roofs of the mansions of the gods, and celestial fans fill the skies.

Instruments of the gods make melodious sounds
while daughters of the gods perform a play of dances.
It completely has all the enjoyments one wishes for,
marvelous treasures pervading the earth and sky.
Without decline, everything is filled,
like an ocean of treasures blanketing the golden ground.

This concludes a concise explanation of how to take the qualities of the environment of Sukhavati to mind.

The Common Qualities of the Residents Beautifully Adorning the Fields

Further, without differentiating among the beings of the three lower states of rebirth and demigods, whoever gets reborn in this [pure land] will never fall back into those four types of rebirth. One will also not have the other [four] non-leisures. Sentient beings [born in this pure land] will not be indefinite in nor be able to lose [the Mahayana lineage]. This is reality and definite by itself.

One will only be reborn by the power of prayer and not by the power of karma and afflictions. Sentient beings in this [pure land] are only born miraculously from a precious lotus and belong to the rebirths of humans and gods. This is only a mere conventional expression of "humans and gods" because the enjoyments are miraculously made manifest, like those in the god realms. All the bodies of the beings are adorned with the thirty-two signs.

[When born in this pure land], one will obtain all five types of clairvoyance. One will have the miraculous clairvoyance, knowing a multitude of more than hundreds of thousands of buddhafields in one single moment of mind. One will have clairvoyance of previous lives, remembering a multitude of hundreds of thousands of eons of previous births. One will have the clairvoyance of the divine eye, seeing a multitude of hundreds of thousands of world systems. One will have divine ear, hearing the Dharma of a multitude of hundreds of thousands of buddhafields in one moment. One will have the clairvoyance of others' thoughts, knowing the minds of sentient beings in the multitude of hundreds of thousands of buddhafields.

In the morning one can visit other buddhafields, and one has the opportunity to offer respect and make offerings of all the offering substances [available in those pure lands], created by the power of the buddhas, to a multitude of many hundreds of thousands of buddhas. This is not possible for sentient beings who have doubt [about the rebirth in this pure land]. Those beings, because of such doubt, are not able to go to other pure lands and offer to the ones gone to bliss, they don't have clairvoyance, and owing to the power of their karma, they have to stay for a long time in the lotus [in which they are born].

The sentient beings [in this pure land] don't take coarse food, like that made of the elements; whatever the beings wish for [appears] and can be taken. As has been explained before, the different cloths and ornaments can be found by the mere wish, and wearing them gives satisfaction.

Being adorned with cloths and ornaments, one enjoys a multitude of hundreds of thousands of pleasant melodies of divine songs, beyond satisfaction, coming from the musical instruments of expert musicians who have arisen out of great streams. An assembly of emanations in the form of birds [arisen from these waters] spread similar sounds in the directions of this buddhafield. These [sounds, which are sounds of the Dharma,] cause the bodhisattvas to always remember and never be separated from the buddhas.

As explained before, sentient beings are pleased with meeting everything they wish for, and when in front of celestial mansions, retinues of seven thousand sons and daughters of the gods show them a divine play that pleases beings.

Initially, the qualities of the residents in these pure lands are expressed so as to generate strong aspiration for rebirth in these [lands] and so that the different prayers for rebirth in these places can come [to fruition].

> The pure sentient beings [in this land] are emanated from good karma.
> Their bodies are extremely beautiful, adorned with the [thirty-two] signs.
> They have perfectly generated various qualities in their mindstreams
> and are always taken care of by the enjoyment of the Dharma.

Their magical [bodies] travel as fast as lightning without
   obstruction,
they can travel to many buddhafields, and they have
the five [wisdom] eyes of the victorious ones.
Moreover, having generated the boundless two accumulations,
they perform the play of happiness and bliss in the pure lands.

The Qualities of the Retinues
The victorious ones in this buddhafield have a retinue of shravakas and bodhisattvas. There are three different assemblies of shravakas. The qualities of the first retinue of the shravakas [is as follows]: While a child of the gods can calculate all the stars of a billionfold world systems in a day and a night, the immeasurable magical emanations of [such a shravaka] like Maudgalyayana cannot even be counted in a multitude of hundreds of thousands of years. If counted, only a mere portion can be determined; [one can] never arrive at the fixed number. If this is true for the first assembly, how can the second and third assembly be counted? In this way the retinues of the shravakas are uncountable. Each emanation possesses an aura of light the width of one arm span.

The retinues of the bodhisattvas are immeasurable, and their qualities are boundless and limitless. They have equanimity, a wish to benefit, and loving kindness toward all sentient beings. They have a mind like Mount Meru and wisdom as vast as an ocean, thoroughly engaged in the nature of the illusion of consciousness itself. They have an accumulation of various qualities and a direct exalted wisdom of the noble ones that is like Mount Meru. [Their consciousness] being unmistaken, they are like great oceans. They are like [stable] grounds, having patience with the virtue and nonvirtue of sentient beings.

Washing away the stains of the afflictions, they are like waterfalls.

They are like kings of fire, burning away all afflictions and conceited minds toward all phenomena. Not attached to the worldly, they are like wind. They are like the sky, free of concepts and penetrating all phenomena thoroughly. Without being polluted with the faults of the world, they are like lotuses. By clearly proclaiming [the distinction between] Dharma and not Dharma at particular times, they are like great thunder dragons. They are like large clouds directly letting the

[11] TALK ABOUT AMITABHA'S PURE LAND, OR HEAVEN

rain of Dharma fall. They are like chief leaders of humans, surpassing great difficulties.

They are like elephants, supremely subdued, and like precious horses, having an utmost subdued mind. They are like forceful, powerful, and fearless lions, kings of animals, and like trees they give complete refuge to all sentient beings. They are like Mount Meru, immovable, not moved by the wrong arguments of others. Like the sky they meditate on immeasurable loving kindness, and like the great Brahma they have accumulated all virtue. Giving up the accumulation of abodes they are like birds, and having conquered all wrong arguments they are like eagles, the king of birds. Because they are a rare occurrence, they are like the udumbara flower. They beat Dharma drums, blow Dharma conches, lift up victorious banners of the Dharma, hold Dharma pendants, and light great Dharma lamps. They cause delight in the minds of a multitude of many hundreds of thousands of buddhas and are praised by all the victorious ones. With great effort in faultless morality they have pure minds, being like lapis lazuli, and, like oceans, they have heard all the Dharma. Each bodhisattva possesses a radiance of a multitude of a hundred thousand leagues. The two chief disciples, the great beings, great bodhisattvas Avalokiteshvara and Vajrapani, have a radiance pervading whole world systems.

> You are like exalted wisdom oceans, oceans for sentient beings.
> Having the armor of an ocean, like courage lacking cowardice,
> you generated bodhichitta in the presence of an ocean of victorious ones
> then searched for an ocean of learning without contentment,
> and having examined the complete Dharma, you became excellent scholars.
> You realized the essence of the instructions of the supramundane,
> fearlessly practiced the Dharma instructions,
> and through effort you always liberate sentient beings.
> With your principal guide, Amitabha,
> you entered the lineage of the Supreme Sage.

You are great heroes, renowned successors of the victorious
   one,
bodhisattvas of the pure lands.

The Main Qualities of the Pure Land

The supreme pure land has marvelous qualities of beings and their environment. In its center is a tree of enlightenment, a large bodhi tree, 1,600 leagues tall. Its branches, leaves, and petals spread out for 800 leagues, and the circumference at the root is 500 leagues. Its leaves, flowers, and fruits spread out throughout, and the tree has a variety of a hundred thousand different colors with diverse leaves, flowers, and fruits.

It has a clear moon-like appearance of precious jewels. It is adorned with precious jewels like those held by Indra. Golden strings, beautiful ornaments made of pearls, bouquets of precious jewels, separate necklaces, ornament garlands of blue and red pearl, and ribbons hang from the mouths of [decorative] lions. All the precious jewels are decorated with a network of small bells and canopies, perfectly adorned with sea-monster heads, crescent-shaped auspicious signs, and coiling swastikas. In brief, it is adorned with the objects desired by sentient beings.

When this tree of enlightenment is moved by the wind, a melodious sound arises that can be heard in infinite world systems. If one hears this sound, sees [the form], inhales its fragrance, tastes its fruits, or is touched by its lights, one will never have an illness of the ear, eye, nose, tongue, or body until enlightenment is achieved. If one takes the tree to mind, then until enlightenment is achieved, one's mind will never get distracted. Bhagavan Amitabha, the one gone to bliss, the foe destroyer, the complete fully enlightened being, the pure one free from passion, is sitting in front of this tree, teaching the Dharma amid an ocean-like retinue, which fosters and respects him. He is called Victorious One of Boundless Life (Amitayus) because his life cannot be measured, and he can remain from hundreds of eons up to a multitude of hundreds of thousands of eons.

Amitabha is also called the Victorious One of Boundless Light (Amitabha) because his radiance pervades a multitude of hundreds of thousands of buddhafields in the ten directions, equaling the particles of sand of the river Ganges, and therefore his light rays cannot be measured. This is true, but depending on the need of sentient beings, he can also show the aspect of having light rays the length of an arm span.

The light rays are like stainless crystal, as vast as the sky, and they generate bliss in the body and happiness in the mind, supreme happiness in the mind, of whichever sentient being is touched by them. The play of this limitless collection of light is like a golden mountain surrounded [by this brightness].

The glorious body of the great sage Amitabha is completely surrounded in a similar way. He surpasses the complete assembly of bodhisattvas and shravakas in his retinue. He is beyond samsara, luminous and clear, like a jewel, shining bright in all directions; he is similar to the victorious Mount Meru, being in the center of all other mountains.

Merely seeing this great and supreme buddha, an eminent being with the thirty-two major and eighty minor marks, pleases one's mind. These major and minor marks came into being by countless roots of virtue accumulated over immeasurable eons. Having created these causes, Amitabha established this complete beautified body beyond all dimensions.

The sky on autumn nights is free of clouds and totally pervaded by moonlight amid constellations of glittering pearl-like stars. Similarly, [Amitabha] is amid an immeasurable retinue of bodhisattvas with brilliant appearance and having completely matured their mindstreams and senses through a vast accumulation of roots of virtue. Amitabha is also in the center of hundreds of thousands of compassionate arhats, leaders of humans, followed by their disciples, all acting with great tranquility, possessing divine eyes, magical powers, and clairvoyance.

[Amitabha, you] know all objects of knowledge without obstruction, courageously and indefatigably teaching the Dharma in accordance with the need of trainees. Heroically, you depend on great compassion and work only for the benefit of limitless sentient beings. Being fearless like a powerful lion, king of animals, amid a great assembly of living beings, you spread the sound of the lion's roar in all directions. Similarly, in the center of immeasurable retinues, you free beings from all fears of enemies, spreading the lion-like sound of the vast and profound [teachings] without interruption.

I pay homage to Amitabha!
You, who sit in front of the tree of enlightenment
with a magnificent body [arisen from] limitless merit
    surrounded by a great assembly,
you are the refuge for those who wish to go to Sukhavati.
Lord, your mass of light fills world systems.
Ah, the buddhafield of the victorious ones
is extremely vast, with spacious dimensions.
Having the complete qualities of all the victorious ones,
your activities are fearless,
working only for the purpose of all sentient beings,
who are saturated with the wrongdoings of the five
    degenerations.

You are like an enormous, powerful mountain.
Your supreme vigorous [face] is like a moon,
with extremely beautiful blue eyes like utpala flowers.
Whatever has the most excellence is similar to you.
You blaze with splendor, having all the qualities of
    knowledge and compassion.
Your eloquent speech is a delight for the assembly
    surrounding you.
Staying until the end of existence for the purpose of others,
you are in all circumstances the protector of all migrators.

This is a brief explanation of how to take the qualities of the beings [in the pure land] to mind. If one does it more elaborately, think that one is in front of the Victorious One [Amitabha], the master of the world, and make prayers related to this pure land. Complete the vast practices of the bodhisattvas and conclude by reflecting on all the qualities of this pure land, as referred to in prayers, by studying the clear explanations of the sutras.

It is vital to have strong aspiration to be born there; try to generate this strong aspiration again and again by focusing on the qualities of the pure land as explained in brief above. The benefits of this are explained in the *Display of the Pure Land of Sukhavati Sutra*:

[11] TALK ABOUT AMITABHA'S PURE LAND, OR HEAVEN

If all the subtle particles that can be found in the world
are cut and broken down into smaller particles,
and if world systems greater in number than this
are filled with jewels [and offered],
the merit of the practice of generosity of such [an amount
  of] precious jewels
becomes never equal to the amount of merit that is created
  with
joyfully listening with folded hands
to the immeasurable characteristics of the light
and all other special qualities of Sukhavati.
Therefore one should generate the strong aspiration to go
to the supreme world of Sukhavati
by generating devotion and faith through listening to the
  qualities
of [Amitabha,] the One Gone to Bliss.

Whoever hears the name of the world of Sukhavati
[creates] more merit than the parts of this supreme vast
  pure land;
the [magnitude] can never be illustrated with examples.
Knowing the perfect teachings of the Buddha,
which possesses wisdom,
one's merit will increase.
Therefore one should listen and clear all doubts
and, with the root of faith, obtain the ultimate.

The Buddha explained the qualities of the pure land and how to create causes to be reborn there, witnessed by the exalted wisdom of the victorious ones. It is important to generate strong faith without the slightest doubt. It is said that if one has doubt and establishes the causes to be reborn there, one will have the great misfortune to be reborn in this pure land but with obstruction and will have to stay in the womb of the lotus for five hundred years without being able to see the buddhas or listen to the Dharma.

The mere expression of the qualities of the pure land, seen as an object of aspiration, as explained once before, is more than enough for the intelligent ones, who easily understand [the need and way to be reborn there]. But for people like us who are of lesser intelligence, it is said that if there is no [elaborate] explanation, one will not generate the wish to be reborn there, will not see this object of aspiration. If one doesn't observe this [pure land] well, seeing only some of its qualities, one will never generate a strong and vast aspiration, and it will only remain as a mere minor thought.

The way to supplicate the Conqueror in order to easily establish [the rebirth] in the dwelling of the ripening result of the victorious ones and their retinue is [to recite the prayer to be reborn there. See practice 66].

Colophon for the English Translation
Translated by Geshe Tenzin Namdak, Sera Je Monastery, Sakadawa, June, 2014. The most compassionate and kind lama, Kyabje Thubten Zopa Rinpoche, asked me to translate this text.

By any merit created through this translation, may His Holiness the Dalai Lama, Kyabje Lama Zopa Rinpoche, and all of our other precious gurus have long and healthy lives. May their holy wishes be spontaneously fulfilled, may they, at the time of our deaths, lead us to the pure land of Sukhavati and may we quickly obtain the state of full enlightenment for the benefit of all mother sentient beings.

With many thanks to Ven. Gyalten Lekden for proofreading this text.

> Being unrealized, low in acquired knowledge and learning,
> Saturated with wrong views and defilements,
> Taking the lamas and deities as my witness,
> I confess my mistakes to the wise.

TALK ABOUT YOUR LOVED ONE'S GOOD QUALITIES [12]

See chapters 14 and 18.

Emphasize all the good, positive things the dying person has done during their life and do not dwell on what they consider to be failures or weaknesses. Tell them: "You have lived a good life, sincere, and you have done many good things."

Use whatever compassion your loved one has experienced during their life to show how important compassion is, and encourage them to feel compassion and loving kindness even as they are dying.

TALK ABOUT COMPASSION, BODHICHITTA [13]

See chapters 14 and 18.
See also practices 21, 38, and 42.

His Holiness the Dalai Lama says that the best way to die is to die with the thought of benefiting others—a "self-supporting death," His Holiness calls it.

It is your responsibility to help your loved one develop compassion. Thinking of the happiness of others as they die rather than their own terrible circumstances is an amazing thing. Compassion is the ultimate attitude to bring to the next life. If the person could remember this, they will without one single doubt be saved from the lower realms.

On the basis of realizing that sentient beings have so much suffering, and on the basis of realizing that sentient beings are so precious, so kind, that they are the ones from whom the dying person has received all their own past, present, and future happiness—on the basis of this, great loving kindness and great compassion arise: the wish that other sentient beings have happiness and that they, the dying person, will give it to them, and the wish that others be free of suffering and that they, the dying person, will free them. On the basis of this understanding, your loved one will be able to enjoy the experience of death for others, for all sentient beings. Psychologically that is how it works.

Even if your loved one doesn't have a religion, explain that so many others are dying right now, that everyone has to go through this experience. Help them think in a broad way instead of thinking only of themselves.

RECITE THE NAMES OF THE SEVEN MEDICINE BUDDHAS [14]

See chapters 15, 18, 20, 21, 22, 23, and 27.
See also other practices related to the Medicine Buddha: 22, 36, 59, and 78.

The Medicine Buddha promised that whoever chants his name or mantra will have all their prayers and wishes fulfilled. In the past, when the Medicine Buddha was a bodhisattva, with unbearable compassion that encompasses all us sentient beings, he made countless prayers that we pacify our many problems and achieve all temporary and ultimate happiness, especially during the time of the five degenerations. That time has come; this is our time. Therefore all the prayers that the Medicine Buddha made in the past will now be fulfilled.

Recite the names of the Seven Medicine Buddhas as many times as you like.

1. Buddha Renowned Glorious King of Excellent Signs
2. Buddha King of Melodious Sound, Brilliant Radiance of Skill, Adorned with Jewels, Moon, and Lotus
3. Buddha Stainless Excellent Gold
4. Buddha Supreme Glory Free from Sorrow
5. Buddha Melodious Ocean of Dharma Proclaimed
6. Buddha Delightful King of Clear Knowing
7. Buddha Medicine Guru, Great King with the Radiance of a Lapis Jewel

RECITE THE NAMES OF THE THIRTY-FIVE BUDDHAS OF CONFESSION [15]

See chapters 15, 18, 20, 21, 22, and 23.
See also practice 49.

Merely hearing the names of the Thirty-Five Buddhas of Confession purifies many thousands of eons of negative karma and makes it impossible to be reborn in the lower realms.

Recite the names as many times as you like.

See also the full practice of prostrations to the Thirty-Five Buddhas of Confession and the four opponent powers (practice 49).

Shakyamuni Buddha
1. To the Founder, Bhagavan, Tathagata, Arhat, Perfectly Completed Buddha, Glorious Conqueror Shakyamuni Buddha, I prostrate.

First Row, Blue, in the Aspect of Akshobhya
2. To Tathagata Thoroughly Destroying with Vajra Essence, I prostrate.
3. To Tathagata Radiant Jewel, I prostrate.
4. To Tathagata King, Lord of the Nagas, I prostrate. [with a white face]
5. To Tathagata Army of Heroes, I prostrate.
6. To Tathagata Delighted Hero, I prostrate.
7. To Tathagata Jewel Fire, I prostrate.

Second Row, White, in the Aspect of Vairochana
8. To Tathagata Jewel Moonlight, I prostrate.
9. To Tathagata Meaningful to See, I prostrate.
10. To Tathagata Jewel Moon, I prostrate.
11. To Tathagata Stainless One, I prostrate.
12. To Tathagata Bestowed with Courage, I prostrate.
13. To Tathagata Pure One, I prostrate.
14. To Tathagata Bestowed with Purity, I prostrate.

[15] NAMES OF THE THIRTY-FIVE BUDDHAS OF CONFESSION

Third Row, Yellow, in the Aspect of Ratnasambhava
15. To Tathagata Water God, I prostrate.
16. To Tathagata Deity of the Water God, I prostrate.
17. To Tathagata Glorious Goodness, I prostrate.
18. To Tathagata Glorious Sandalwood, I prostrate.
19. To Tathagata Infinite Splendor, I prostrate.
20. To Tathagata Glorious Light, I prostrate.
21. To Tathagata Sorrowless Glory, I prostrate.

Fourth Row, Red, in the Aspect of Amitabha
22. To Tathagata Son of Non-craving, I prostrate.
23. To Tathagata Glorious Flower, I prostrate.
24. To Tathagata Pure Light Rays Clearly Knowing by Play, I prostrate.
25. To Tathagata Lotus Light Rays Clearly Knowing by Play, I prostrate.
26. To Tathagata Glorious Wealth, I prostrate.
27. To Tathagata Glorious Mindfulness, I prostrate.
28. To Tathagata Glorious Name Widely Renowned, I prostrate.

Fifth Row, Green, in the Aspect of Amoghasiddhi
29. To Tathagata King Holding the Victory Banner of Foremost Power, I prostrate.
30. To Tathagata Glorious One Totally Subduing, I prostrate.
31. To Tathagata Utterly Victorious in Battle, I prostrate.
32. To Tathagata Glorious Transcendence Through Subduing, I prostrate.
33. To Tathagata Glorious Manifestations Illuminating All, I prostrate.
34. To Tathagata All-Subduing Jewel Lotus, I prostrate.
35. To Tathagata, Arhat, Perfectly Completed Buddha, King, Lord of the Mountains Firmly Seated on Jewel and Lotus, I prostrate.

RECITE THE MANTRA OF BEAM OF COMPLETELY PURE STAINLESS LIGHT AND THE MANTRA TAUGHT BY BUDDHA DRODEN GYALWA CHÖ [16]

See chapter 15.
See also practice 29.

It is extremely beneficial for you and other helpers to recite these two mantras a few times every day in the months and weeks before death. As a result, anyone who hears, sees, or touches you has all their negative karma purified. In addition, whatever you touch becomes a holy object.

It is not necessary to recite them at the time of death.

The Mantra of Beam of Completely Pure Stainless Light

NAMA NAVATINAM TATHAGATA GANGANAM DIVA LUKANAM / KOTI NIYUTA SHATA SAHASRANAM / OM VOVORI / CHARI NI* CHARI / MORI GOLI CHALA VARI SVAHA

[*indicates a high tone]

The Mantra Taught by Buddha Droden Gyalwa Chö

OM HRI YA DHE SARVA TATHAGATA HRIDAYA GARBHE / JVALA DHARMADHATU GARBHE / SAMTARANA AYU SAMSHODHAYA / PAPAM SARVA TATHAGATA SAMENDRA USHNISHA VIMALE VISHUDDHE SVAHA

RECITE THE MANTRA FOR ALLEVIATING FEAR OR PAIN [17]

See chapter 15.

This mantra, which includes the name of one of the eight bodhisattvas, can alleviate pain and calm fears. You can recite the mantra and help your loved one learn it. If they recite the mantra at least seven times every day, they won't have a difficult death, they won't experience frightening karmic appearances. They will die without fear.

Then it's easy for the people taking care of them. If the person is fearful, you will also be scared or worried, and then you can't help them; you won't know what to do.

OM SHAVA DE VADA VISALI NE SVAHA

RECITE THE NAME MANTRA OF HIS HOLINESS THE DALAI LAMA OR OF YOUR LOVED ONE'S OWN GURU [18]

See chapters 15, 18, 20, 21, 22, and 23.
See also other practices related to the guru: 1, 10, 35, 43, 47, 60, 72, and 85.

You could have the dying person recite His Holiness the Dalai Lama's name mantra or their own root guru's mantra. While they recite it, they could visualize His Holiness or their guru and imagine purifying all their negative karma and defilements.

You can also recite it for them.

Name Mantra of His Holiness the Dalai Lama

OM AH GURU VAJRADHARA BHATTARAK MANJUSHRI VAGINDRA SUMATI JÑANA SHASANADHARA SAMUDRA SHRIBHADRA SARVASIDDHI HUM HUM

RECITE THE NAME MANTRA OF THE BUDDHA WHO PROTECTS FROM THE LOWER REALMS [19]

See chapters 15, 18, 20, 21, 22, and 23.
See also practice 3.

The Buddha who protects from the lower realms is Rinchen Tsuktorchen (Sanskrit: Ratna Shikhin). Having heard this mantra, it is impossible for any animal or person to be reborn in the lower realms. So don't just recite it to yourself, and don't mumble it: say it loudly so that your loved one can hear it.

If you come across an animal who is dying, this is the first thing you would recite into their ear.

Tibetan
CHOMDENDÉ DEZHIN SHEKPA DRACHOMPA YANGDAKPAR DZOKPAI SANGYÉ RINCHEN TSUKTOR CHEN LA CHAK TSAL LO

Sanskrit
NAMO BHAGAVAN TATHAGATA ARHAT SAMYAK SAMBUDDHA RATNA SHIKHIN

English
To the conqueror, the tathagata, the arhat, the perfectly enlightened Buddha Ratna Shikhin, I bow down.

RECITE OTHER MANTRAS, SUCH AS AMITABHA BUDDHA'S [20]

See chapters 15, 18, 20, 21, 22, and 23.
See also chapter 6 and other practices related to Amitabha: 11, 64, 66, and 81.

There are many mantras of the various buddhas, such as Amitabha. Or you could recite a very special mantra that fulfills all wishes: The Great Increasing Jewel Fathomless Celestial Mansion Extremely Well-Abiding Secret Holy Mantra.

Mantra of Amitabha Buddha

OM AMI DEWA HRIH

The Great Increasing Jewel Fathomless Celestial Mansion Extremely Well-Abiding Secret Holy Mantra
In Sanskrit, the name of this mantra is *Arya mahamani vipulavi manavishva supratishthita guhya paramarahasya kalparaja nama dharani*, or the "Mahamani mantra," for short.

OM VIPULA GARBHE MANI PRABHE / TATHAGATA NIRDESHA NE / MANI MANI / SUPRABHE / VIMALE / SAGARA GAMBHIRE / HUM HUM / JVALA JVALA / BUDDHA VILOKITE / GUHYA ADHISH THITÉ / GARBHE SVAHA

Near Heart Mantra
OM MANI VAJRE HUM

Heart Mantra
OM MANI DHIRI HUM

RECITE THE COMPASSION BUDDHA MANTRA [21]

See chapters 15, 18, 20, 21, 22, and 23.
See also other practices related to the Compassion Buddha: 13, 38, and 73.

The First of the Ten Powerful Mantras
The benefits of reciting the mantra of the Compassion Buddha (Tibetan: Chenrezik; Sanskrit: Avalokiteshvara) are infinite, like the limitless sky. If your loved one doesn't have much intellectual understanding of Dharma and the only thing they know is this mantra, and free of attachment to this life, they have spent their life chanting it, that is enough.

Short Mantra
OM MANI PADME HUM

Long Mantra
NAMO RATNA TRAYAYA / NAMA ARYA JÑANA SAGARA / VAIROCHANA VYUHA RAJAYA / TATHAGATAYA / ARHATE SAMYAK SAMBUDDHAYA / NAMA SARVA TATHAGATABHYAH / ARHATEBHYAH / SAMYAK SAMBUDDHEBHYAH / NAMAH ARYA AVALOKITESHVARAYA / BODHISATTVAYA / MAHASATTVAYA / MAHAKARUNIKAYA / TADYATHA / OM DHARA DHARA / DHIRI DHIRI / DHURU DHURU / ITTI VATTE / CHALE CHALE / PRACHALE PRACHALE / KUSUME KUSUME VARE / ILI MILI / CHITI JVALAM / APANAYE SVAHA

RECITE THE MEDICINE BUDDHA MANTRA [22]

See chapters 15, 18, 20, 21, 22, 23, and 27.
See also other practices related to the Medicine Buddha: 14, 36, 59, and 78.

The Second of the Ten Powerful Mantras
The Medicine Buddha promised that whoever chants his name or mantra will have all their prayers and wishes fulfilled. Have your loved one recite the mantra with full trust in Medicine Buddha, or you recite it so they can hear it. Explain that Medicine Buddha is always with them—in their heart, on their crown, in front of them. Tell them that there is not one second Medicine Buddha does not see them or have compassion for them.

Short Mantra
TADYATHA / OM BHAISHAJYE BHAISHAJYE MAHA BHAISHAJYE [BHAISHAJYE] / RAJA SAMUDGATE SVAHA

Common Pronunciation
TAYATA OM BEKANZE BEKANZE MAHA BEKANZE [BEKANZE] RADZA SAMUNGATE SOHA

Long Mantra
OM NAMO BHAGAVATE BHAISHAJYE / GURU VAIDURYA / PRABHA RAJAYA / TATHAGATAYA / ARHATE SAMYAKSAM BUDDHAYA / TADYATHA / OM BHAISHAJYE BHAISHAJYE MAHA BHAISHAJYE [BHAISHAJYE] / RAJA SAMUDGATE SVAHA

RECITE THE LOTUS PINNACLE OF AMOGHAPASHA MANTRA [23]

See chapters 15, 18, 20, 21, 22, and 23.
See also practice 31.

The Third of the Ten Powerful Mantras

Reciting this mantra of Buddha Pema Tsuktor (Sanskrit: Padmoshnisha) seven times every day with the thought to benefit others creates the cause to be reborn in the pure lands.

OM PADMOSHNISHA VIMALE HUM PHAT

RECITE THE MITRUKPA MANTRA [24]

See chapters 15, 18, 20, 21, 22, and 23.
See also other practices related to Mitrukpa: 2, 31, 58, and 87.

The Fourth of the Ten Powerful Mantras

The mantra of Mitrukpa (Sanskrit: Akshobhya) is for purifying karmic obscurations. As I mentioned in practice 2, merely seeing it purifies the heaviest of the very heavy negative karmas, avoiding the holy Dharma, which is heavier than destroying all the monasteries, all the statues, stupas, scriptures, every single holy object that exists in this world.

Reciting or seeing it also purifies the negative karma of having taken things from the Sangha without permission or having deprived them of receiving things—karmas like that. No question then about all other negative karmas.

NAMO RATNA TRAYAYA / OM KAMKANI KAMKANI / ROCHANI ROCHANI / TROTANI TROTANI / TRASANI TRASANI / PRATIHANA PRATIHANA / SARVA KARMA PARAM PARA NI ME SARVA SATTVA NANCHA SVAHA

RECITE THE NAMGYALMA MANTRA [25]

See chapters 15, 18, 20, 21, 22, and 23.
See also other practices related to Namgyalma: 8, 31, 58, and 77.

The Fifth of the Ten Powerful Mantras
Namgyalma (Sanskrit: Ushnishavijaya) is a deity for long life and purification. The mantra has infinite benefits. It is said to be so powerful that for anyone who hears it, this life will be their last birth from a womb. And if animals hear it, they will not be born in the lower realms.

Short Mantra
OM BHRUM SVAHA / OM AMRITA AYUR DADAI SVAHA

Long Mantra
OM NAMO BHAGAVATE / SARVA TRAILOKYA PRATIVISHISHTAYA / BUDDHAYA TE NAMAHA / TADYATHA / OM BHRUM BHRUM BHRUM / SHODHAYA SHODHAYA / VISHODHAYA VISHODHAYA / ASAMA SAMANTA / AVABHASA SPHARANA GATI / GAGANA SVABHAVA VISHUDDHE / ABHISHINCHATU MAM / SARVA TATHAGATA / SUGATA PRAVACHANA / AMRITA ABHISHEKAIRA / MAHAMUDRA / MANTRAPADE / AHARA AHARA / MAMA AYUR SAMDHARANI / SHODHAYA SHODHAYA / VISHODHAYA VISHODHAYA / GAGANA SVABHAVA / VISHUDDHE USHNISHA VIJAYA PARISHUDDHE / SAHASRAR ASMIN CHODITE / SARVA TATHAGATA AVALOKINI / SHAT PARAMITA PARIPURANI / SARVA TATHAGATA MATE / DASHA BHUMI PRATISHTHITE / SARVA TATHAGATA HRIDAYA / ADHISHTHANA ADHISHTHITE / MUDRE MUDRE MAHA MUDRE / VAJRAKAYA SAMHATANA PARISHUDDHE / SARVA KARMA AVARANA VISHUDDHE / PRATINIVARTAYA MAMA AYUR / VISHUDDHE SARVA TATHAGATA / SAMAYA ADHISHTHANA ADHISHTHITE / OM MUNI MUNI MAHA MUNI / VIMUNI VIMUNI MAHA VIMUNI / MATI MATI MAHA MATI / MAMATI SUMATI TATHATA / BHUTAKOTI PARISHUDDHE / VISPHUTA BUDDHE SHUDDHE / HE HE JAYA JAYA / VIJAYA VIJAYA / SMARA SMARA / SPHARA SPHARA / SPHARAYA SPHARAYA / SARVA BUDDHA

ADHISHTHANA ADHISHTHITE / SHUDDHE SHUDDHE / BUDDHE BUDDHE / VAJRE VAJRE MAHAVAJRE / SUVAJRE VAJRA GARBHE JAYA GARBHE / VIJAYA GARBHE / VAJRA JVALA GARBHE / VAJRODBHAVE / VAJRA SAMBHAVE / VAJRE VAJRINI / VAJRAM BHAVATU MAMA SHARIRAM / SARVA SATTVA NANCHA KAYA PARISHUDDHIR BHAVATU / ME SADA SARVA GATI / PARISHUDDHISHCHA / SARVA TATHAGATASHCHA MAM SAMASH VASAYANTU / BUDDHYA BUDDHYA / SIDDHYA SIDDHYA / BODHAYA BODHAYA / VIBODHAYA VIBODHAYA / MOCHAYA MOCHAYA / VIMOCHAYA VIMOCHAYA / SHODHAYA SHODHAYA / VISHODHAYA VISHODHAYA / SAMANTA RASMI PARISHUDDHE / SARVA TATHAGATA HRIDAYA / ADHISHTHANA ADHISHTHITE / MUDRE MUDRE MAHAMUDRE / MANTRAPADAHI SVAHA

After reciting either mantra, say a few times:
OM AMITE / AMITOD BHAVE / AMITA SAMBHAVA / AMITE VIKRANTE / AMITA GATRE / AMITE GAMINI / AMITA AYUR DADAI GAGANA KIRTI KARE / SARVA KLESHA KSHAYAM KARI YE SVAHA

RECITE GURU RINPOCHE PADMASAMBHAVA'S MANTRA [26]

See chapters 15, 18, 20, 21, 22, and 23.

The Sixth of the Ten Powerful Mantras
According to Guru Rinpoche himself, whoever recites his mantra "will meet with me again and again in this life, in future lives, and in the intermediate state between death and rebirth."

OM AH HUM VAJRA GURU PADMA SIDDHI HUM

RECITE THE KUNRIK MANTRA [27]

See chapters 15, 18, 20, 21, 22, and 23.
See also other practices related to Kunrik: 31, 58, and 78.

The Seventh of the Ten Powerful Mantras
Kunrik (Sanskrit: Vairochana), who is white, has three faces, and holds a Dharma wheel, is known as "the king of deities for purifying the lower realms." It is said that Kunrik practice can even liberate someone who is already in the lower realms.

Kirti Tsenshab Rinpoche has explained that laypeople in Amdo prepare for their death by taking an initiation of Kunrik. Because the Amdo people have faith that they have purified everything, they are not worried when death comes; they are relaxed, comfortable.

OM NAMO BHAGAVATE / SARVA DURGATI PARI SHODHANA RAJAYA / TATHAGATAYA / ARHATE SAMYAKSAM BUDDHAYA / TADYATHA / OM SHODHANI / SHODHANI / SARVA PAPAM VISHODHANI / SHUDHE VISHUDHE / SARVA KARMA AVARANA VISHODHANI SVAHA

RECITE THE MILAREPA MANTRA [28]

See chapters 15, 18, 20, 21, 22, and 23.

The Eighth of the Ten Powerful Mantras
Milarepa himself said that merely remembering his name and thinking about him will cause us to be born in a pure land, where we will meet him and receive teachings. He generated this very special bodhichitta in order to offer extensive benefit to sentient beings.

Depending on the level of our devotion, we can even receive instructions from Milarepa in our dreams.

OM AH GURU HASA VAJRA SARVA SIDDHI PHALA HUM

RECITE THE MANTRA OF THE BEAM OF COMPLETELY PURE STAINLESS LIGHT [29]

See chapters 15, 18, 20, 21, 22, and 23.
See also practices 6 and 16.

The Ninth of the Ten Powerful Mantras

As I mentioned in practice 16, whoever hears, sees, or touches a person who has recited this mantra will have their negative karma purified.

NAMA NAVATINAM TATHAGATA GANGANAM DIVA LUKANAM / KOTI NIYUTA SHATA SAHASRANAM / OM VOVORI / CHARI NI* CHARI / MORI GOLI CHALA VARI SVAHA

[*indicates a high tone]

RECITE THE MAITREYA BUDDHA MANTRA [30]

See chapters 15, 18, 20, 21, 22, and 23.
See also other practices related to Maitreya: 69, 70, and 71.

The Tenth of the Ten Powerful Mantras
Reading and reciting the mantra of Maitreya Buddha's promise, contemplating the meaning, or merely hearing it—this includes animals—causes one not to be reborn in the lower realms. One will follow the path of the ten virtuous actions and receive all the enjoyments one seeks. And when Maitreya Buddha shows the twelve deeds of a Buddha, he will lead this sentient being from poverty.

Maitreya will definitely find even the sentient beings in a hell and give them the prediction of the time of their enlightenment.

Mantra of Maitreya Buddha's Promise
NAMO RATNA TRAYAYA / NAMO BHAGAVATE SHAKYAMUNIYE / TATHAGATAYA / ARHATE SAMYAKSAM BUDDHAYA / TADYATHA / OM AJITE AJITE APARAJITE / AJITAÑCHAYA HA RA HA RA MAITRI AVALOKITE KARA KARA MAHA SAMAYA SIDDHI BHARA BHARA MAHA BODHI MANDA BIJA SMARA SMARA AHSMA KAM SAMAYA BODHI BODHI MAHA BODHI SVAHA

Heart Mantra
OM MOHI MOHI MAHA MOHI SVAHA

Near Heart Mantra
OM MUNI MUNI SMARA SVAHA

RECITE THE FIVE GREAT MANTRAS [31]

See chapters 15, 18, 20, 21, 22, and 23.
See also practices 23, 24, 25, 27, and 58.

Four of the five great mantras are among the ten powerful mantras; the fifth is the mantra of Buddha Stainless Pinnacle (Tibetan: Drimé Tsuktor; Sanskrit: Ushnishavimala).

> Kunrik [27]
> Mitrukpa [24]
> Namgyalma [25]
> Stainless Pinnacle
> Lotus Pinnacle of Amoghapasha [23]

The Heart Mantra of Stainless Pinnacle

> OM NAMASTRAIYA DHVIKANAM / SARVA TATHAGATA HRIDAYA GARBHE JVALA JVALA / DHARMADHATU GARBHE / SAMBHARA MAMA AYU / SAMSHODHAYA MAMA SARVA PAPAM / SARVA TATHAGATA SAMANTOSHNISHA VIMALE VISHUDDHE / HUM HUM HUM HUM / AM VAM SAM JA SVAHA

RECITE THE SUTRA FOR ALLEVIATING PAIN [32]

See chapters 15 and 18.

It is said that listening to the *Noble Great Sutra on Entering the City of Vaishali* can help alleviate the pain of those who are sick or dying.

THE NOBLE GREAT SUTRA ON ENTERING THE CITY OF VAISHALI

In the language of India: *Arya vaishali pravesha mahasutra*
In Tibetan: *Phakpa yangpai drongkhyer du jukpai do chenpo*

Homage to all the buddhas and bodhisattvas!

Thus have I heard. At one time the Bhagavan was residing in a boathouse in the middle of a swamp. Then the Bhagavan spoke to the venerable Ananda: "Ananda, let's proceed to where the city of Vaishali is."

"Let's do accordingly, Venerable Sir." Thus replying, Ananda followed the instructions of the Bhagavan.

Then the Bhagavan traveled through the country of Libriza, arrived at its city of Vaishali, and was sojourning at the Mango Grove of the city of Vaishali.

Then, at that time the Bhagavan spoke to Ananda: "Ananda, go into the city of Vaishali. Place your feet on the doorsills of homes and recite the foundations of these secret mantras and these verses:

VISARATA / VISARATA / VISARATA / VISARATA
[VISARATA *means to pacify thoroughly, in this case to pacify epidemics.*]

"The Buddha, who has loving kindness toward the world, spoke thus! It is the noble intent of all the buddhas, the intent of all the pratyekabuddhas, the intent of all the arhats, and the intent of all those on the learners' paths. It is the intent of all shravakas, the intent of all those who abide by truthful speech, the intent of Dharma teachings, the intent of Brahma kings, the intent of individual Brahmas, the intent of Shiva of the desire realm, the intent of Indra, the intent of the gods, the intent of the king of demigods, the intent of all demigods, the intent of messengers of demigods, and the intent of the host of jungpo spirits!

VISARATA / VISARATA / VISARATA / VISARATA

"The Buddha, who has loving kindness toward the world, spoke thus!

MUNCHATA / MUNCHATA
[MUNCHATA *means depart, commanding spirits carrying epidemics to depart or go away.*]

"Go away! May all epidemics be thoroughly pacified!

NIRGACHATA / NIRGACHATA / NIRGACHATA / NIRGACHATA
[NIRGACHATA *also means to depart.*]

"The Buddha, the Great God, the God of Gods, the Guru of Gods has arrived! Therefore, gods together with Indra, gods together with Brahma, gods together with Ishana, and people together with their kings will also come. The kings of the four quarters will also come. Hundreds and thousands of gods, the kings of demigods, and hundreds and thousands of demigods will also come. Hundreds and thousands of jungpo spirits who have great devotion to the Bhagavan Buddha will also come for the benefit of all sentient beings. These [gods and spirits] may bring about great harm to you. As such:

NIRGACHATA / NIRGACHATA / NIRGACHATA / NIRGACHATA

"Leave immediately! Among you all, may those who harbor hatred be vanquished! May those who possess loving minds and who do not want to harm but rather want to engage in protecting others stay and also assume physical forms!

"The Buddha, who has loving kindness toward the world, spoke:

[32] RECITE THE SUTRA FOR ALLEVIATING PAIN

SUMU SUMU SUMU SUMU / SUMURU SUMURU SUMURU SUMURU
SUMURU SUMURU SUMURU SUMURU / MURU MURU MURU MURU
MURU MURU MURU MURU MURU / MIRI MIRI MIRI MIRI MIRI MIRI
MIRI MIRI MIRI / MURU MIRI MURU RIMI MURU RIMI MURU RIMI
MURU RIMI / MURU MIRI MURU RIMI MURU RIMI MURU RIMI /
MURU MIRI MURU / MIRI MURU MIRI MURU MIRI / MIRU RI TI /
RI RI RI RI RI RI / RĪ RĪ RĪ RĪ RĪ RĪ / TIMIRI / MIRI MIRI MIRI MIRI
MIRI MIRI / MIRITI HASIMIRITI MIIRITI MITI SISĪ SIMĪ / KAMKARA
KAMKARATA KAMKARA KAMKARATSA / KAMKARĀ KAMKARĀ
KAMKARĀ KAMKARĀ KAMKARĀ KAMKARĀ KAMKARĀ KAMKARĀ
KAMKARĀ KAMKARĀ KAMKARĀ KAMKARĀ KAMKARĀ KAMKARĀ
KAMKARĀ KAMKARĀ KAMKARĀ / KAMKA ROTĪTI KURI SHO KAM
KARAA / KAMKARISHI / RI RI RI RI RI RI / TIRI TEPHU SVAHA /
RIPHU RIPHU RIPHU RIPHU RIPHU RIPHU RIPHU RIPHU / NAA
THĀ NĀ NĀ THĀ THA RIPHU RIPHU / NIRGACHATA RIPHU RIPHU
NIRGACHATA PĀLAYATA RIPHU RIPHU PĀLAYATA

"The Buddha who has a compassionate mind toward the world, who possesses exceptional intent to benefit all beings, who abides in love, who possesses compassion, who abides in joy, and who abides in equanimity will be coming."

KSHIPRANA NIRGACHATA SVAHA

Taught by the Buddha through his supreme enlightened wisdom and through the power of truth, the foundations of these secret mantras have been established! These verses have been established!

He who has eliminated the miserliness of attachment,
who thoroughly eliminated stains,
and whose mind is without any harmful intent:
he will bring happiness and benefit to you!

The guide who leads sentient beings
on the path of liberation
and who teaches all aspects of the Dharma:
he will bring happiness and benefit to you!

The teacher on whom all migratory beings rely
and who, for the sake of all sentient beings,
attained the state of bliss:
he will bring happiness and benefit to you!

The protector who, with a loving mind,
looks after all these sentient beings eternally
like his only son:
he will bring happiness and benefit to you!

Who, for those sentient beings circling in samsara,
has become an object that can be relied upon
and who has become an island, savior, and a friend:
he will bring happiness and benefit to you!

For whom all phenomena have become the object of
    direct perception,
who is pure and does not mislead,
and who maintains the purity of his stainless speech:
he will bring happiness and benefit to you!

The great hero whose birth
brought auspiciousness and meaning,
accomplishing many purposes:
he will bring happiness and benefit to you!

Who, when he was born,
the earth together with its forests mightily shook,
bringing joy and happiness to all beings:
he will bring happiness and benefit to you!

When he attained the essence of buddhahood,
six times the earth mightily shook,
making the demonic forces unhappy:
he will bring happiness and benefit to you!

[32] RECITE THE SUTRA FOR ALLEVIATING PAIN

When turning the wheel of Dharma,
his teachings on the noble truths
were powerful and melodious:
he will bring happiness and benefit to you!

The stunner who defeated all heretics
with Dharma teachings
and conquered all crowds:
he will bring happiness and benefit to you!

May the Buddha bring you happiness and benefit!
May the happiness and well-being of Indra together with gods
and the happiness and well-being of all classes of jungpo
    spirits
eternally be bestowed upon you!

By the merit and power of the buddhas,
and because of the intents of gods,
may whatever aspirations you have
be fulfilled today!

May you, the two-legged ones, have happiness and
    well-being!
May you, the four-legged ones, have happiness and
    well-being!
May those of you who are going away have happiness and
    well-being!
May those of you who are returning also have happiness
    and well-being!

May you enjoy happiness and well-being during the day
    and during the night!
May you enjoy happiness and well-being at noon!
May you enjoy happiness and well-being at all times!
May you not engage in negative actions!

The Buddha has come,
completely surrounded by thousands of gods.
As such, may those with intent to harm depart!
May those with compassion remain!

By the power of the truth of the words of the Buddha,
of pratyekabuddhas, arhats, and those on the learner's paths,
may those who destroy the well-being of this world
disappear in this very city!

May all beings and insects,
all spirits, and all of you
enjoy only happiness!
May everyone be pacified of all diseases!
May everyone see goodness,
and may none engage in negativities!

Those spirits who have come here,
dwelling on the land and in the space,
may you have loving compassion toward the humans!
May you also practice Dharma day and night!

Thus the Buddha spoke. The venerable Ananda responded, "I will do accordingly."

Thus, in accordance with the instructions of the Bhagavan, he went to the city of Vaishali. Placing his feet on the doorsills of homes, he uttered these mantras and these verses:

VISARATA / VISARATA / VISARATA / VISARATA

The Buddha, who has loving kindness toward the world, spoke thus! It is the noble intent of all the buddhas, the intent of all the pratyekabuddhas, the intent of all the arhats, and the intent of all those on the learner's paths. It is the intent of all shravakas, the intent of all those who abide by truthful speech, the intent of Dharma teachings, the intent of Brahma kings, the intent of individual Brahmas, the intent of Shiva of the desire realm, the intent of Indra, the intent of the gods, the

[32] RECITE THE SUTRA FOR ALLEVIATING PAIN

intent of the king of demigods, the intent of all demigods, the intent of messengers of demigods, and the intent of the host of jungpo spirits!

VISARATA / VISARATA / VISARATA / VISARATA

The Buddha, who has loving kindness toward the world, spoke thus!

MUNCHATA / MUNCHATA

Go away! May all epidemics be thoroughly pacified!

NIRGACHATA / NIRGACHATA / NIRGACHATA / NIRGACHATA

The Buddha, the Great God, the God of Gods, the Guru of Gods has arrived! Therefore, gods together with Indra, gods together with Brahma, gods together with Ishana, and people together with their kings will also come. The kings of the four quarters will also come. Hundreds and thousands of gods, the kings of demigods, and hundreds and thousands of demigods will also come. Hundreds and thousands of jungpo spirits who have great devotion to the Bhagavan Buddha will also come for the benefit of all sentient beings. These [gods and spirits] may bring about great harm to you. As such:

NIRGACHATA / NIRGACHATA / NIRGACHATA / NIRGACHATA

Leave immediately! Among you all, may those who harbor hatred be vanquished! May those who possess loving minds and who do not want to harm but rather want to engage in protecting others stay and also assume physical forms!

The Buddha who has loving kindness toward the world spoke:

SUMU SUMU SUMU SUMU / SUMURU SUMURU SUMURU SUMURU
SUMURU SUMURU SUMURU SUMURU / MURU MURU MURU MURU
MURU MURU MURU MURU MURU / MIRI MIRI MIRI MIRI MIRI
MIRI MIRI MIRI MIRI / MURU MIRI MURU RIMI MURU RIMI MURU
RIMI MURU RIMI / MURU MIRI MURU RIMI MURU RIMI MURU
RIMI / MURU MIRI MURU / MIRI MURU MIRI MURU MIRI / MIRU

RI TI / RI RI RI RI RI RI / RĪ RĪ RĪ RĪ RĪ RĪ / TIMIRI / MIRI MIRI MIRI MIRI MIRI MIRI / MIRITI HASIMIRITI MIIRITI MITI SISĪ SIMĪ / KAMKARA KAMKARATA KAMKARA KAMKARATSA / KAMKARĀ KAMKARĀ KAMKARĀ KAMKARĀ KAMKARĀ KAMKARĀ KAMKARĀ KAMKARĀ KAMKARĀ KAMKARĀ KAMKARĀ KAMKARĀ KAMKARĀ KAMKARĀ KAMKARĀ KAMKARĀ / KAMKA ROTĪTI KURI SHO KAM KARAA / KAMKARISHI / RI RI RI RI RI RI / TIRI TEPHU SVAHA / RIPHU RIPHU RIPHU RIPHU RIPHU RIPHU RIPHU RIPHU / NAA THĀ NĀ NĀ THĀ THA RIPHU RIPHU / NIRGACHATA RIPHU RIPHU NIRGACHATA PĀLAYATA RIPHU RIPHU PĀLAYATA

The Buddha who has compassionate mind toward the world, who possesses exceptional intent to benefit all beings, who abides in love, who possesses compassion, who abides in joy, and who abides in equanimity will be coming.

KHIPRANA NIRGACHATA SVAHA

Taught by the Buddha through his supreme enlightened wisdom and through the power of truth, the foundations of these secret mantras have been established! These verses have been established!

He who has eliminated the miserliness of attachment,
who thoroughly eliminated stains,
and whose mind is without any harmful intent:
he will bring happiness and benefit to you!

The guide who leads sentient beings
on the path of liberation
and who teaches all aspects of the Dharma:
he will bring happiness and benefit to you!

The teacher on whom all migratory beings rely
and who, for the sake of all sentient beings,
attained the state of bliss:
he will bring happiness and benefit to you!

[32] RECITE THE SUTRA FOR ALLEVIATING PAIN

The protector who, with a loving mind,
looks after all these sentient beings eternally
like his only son:
he will bring happiness and benefit to you!

Who, for those sentient beings circling in samsara,
has become an object that can be relied upon
and who has become an island, savior, and a friend:
he will bring happiness and benefit to you!

For whom all phenomena have become the object of
    direct perception,
who is pure and does not mislead,
and who maintains the purity of his stainless speech:
he will bring happiness and benefit to you!

The great hero whose birth
brought auspiciousness and meaning,
accomplishing many purposes:
he will bring happiness and benefit to you!

Who, when he was born,
the earth together with its forests mightily shook,
bringing joy and happiness to all beings:
he will bring happiness and benefit to you!

When he attained the essence of buddhahood,
six times the earth mightily shook,
making the demonic forces unhappy:
he will bring happiness and benefit to you!

When turning the wheel of Dharma,
his teachings on the noble truths
were powerful and melodious:
he will bring happiness and benefit to you!

The stunner who defeated all heretics
with Dharma teachings
and conquered all crowds:
he will bring happiness and benefit to you!

May the Buddha bring you happiness and benefit!
May the happiness and well-being of Indra together with
   gods
and the happiness and well-being of all classes of jungpo
   spirits
eternally be bestowed upon you!

By the merit and power of the buddhas,
and because of the intents of gods,
may whatever aspirations you have
be fulfilled today!

May you, the two-legged ones, have happiness and
   well-being!
May you, the four-legged ones, have happiness and
   well-being!
May those of you who are going away have happiness and
   well-being!
May those of you who are returning also have happiness
   and well-being!

May you enjoy happiness and well-being during the day
   and during the night!
May you enjoy happiness and well-being at noon!
May you enjoy happiness and well-being at all times!
May you not engage in negative actions!

The Buddha has come,
completely surrounded by thousands of gods.
As such, may those with intent to harm depart!
May those with compassion remain!

[32] RECITE THE SUTRA FOR ALLEVIATING PAIN

By the power of the truth of the words of the Buddha,
of pratyekabuddhas, arhats, and those on the learner's
  paths,
may those who destroy the well-being of this world
disappear in this very city!

May all beings and insects,
all spirits, and all of you
enjoy only happiness!
May everyone be pacified of all diseases!
May everyone see goodness,
and may none engage in negativities!

Those spirits who have come here,
dwelling on the land and in the space,
may you have loving compassion toward the humans!
May you also practice Dharma day and night!

Thus ends the *Noble Great Sutra on Entering the City of Vaishali*.

Colophon
Translated into English from the Tibetan by Tenzin Bhuchung Shastri.

RECITE THE HEART SUTRA [33]

See chapters 15, 18, 20, 21, 22, 23, and 29.
See also practice 34.

It is mentioned in a sutra called *Roar of the Lion* that the merit of merely listening to teachings on emptiness, the perfection of wisdom, is far greater than practicing the other five perfections for ten thousand eons. Even having faith in emptiness can purify the heaviest of negative karmas.

The minute you have even the mere idea of the understanding of dependent arising—that's the reason things are empty—you begin to liberate yourself from all the sufferings of samsara.

THE HEART OF THE PERFECTION OF WISDOM SUTRA

In the language of India: *Prajnaparamita hridaya sutra*
In Tibetan: *Sherab kyi pharoltu chinpai nyingpoi do*

I prostrate to all the buddhas and bodhisattvas.

Thus did I hear at one time. The Bhagavan was dwelling on Mass of Vultures Mountain in Rajagriha together with a great community of monks and a great community of bodhisattvas. At that time, the Bhagavan was absorbed in the concentration on the categories of phenomena called *profound perception*. Also, at that time, the bodhisattva great being Noble Avalokiteshvara looked upon the very practice of the profound perfection of wisdom and beheld those five aggregates also as empty of inherent nature.

Then, through the power of Buddha, the venerable Shariputra said this to the bodhisattva great being Noble Avalokiteshvara:

"How should any son of the lineage train who wishes to practice the activity of the profound perfection of wisdom?"

He said that, and the bodhisattva great being Noble Avalokiteshvara said this to the venerable Sharadvatiputra.

"Shariputra, any son of the lineage or daughter of the lineage who wishes to practice the activity of the profound perfection of wisdom should look upon it like this, correctly and repeatedly beholding those five aggregates also as empty of inherent nature.

"Form is empty. Emptiness is form. Emptiness is not other than form; form is also not other than emptiness.

"In the same way, feeling, discrimination, compositional factors, and consciousness are empty.

"Shariputra, likewise, all phenomena are emptiness; without characteristic; unproduced, unceased; stainless, not without stain; not deficient, not fulfilled.

"Shariputra, therefore, in emptiness there is no form, no feeling, no discrimination, no compositional factors, no consciousness.

"No eye, no ear, no nose, no tongue, no body, no mind.

"No visual form, no sound, no odor, no taste, no object of touch, and no phenomenon.

"There is no eye element and so on up to and including no mind element and no mental consciousness element.

"There is no ignorance, no extinction of ignorance, and so on up to and including no aging and death and no extinction of aging and death.

"Similarly, there is no suffering, origination, cessation, and path. There is no exalted wisdom, no attainment, and also no nonattainment.

"Shariputra, therefore, because there is no attainment, bodhisattvas rely on and dwell in the perfection of wisdom, the mind without obscuration and without fear. Having completely passed beyond error, they reach the endpoint of nirvana.

"All the buddhas who dwell in the three times also manifestly, completely awaken to unsurpassable, perfect, complete enlightenment in reliance on the perfection of wisdom.

"Therefore the mantra of the perfection of wisdom, the mantra of great knowledge, the unsurpassed mantra, the mantra equal to the unequaled, the mantra that thoroughly pacifies all suffering, should be known as truth since it is not false.

"The mantra of the perfection of wisdom is declared:

TADYATHA [OM] GATE GATE PARAGATE PARASAMGATE BODHI SVAHA

"Shariputra, the bodhisattva great being should train in the profound perfection of wisdom like that."

Then the Bhagavan arose from that concentration and commended the bodhisattva great being Noble Avalokiteshvara saying: "Well said, well said, child of the lineage, it is like that. It is like that; one should practice the profound perfection of wisdom just as you have indicated; even the tathagatas rejoice."

The Bhagavan having thus spoken, the venerable Sharadvatiputra, the bodhisattva great being Noble Avalokiteshvara, and those surrounding in their entirety along with the world of gods, humans, demigods, and gandharvas were overjoyed and highly praised that spoken by the Bhagavan.

This completes the *Heart of the Perfection of Wisdom Sutra*.

Colophon for the English Translation
Translated from the Tibetan by Gelong Thubten Tsultrim (the American monk George Churinoff), the first day of Saka Dawa, 1999, at Tushita Meditation Centre, Dharamsala, India.

RECITE THE VAJRA CUTTER SUTRA [34]

See chapters 15, 18, 20, 21, 22, 23, and 29.
See also practice 33.

As I mentioned in practice 33, even having faith in emptiness can purify the heaviest of negative karmas. The minute you have even the mere idea of the understanding of dependent arising—that's the reason things are empty—you begin to liberate yourself from all the sufferings of samsara.

THE VAJRA CUTTER: AN EXALTED MAHAYANA SUTRA ON THE WISDOM GONE BEYOND

In the language of India: *Arya prajnaparamita nama vajracchedika mahayana sutra*
In Tibetan: *Pakpa sherab kyi paroltuchinpa dorje chöpa shejawa tekpa chenpoi do*

I prostrate to all the buddhas and bodhisattvas.

Thus did I hear at one time. The Bhagavan was dwelling at Shravasti, in the grove of Prince Jeta, in the garden of Anathapindada, together with a great Sangha of 1,250 bhikshus and a great many bodhisattva great beings.

Then, in the morning, having put on the lower and upper Dharma robes and carried the begging bowl, the Bhagavan entered the great city of Shravasti to request alms. Then, having gone to the great city of Shravasti to request alms, the Bhagavan afterward enjoyed the alms food, and having performed the activity of food, since he had given up alms of later food, put away the begging bowl and upper robe. He washed his feet, sat upon the prepared cushion, and having assumed the cross-legged posture, straightened the body upright and placed mindfulness in front. Then many bhikshus approached the place where the Bhagavan was and, having reached there, bowing their heads to the Bhagavan's feet, circumambulated three times, and sat to one side.

Also at that time, the venerable Subhuti, joining that very assembly, sat down. Then the venerable Subhuti rose from the seat, placed the upper robe over one shoulder, set his right knee on the ground, bowed with joined palms toward the Bhagavan, and said this: "Bhagavan, the extent to which the Tathagata Arhat Perfectly Enlightened Buddha has benefited the bodhisattva great beings with highest benefit, the extent to which the Tathagata has entrusted the bodhisattva great beings with highest entrustment—Bhagavan, it is astonishing; Sugata, it is astonishing. Bhagavan, how should one who has correctly entered the bodhisattva's vehicle abide, how should they practice, how should they control the mind?"

That was said, and the Bhagavan said to the venerable Subhuti, "Subhuti, well said, well said. Subhuti, it is so; it is so. The Tathagata has benefited the bodhisattva great beings with the highest benefit. The Tathagata has entrusted the bodhisattva great beings with the highest entrustment. Therefore, Subhuti, listen and properly retain it in mind, and I will explain to you how one who has correctly entered the bodhisattva's vehicle should abide, should practice, should control the mind."

Having replied, "Bhagavan, so be it," the venerable Subhuti listened in accordance with the Bhagavan, and the Bhagavan said this: "Subhuti, here, one who has correctly entered the bodhisattva's vehicle should generate the mind [of enlightenment] thinking this: 'As many as are included in the category of sentient being—born from egg, born from the womb, born from heat and moisture, born miraculously; with form, without form, with discrimination, without discrimination, without discrimination but not without [subtle] discrimination—the realm of sentient beings, as many as are designated by imputation as sentient beings, all those I shall cause to pass completely beyond sorrow into the realm of nirvana without remainder of the aggregates. Although limitless sentient beings have thus been caused to pass completely beyond sorrow, no sentient being whatsoever has been caused to pass completely beyond sorrow.'

"Why is that? Subhuti, because if a bodhisattva engages in discriminating a sentient being, he is not to be called a 'bodhisattva.' Why is that? Subhuti, if anyone engages in discriminating a sentient being, or engages in discriminating a living being, or engages in discriminating a person, they are not to be called a 'bodhisattva.'

"Further, Subhuti, a bodhisattva gives a gift without abiding in a thing; gives a gift without abiding in any phenomenon whatsoever. A gift should be given not abiding in visual form; a gift should be given not abiding in sound, smell, taste, tactility, or phenomenon either. Subhuti, without abiding in discriminating anything whatsoever as any sign, thus does a bodhisattva give a gift. Why is that? Subhuti, because the heap of merit of that bodhisattva who gives a gift without abiding, Subhuti, is not easy to take the measure of.

"Subhuti, what do you think about this? Do you think it is easy to take the measure of space in the east?"

Subhuti replied, "Bhagavan, it is not so."

The Bhagavan said, "Subhuti, similarly, do you think it is easy to take the measure of space in the south, west, north, above, below, the intermediate directions, and the ten directions?"

Subhuti replied, "Bhagavan, it is not so."

The Bhagavan said, "Subhuti, similarly, the heap of merit of that bodhisattva who gives a gift without abiding is also not easy to take the measure of.

"Subhuti, what do you think about this? Is one viewed as the Tathagata due to the perfect marks?"

Subhuti replied, "Bhagavan, it is not so; one is not viewed as the Tathagata due to the perfect marks. Why is that? Because that itself which the Tathagata called perfect marks are not perfect marks."

He replied thus, and the Bhagavan said this to the venerable Subhuti: "Subhuti, to the degree there are perfect marks, to that degree there is deception. To the degree there are no perfect marks, to that degree there is no deception. Thus view the Tathagata as marks and no marks."

He said that, and the venerable Subhuti replied to the Bhagavan, "Bhagavan, in the future period, at the end of the five hundred, when the holy Dharma will totally perish, will any sentient beings produce correct discrimination upon the words of sutras such as this being explained?"

The Bhagavan said, "Subhuti, do not say what you have said, '. . . in the future period, at the end of the five hundred, when the holy Dharma will totally perish, will any sentient beings produce correct discrimination upon the words of sutras such as this being explained...' Moreover, Subhuti, in the future period, at the end of the five hundred, when the holy Dharma will totally perish, there will be bodhisattva great beings, endowed with morality, endowed with qualities, endowed with wisdom. Subhuti, those bodhisattva great beings moreover will not have made homage to just a single buddha; they will not have produced roots of virtue to just a single buddha. Subhuti, there will be bodhisattva great beings who have made homage to many hundred thousands of buddhas and produced roots of virtue to many hundred thousands of buddhas.

"Subhuti, those who will acquire merely a single mind of faith upon the words of such sutras as this being explained, Subhuti, the Tathagata knows. Subhuti, they are seen by the Tathagata; Subhuti, all those sentient beings will produce and perfectly collect an unfathomable heap of merit. Why is that? Subhuti, because those bodhisattva great beings will not engage in discriminating a self and will not discriminate a sentient being, will not discriminate a living being, will not engage in discriminating a person.

"Subhuti, those bodhisattva great beings will not engage in discriminating phenomena nor discriminating non-phenomena; nor will they engage in discrimination or non-discrimination. Why is that? Subhuti, because if those bodhisattva great beings engage in discriminating phenomena, that itself would be of them grasping a self and grasping a sentient being, grasping a living being, grasping a person. Because even if they engage in discriminating phenomena as nonexistent, that would be of them grasping a self and grasping a sentient being, grasping a living being, grasping a person.

"Why is that? Further, Subhuti, because a bodhisattva should not wrongly grasp phenomena, nor grasp non-phenomena."

Therefore, thinking of that, the Tathagata said, "If, by those who know this Dharma treatise as like a boat, even dharmas should be given up, what need is there to mention non-dharmas?"

Further, the Bhagavan said to the venerable Subhuti, "Subhuti, what do you think about this? Does that Dharma that was manifestly and completely realized by the Tathagata, unsurpassed perfect and complete enlightenment, exist whatsoever? Has any Dharma been taught by the Tathagata?"

He said that, and the venerable Subhuti replied to the Bhagavan, "Bhagavan, as I understand this meaning that was taught by the

Bhagavan, that dharma that was manifestly and completely realized by the Tathagata, unsurpassed perfect and complete enlightenment, does not exist whatsoever. That Dharma that was taught by the Tathagata does not exist whatsoever. Why is that? Because any dharma manifestly and completely realized or taught by the Tathagata is not to be grasped, not to be expressed; it is not dharma nor is it non-dharma. Why is that? Because arya beings are differentiated by the uncompounded."

The Bhagavan said to the venerable Subhuti, "Subhuti, what do you think about this? If some son of the lineage or daughter of the lineage were to give gifts completely filling this billionfold world system with the seven types of precious things, do you think that son of the lineage or daughter of the lineage would produce an immense heap of merit on that basis?"

Subhuti replied, "Bhagavan, immense. Sugata, immense. That son of the lineage or daughter of the lineage would produce an immense heap of merit on that basis. Why is that? Bhagavan, because that very heap of merit is not a heap; therefore the Tathagata says, 'heap of merit, heap of merit.'"

The Bhagavan said, "Subhuti, compared to any son of the lineage or daughter of the lineage who were to give gifts completely filling this billionfold world system with the seven types of precious things, if someone, having taken even as little as one stanza of four lines from this discourse of Dharma, also were to explain and correctly and thoroughly teach it to others, the heap of merit produced on that basis would be much greater, incalculable, unfathomable. Why is that? Subhuti, because the unsurpassed perfectly completed enlightenment of the tathagata arhat perfectly completed buddhas arises from it; the buddha bhagavans also are produced from it. Why is that? Subhuti, because the Buddhadharmas called *Buddhadharmas* are those Buddhadharmas taught by the Tathagata as nonexistent; therefore, they are called *Buddhadharmas*.

"Subhuti, what do you think about this? Does the stream enterer think, 'I have attained the result of stream entry'?"

Subhuti replied, "Bhagavan, it is not so. Why is that? Bhagavan, because one does not enter into anything whatsoever; therefore, one is called *stream enterer*. One has not entered into form, nor entered into sound, nor into smell, nor into taste, nor into tactility, nor entered into a phenomenon; therefore, one is called *stream enterer*. Bhagavan, if that stream enterer were to think 'I have attained the result of stream entry,' that itself would be a grasping of that as a self, grasping as a sentient being, grasping as a living being, grasping as a person."

The Bhagavan said, "Subhuti, what do you think about this? Does the once-returner think, 'I have attained the result of once-returner'?"

Subhuti replied, "Bhagavan, it is not so. Why is that? Because the phenomenon of entry into the state of the once-returner does not exist whatsoever. Therefore, one says, 'once-returner.'"

The Bhagavan said, "Subhuti, what do you think about this? Does the nonreturner think, 'I have attained the result of nonreturn'?"

Subhuti replied, "Bhagavan, it is not so. Why is that? Because the phenomenon of entry into the state of the nonreturn does not exist whatsoever. Therefore, one says, 'nonreturner.'"

The Bhagavan said, "Subhuti, what do you think about this? Does the arhat think, 'I have attained the result of arhatship'?"

Subhuti replied, "Bhagavan, it is not so. Why is that? Because the phenomenon called *arhat* does not exist whatsoever. Bhagavan, if the arhat were to think, 'I have attained the result of arhatship,' that itself would be a grasping of that as a self, grasping as a sentient being, grasping as a living being, grasping as a person.

"Bhagavan, I was declared by the Tathagata Arhat Perfectly Completed Buddha as the foremost of those who abide without afflictions. Bhagavan, I am an arhat, free of attachment; but, Bhagavan, I do not think, 'I am an arhat.' Bhagavan, if I were to think, 'I have attained arhatship,' the Tathagata would not have made the prediction about me saying, 'The son of the lineage Subhuti is the foremost of those who abide without afflictions. Since not abiding in anything whatsoever, he abides without affliction, he abides without affliction.'"

The Bhagavan said, "Subhuti, what do you think about this? Does that Dharma that was received by the Tathagata from the Tathagata Arhat Perfectly Completed Buddha Dipankara exist whatsoever?"

Subhuti replied, "Bhagavan, it is not so. That Dharma that was received by the Tathagata from the Tathagata Arhat Perfectly Completed Buddha Dipankara does not exist whatsoever."

The Bhagavan said, "Subhuti, if some bodhisattva were to say, 'I shall actualize arranged fields,' they would speak untruly. Why is that?

Subhuti, because arranged fields called *arranged fields*, those arrangements are taught by the Tathagata as nonexistent; therefore, they are called *arranged fields*. Subhuti, therefore the bodhisattva great being should generate the mind without abiding, should generate the mind not abiding in anything. They should generate the mind not abiding in form, should generate the mind not abiding in sound, smell, taste, tactility, or phenomenon.

"Subhuti, it is like this: if, for example, the body of a being were to become thus, were to become like this, as big as Meru, the king of mountains, Subhuti, what do you think about this? Would that body be big?"

Subhuti replied, "Bhagavan, that body would be big. Sugata, that body would be big. Why is that? Because it is taught by the Tathagata as not being a thing; therefore it is called a *body*. Since it is taught by the Tathagata as not being a thing; therefore it is called a *big body*."

The Bhagavan said, "Subhuti, what do you think about this? If there were also just as many Ganges rivers as there are grains of sand in the river Ganges, would their grains of sand be many?"

Subhuti replied, "Bhagavan, if those very Ganges rivers were many, there is no need to mention their grains of sand."

The Bhagavan said, "Subhuti, you should appreciate; you should understand. If some man or woman, completely filling with the seven kinds of precious things as many world systems as there are grains of sand of those rivers Ganges, were to offer that to the Tathagata Arhat Perfectly Completed Buddha, Subhuti, what do you think about this? Would that man or woman produce much merit on that basis?"

Subhuti replied, "Bhagavan, much. Sugata, much. That man or woman would produce much merit on that basis."

The Bhagavan said, "Subhuti, compared to someone who, completely filling that many world systems with the seven types of precious things, were to give gifts to the Tathagata Arhat Perfectly Completed Buddha, if someone, having taken even as little as a stanza of four lines from this discourse of Dharma, were to explain it and correctly and thoroughly teach it also to others, the merit that itself would produce on that basis would be much greater, incalculable, unfathomable.

"Furthermore, Subhuti, if, at whatever place on earth even a stanza of four lines from this discourse on Dharma is recited or taught, that place on earth is a real shrine of the world with gods, humans, and demigods, what need to mention that whoever takes up this discourse of Dharma, memorizes, reads, understands, and properly takes to mind will be most astonishing. At that place on earth [where] the Teacher resides, other levels of gurus also abide."

He said that, and the venerable Subhuti replied to the Bhagavan, "Bhagavan, what is the name of this discourse of Dharma? How should it be remembered?"

He said that and the Bhagavan replied to the venerable Subhuti, "Subhuti, the name of this Dharma discourse is the 'wisdom gone beyond'; it should be remembered like that. Why is that? Subhuti, because the very same wisdom gone beyond that is taught by the Tathagata is not gone beyond; therefore it is called 'wisdom gone beyond.'

"Subhuti, what do you think about this? Does the Dharma that is taught by the Tathagata exist whatsoever?"

Subhuti replied, "Bhagavan, the Dharma that is taught by the Tathagata does not exist whatsoever."

The Bhagavan said, "Subhuti, what do think about this? Are the quantities of particles of earth that exist in a billionfold world system many?"

Subhuti replied, "Bhagavan, the particles of earth are many. Sugata, they are many. Why is that? Bhagavan, because that which is a particle of earth was taught by the Tathagata as not being a particle; therefore it is called 'particle of earth.' That which is a world system was taught by the Tathagata as not being a world system; therefore it is called a 'world system.'"

The Bhagavan said, "Subhuti, what do you think about this? Is one to be viewed as the Tathagata Arhat Perfectly Completed Buddha due to those thirty-two marks of a great being?"

Subhuti replied, "Bhagavan, it is not so. Why is that? Bhagavan, because those thirty-two marks of a great being that are taught by the Tathagata are taught by the Tathagata as no marks; therefore they are called 'thirty-two marks of the Tathagata.'"

The Bhagavan said, "Further, Subhuti, compared with some man or woman completely giving up bodies numbering the grains of sand of the river Ganges, if someone, taking even as little as a stanza of four lines from this discourse of Dharma, also were to teach it to others, they would produce on that basis many greater merits, incalculable, unfathomable."

Thereupon the venerable Subhuti, due to the impact of the Dharma, shed tears. Having wiped away the tears, he replied to the Bhagavan, "Bhagavan, this discourse on Dharma taught thus by the Tathagata, Bhagavan, is astonishing. Sugata, it is astonishing. Bhagavan, since my production of exalted wisdom, I have never before heard this discourse on Dharma. Bhagavan, those sentient beings who will produce correct discrimination upon this sutra being explained will be most astonishing. Why is that? Bhagavan, because that which is correct discrimination is not discrimination; therefore correct discrimination was taught by the Tathagata saying 'correct discrimination.' Bhagavan, upon this Dharma discourse being explained, that I imagine and appreciate it does not astonish me. Bhagavan, in the final time, in the final age, at the end of the five hundred, those sentient beings who take up this Dharma discourse and memorize, read, and understand it will be most astonishing. Furthermore, Bhagavan, they will not engage in discriminating a self; they will not engage in discriminating a sentient being, discriminating a living being, discriminating a person. Why is that? Bhagavan, because that itself which is discrimination as a self, discrimination as a sentient being, discrimination as a living being, and discrimination as a person is not discrimination. Why is that? Because buddha bhagavans are free of all discrimination."

He said that, and the Bhagavan replied to the venerable Subhuti, "Subhuti, it is so; it is so. Upon this sutra being explained, those sentient beings who are unafraid, unterrified, and will not become terrified will be most astonishing. Why is that? Subhuti, because this highest wisdom gone beyond, taught by the Tathagata, the highest wisdom gone beyond that is taught by the Tathagata, was also taught by unfathomable buddha bhagavans—therefore it is called 'highest wisdom gone beyond.'

"Further, Subhuti, that itself which is the patience gone beyond of the Tathagata has not gone beyond. Why is that? Subhuti, because when the king of Kalinga cut off my limbs and appendages, at that time there did not arise in me discrimination as a self, discrimination as a sentient being, discrimination as a living being, nor discrimination as a person, and in me there was no discrimination whatsoever, yet there was also no non-discrimination. Why is that? Subhuti, because, if at that time there had arisen in me discrimination as a self, at that time there would also have arisen discrimination of malice; if there had arisen discrimination as a sentient being, discrimination as a living being, discrimination as a person, at that time there would also have arisen discrimination of malice.

"Subhuti, I know with clairvoyance that in the past period, during five hundred lifetimes, I was the sage called Preacher of Patience; even then there did not arise in me the discrimination as a self; there did not arise the discrimination as a sentient being, discrimination as a living being, discrimination as a person. Subhuti, therefore the bodhisattva great being, completely abandoning all discrimination, should generate the mind for unsurpassed perfectly complete enlightenment. One should generate the mind not abiding in form. One should generate the mind not abiding in sound, smell, taste, tactility, or phenomena. One should generate the mind not abiding in non-phenomena either. One should generate the mind not abiding in anything whatsoever. Why is that? Because that itself which is abiding does not abide. Therefore the Tathagata taught, 'The bodhisattva should give gifts not abiding.'

"Further, Subhuti, the bodhisattva should thus totally give away gifts for the welfare of all sentient beings. However, that itself which is discrimination as a sentient being is non-discrimination. Those themselves who were taught by the Tathagata saying 'all sentient beings' also do not exist. Why is that? Subhuti, because the Tathagata teaches reality, teaches truth, teaches what is; the Tathagata teaches what is without error.

"Further, Subhuti, the Dharma that is manifestly and completely realized or shown by the Tathagata has neither truth nor falsity. Subhuti, it is like this, for example: if a man with eyes has entered darkness, he does not see anything whatsoever; likewise should one view the bodhisattva who totally gives up a gift by falling to the level of things.

"Subhuti, it is like this, for example: upon dawn and the sun rising, a man with eyes sees various kinds of forms; likewise should one view the bodhisattva who totally gives up a gift by not falling to the level of things.

"Further, Subhuti, those sons of the lineage or daughters of the lineage who take up this Dharma discourse and memorize, read, understand, and correctly and thoroughly teach it to others in detail are known by the Tathagata, they are seen by the Tathagata. All those sentient beings will produce an unfathomable heap of merit.

"Further, Subhuti, compared to some man or woman, at the time of dawn, totally giving up bodies numbering the grains of sand of the river Ganges—also totally giving up bodies numbering the grains of sand of the river Ganges at the time of midday and evening—in such number totally giving up bodies for many hundred thousands of ten million, hundred billion eons, if someone, having heard this Dharma discourse, would not reject it, if they themselves would produce much greater merit on that basis, incalculable, unfathomable, what need to mention someone who, having written it in letters, takes it up, memorizes, reads, understands, and correctly and thoroughly teaches it to others in detail?

"Further, Subhuti, this Dharma discourse is unimaginable and incomparable. This Dharma discourse was taught by the Tathagata for the benefit of sentient beings who have correctly entered into the supreme vehicle, the welfare of sentient beings who have correctly entered into the best vehicle. Those who take up this Dharma discourse and memorize, read, understand, and correctly and thoroughly teach it to others in detail are known by the Tathagata; they are seen by the Tathagata. All those sentient beings will be endowed with an unfathomable heap of merit. Being endowed with an unimaginable heap of merit, incomparable, immeasurable, and limitless, all those sentient beings will hold my enlightenment on the shoulder. Why is that? Subhuti, this Dharma discourse is unable to be heard by those who appreciate the inferior, by those viewing a self, by those viewing a sentient being, by those viewing a living being; those viewing a person are unable to hear, to take up, to memorize, to read, and to understand because that cannot be.

"Further, Subhuti, at whatever place on earth this sutra is taught, that place on earth will become worthy to be paid homage by the world with gods, humans, and demigods. That place on earth will become worthy as an object of prostration and worthy as an object of circumambulation. That place on earth will become like a shrine.

"Subhuti, whatever son of the lineage or daughter of the lineage takes up the words of a sutra like this, memorizes, reads, and understands, they will be tormented; they will be intensely tormented. Why is that? Subhuti, because whatever nonvirtuous actions of former lifetimes that were committed by those sentient beings that would bring rebirth in the lower realms, those nonvirtuous actions of former lifetimes will be purified by torment in this very life, and those [beings] will also attain the enlightenment of a buddha.

"Subhuti, I know with clairvoyance that in the past period, in even more countless of countless eons, much beyond even beyond the Tathagata Arhat Perfectly Completed Buddha Dipankara, there were 8,400 thousands of ten million, hundred billion buddhas whom I pleased, and having pleased, did not upset. Subhuti, from whatever I did, having pleased and not having upset those buddha bhagavans and in the future period, at the end of the five hundred, from someone taking up this sutra, memorizing, reading, and understanding, Subhuti, compared to this heap of merit, the former heap of merit does not approach even a hundredth part, a thousandth part, a hundred-thousandth part; does not withstand enumeration, measure, calculation, similarity, equivalence, or comparison.

"Subhuti, at that time, the sons of the lineage or daughters of the lineage will receive a heap of merit that, if I were to express the heap of merit of those sons of the lineage or daughters of the lineage, sentient beings would go mad, would be disturbed.

"Further, Subhuti, this Dharma discourse being unimaginable, its maturation indeed should also be known as unimaginable."

Then the venerable Subhuti replied to the Bhagavan, "Bhagavan, how should one who has correctly entered the bodhisattva's vehicle abide, how should they practice, how should they control the mind?"

The Bhagavan said, "Subhuti, here, one who has correctly entered the bodhisattva's vehicle should generate the mind thinking this: 'I shall cause all sentient beings to pass completely beyond sorrow into the realm of nirvana without remainder of the aggregates. Although sentient beings were caused to pass completely beyond sorrow like that, no sentient being whatsoever was caused to pass beyond sorrow.' Why is that? Subhuti, because if a bodhisattva engages in discriminating a sentient being, he is not to be called a bodhisattva. Also, if he engages in discriminating a person, he is not to be called a bodhisattva. Why is that? Subhuti, because the dharma called 'one who has correctly entered the bodhisattva's vehicle' does not exist whatsoever.

"Subhuti, what do you think about this? Does that dharma that was manifestly and completely realized by the Tathagata from the Tathagata Dipankara, unsurpassed perfect and complete enlightenment, exist whatsoever?"

He said that, and the venerable Subhuti replied to the Bhagavan, "Bhagavan, that dharma that was manifestly and completely realized by the Tathagata from the Tathagata Dipankara, unsurpassed perfect and complete enlightenment, does not exist whatsoever."

He said that, and the Bhagavan replied to the venerable Subhuti, "Subhuti, it is so. It is so; that dharma that was manifestly and completely realized by the Tathagata from the Tathagata Dipankara, unsurpassed perfect and complete enlightenment, does not exist whatsoever. Subhuti, if that dharma that was manifestly and completely realized by the Tathagata were to exist at all, the Tathagata Dipankara would not have made the prediction to me, saying, 'Young brahman, in a future period you will become the Tathagata Arhat Perfectly Completed Buddha Shakyamuni.' Subhuti, thus, since that dharma that was manifestly and completely realized by the Tathagata, unsurpassed perfect and complete enlightenment, does not exist whatsoever, therefore the Tathagata Dipankara made the prediction to me, saying, 'Young brahman, in a future period you will become the Tathagata Arhat Perfectly Completed Buddha Shakyamuni.' Why is that? Because, Subhuti, *tathagata* is an epithet of the suchness of reality.

"Subhuti, if someone were to say, 'The Tathagata Arhat Perfectly Completed Buddha manifestly and completely realized unsurpassed perfect and complete enlightenment,' they would speak wrongly. Why is that? Subhuti, because that dharma that was manifestly and completely realized by the Tathagata, unsurpassed perfect and complete enlightenment, does not exist whatsoever. Subhuti, that dharma that was manifestly and completely realized by the Tathagata has neither truth nor falsity. Therefore, 'all dharmas are Buddhadharmas' was taught by the Tathagata. Subhuti, 'all dharmas,' all those are non-dharmas.

Therefore it is said that 'all dharmas are Buddhadharmas.' Subhuti, it is like this, for example: as if a human were endowed with a body and the body became large."

The venerable Subhuti replied, "Bhagavan, that taught by the Tathagata, 'a human endowed with a body and a large body,' is taught by the Tathagata as not being a body. Therefore 'endowed with a body and a large body' is said."

The Bhagavan said, "Subhuti, it is so; if some bodhisattva were to say, 'I shall cause sentient beings to completely pass beyond sorrow,' he should not be called a bodhisattva. Why is that? Subhuti, does the dharma that is called *bodhisattva* exist whatsoever?"

Subhuti replied, "Bhagavan, it does not."

The Bhagavan said, "Subhuti, therefore it was taught by the Tathagata that 'all dharmas are without a sentient being, without a living being, without a person.'

"Subhuti, if a bodhisattva were to say, 'I shall actualize arranged fields,' he too should be expressed similarly. Why is that? Subhuti, because the arranged fields called *arranged fields* are those taught by the Tathagata as non-arranged. Therefore they are called *arranged fields*. Subhuti, whatever bodhisattva appreciates that dharmas are selfless, saying 'dharmas are selfless,' he is expressed by the Tathagata Arhat Perfectly Completed Buddha as a bodhisattva called a *bodhisattva*.

"Subhuti, what do you think about this? Does the Tathagata possess the flesh eye?"

Subhuti replied, "Bhagavan, it is so; the Tathagata possesses the flesh eye."

The Bhagavan said, "Subhuti, what do you think about this? Does the Tathagata possess the divine eye?"

Subhuti replied, "Bhagavan, it is so; the Tathagata possesses the divine eye."

The Bhagavan said, "Subhuti, what do you think about this? Does the Tathagata possess the wisdom eye?"

Subhuti replied, "Bhagavan, it is so; the Tathagata possesses the wisdom eye."

The Bhagavan said, "Subhuti, what do you think about this? Does the Tathagata possess the Dharma eye?"

Subhuti replied, "Bhagavan, it is so; the Tathagata possesses the Dharma eye."

The Bhagavan said, "Subhuti, what do you think about this? Does the Tathagata possess the buddha eye?"

Subhuti replied, "Bhagavan, it is so; the Tathagata possesses the buddha eye."

The Bhagavan said, "Subhuti, what do you think about this? If, there being also just as many Ganges rivers as there are grains of sand in the river Ganges, and there were just as many world systems as there are grains of sand of those, would those world systems be many?"

Subhuti replied, "Bhagavan, it is so; those world systems would be many."

The Bhagavan said, "Subhuti, as many sentient beings as exist in those world systems, I totally know their continua of consciousness of different thoughts. Why is that? Subhuti, because a so-called 'continuum of consciousness' is that taught by the Tathagata as a noncontinuum. Therefore it is called a 'continuum of consciousness.' Why is that? Subhuti, because past consciousness does not exist as observable, nor does future consciousness exist as observable, nor does present consciousness exist as observable.

"Subhuti, what do you think about this? If someone were to give gifts, completely filling this billionfold world system with the seven types of precious things, do you think that son of the lineage or daughter of the lineage would produce an enormous heap of merit on that basis?"

Subhuti replied, "Bhagavan, enormous. Sugata, enormous."

The Bhagavan said, "Subhuti, it is so. It is so; that son of the lineage or daughter of the lineage would produce an enormous heap of merit on that basis. Subhuti, if a heap of merit were a heap of merit, the Tathagata would not have taught a heap of merit called a 'heap of merit.'

"Subhuti, what do you think about this? Should one be viewed as the Tathagata due to total achievement of the form body?"

Subhuti replied, "Bhagavan, it is not so; one should not be viewed as the Tathagata due to total achievement of the form body. Why is that? Bhagavan, because 'total achievement of the form body' is that taught by the Tathagata as not being total achievement; therefore it is called 'total achievement of the form body.'"

The Bhagavan said, "Subhuti, what do you think about this? Is one to be viewed as the Tathagata due to perfect marks?"

Subhuti replied, "Bhagavan, it is not so; one is not to be viewed as the

Tathagata due to perfect marks. Why is that? Because that which was taught by the Tathagata as perfect marks was taught by the Tathagata as not being perfect marks; therefore they are called 'perfect marks.'"

The Bhagavan said, "Subhuti, what do you think about this? If it is thought that the Tathagata considers, 'the Dharma is demonstrated by me,' Subhuti, do not view it like that, because the Dharma that is demonstrated by the Tathagata does not exist whatsoever. Subhuti, if someone were to say 'the Dharma is demonstrated by the Tathagata,' Subhuti, he would deprecate me by wrongly seizing what does not exist. Why is that? Subhuti, because that demonstrated Dharma called 'demonstrated Dharma,' which is referred to by saying 'demonstrated Dharma,' does not exist whatsoever."

Then the venerable Subhuti said to the Bhagavan, "Bhagavan, in the future period, will there be any sentient beings who, having heard this demonstration of such a Dharma as this, will clearly believe?"

The Bhagavan said, "Subhuti, they are not sentient beings nor non-sentient beings. Why is that? Subhuti, so-called sentient beings, because they were taught by the Tathagata as non-sentient beings, therefore are called 'sentient beings.'

"Subhuti, what do you think about this? Does that dharma that was manifestly and completely realized by the Tathagata, unsurpassed perfect and complete enlightenment, exist whatsoever?"

The venerable Subhuti replied, "Bhagavan, that dharma that was manifestly and completely realized by the Tathagata, unsurpassed perfect and complete enlightenment, does not exist whatsoever."

The Bhagavan said, "Subhuti, it is so; it is so. For there, even the least dharma does not exist and is not observed, therefore it is called 'unsurpassed perfect and complete enlightenment.'

"Further, Subhuti, that dharma is equivalent since, for it, nonequivalence does not exist whatsoever; therefore it is called 'unsurpassed perfect and complete enlightenment.' That unsurpassed perfect and complete enlightenment—equivalent as selfless, without sentient being, without living being, without person—is manifestly and completely realized through all virtuous dharmas. Subhuti, virtuous dharmas called 'virtuous dharmas,' they, taught by the Tathagata as just non-dharmas, are therefore called 'virtuous dharmas.'

"Further, Subhuti, compared to any son of the lineage or daughter of the lineage collecting a heap of and giving as gifts the seven types of precious things about equaling whatever Meru, king of mountains, exist in a billion world systems, if someone, having taken up even as little as a stanza of four lines from this wisdom gone beyond, were to teach it to others, Subhuti, compared to this heap of merit, the former heap of merit does not approach even a hundredth part, does not withstand comparison.

"Subhuti, what do you think about this? If it is thought that the Tathagata considers, 'Sentient beings are liberated by me,' Subhuti, do not view it like that. Why is that? Subhuti, because those sentient beings who are liberated by the Tathagata do not exist whatsoever. Subhuti, if some sentient being were to be liberated by the Tathagata, that itself would be, of the Tathagata, grasping a self, grasping a sentient being, grasping a living being, grasping a person. Subhuti, so-called 'grasping a self,' that is taught by the Tathagata as non-grasping, yet that is grasped by childish ordinary beings. Subhuti, so-called 'childish ordinary beings,' they were taught by the Tathagata as just non-beings; therefore they are called 'childish ordinary beings.'

"Subhuti, what do you think about this? Is one to be viewed as the Tathagata due to perfect marks?"

Subhuti replied, "Bhagavan, it is not so; one is not viewed as the Tathagata due to perfect marks."

The Bhagavan said, "Subhuti, it is so; it is so. One is not viewed as the Tathagata due to perfect marks. Subhuti, if one were viewed as the Tathagata due to perfect marks, even a chakravartin king would be the Tathagata; therefore one is not viewed as the Tathagata due to perfect marks."

Then the venerable Subhuti said to the Bhagavan, "Bhagavan, as I understand the meaning of what the Bhagavan has said, one is not viewed as the Tathagata due to perfect marks."

Then these verses were spoken by the Bhagavan at that time: "Whoever sees me as form, whoever knows me as sound, has wrongly engaged by abandoning; those beings do not see me. The buddhas are dharmata viewed; the guides are the dharmakaya. Since dharmata is not to be known, it is unable to be known.

"Subhuti, what do you think about this? If one grasps that 'the Tathagata Arhat Perfectly Completed Buddha is due to perfect marks,'

Subhuti, you should not view so. For, Subhuti, the Tathagata Arhat Perfectly Completed Buddha does not manifestly and completely realize unsurpassed perfect and complete enlightenment due to perfect marks.

"Subhuti, if one grasps that 'some dharma has been designated as destroyed or annihilated by those who have correctly entered the bodhisattva's vehicle,' Subhuti, it should not be viewed so; those who have correctly entered the bodhisattva's vehicle have not designated any dharma whatsoever as destroyed or annihilated.

"Further, Subhuti, compared to any son of the lineage or daughter of the lineage who gives gifts, completely filling with the seven kinds of precious things as many world systems as there are grains of sand of the rivers Ganges, if any bodhisattva attained forbearance that dharmas are selfless and unproduced, the heap of merit they themselves would produce on that basis would be much greater. Further, Subhuti, a heap of merit should not be acquired by the bodhisattva."

The venerable Subhuti replied, "Bhagavan, should not a heap of merit be acquired by the bodhisattva?"

The Bhagavan said, "Subhuti, acquire, not wrongly grasp; therefore it is called 'acquire.'

"Subhuti, if someone says, 'The Tathagata goes or comes or stands or sits or lies down,' he does not understand the meaning explained by me. Why is that? Subhuti, because the Tathagata [the 'One Gone Thus'] does not go anywhere and does not come from anywhere; therefore one says, 'the Tathagata Arhat Perfectly Completed Buddha.'

"Further, Subhuti, if some son of the lineage or daughter of the lineage were, for example, to render as many atoms of earth as exist in a billionfold world system into powder like a collection of subtlest atoms, Subhuti, what do you think about this? Would that collection of subtlest atoms be many?"

Subhuti replied, "Bhagavan, it is so. That collection of subtlest atoms would be many. Why is that? Bhagavan, because if there were a collection, the Bhagavan would not have said 'collection of subtlest atoms.' Why is that? Because that collection of subtlest atoms that was taught by the Bhagavan was taught by the Tathagata as no collection; therefore one says 'collection of subtlest atoms.' That billionfold world system that was taught by the Tathagata was taught by the Tathagata as no system; therefore one says 'billionfold world system.' Why is that? Bhagavan, because if there were to be a world system, that itself would be grasping a solid thing. That taught by the Tathagata as grasping a solid thing was taught by the Tathagata as no grasping; therefore one says 'grasping a solid thing.'"

The Bhagavan said, "Subhuti, grasping a solid thing is itself a convention; that dharma does not exist as expressed, yet it is grasped by ordinary childish beings. Subhuti, if someone were to say, 'viewing as a self was taught by the Tathagata and viewing as a sentient being, viewing as a living being, viewing as a person was taught by the Tathagata,' Subhuti, would that be spoken by right speech?"

Subhuti replied, "Bhagavan, it would not. Sugata, it would not. Why is that? Bhagavan, because that which was taught by the Tathagata as viewing as a self was taught by the Tathagata as no viewing; therefore one says, 'viewing as a self.'"

The Bhagavan said, "Subhuti, those who have correctly entered the bodhisattva's vehicle should know, should view, should appreciate all dharmas like this; they should appreciate like this, not abiding whatsoever in any discrimination as a dharma. Why is that? Subhuti, because discrimination as a dharma, called 'discrimination as a dharma,' is taught by the Tathagata as non-discrimination; therefore one says 'discrimination as a dharma.'

"Further, Subhuti, compared to any bodhisattva great being who were to give gifts completely filling unfathomable and incalculable world systems with the seven kinds of precious things, if any son of the lineage or daughter of the lineage who, having taken as little as a stanza of four lines from this perfection of wisdom, were to memorize or read or understand or correctly and thoroughly teach it to others in detail, the merit he himself would produce on that basis would be more, incalculable, unfathomable.

"How should one correctly and thoroughly teach? Just how one would not correctly and thoroughly teach; therefore one says, 'correctly and thoroughly teach.'

"As a star, a visual aberration, a lamp, an illusion, dew, a bubble, a dream, lightning, and a cloud—view all the compounded like that."

That having been said by the Bhagavan, the elder Subhuti, those bodhisattvas, the fourfold disciples—monks, nuns, and lay male and female disciples—and the world with gods, humans, demigods, and gandharvas, overjoyed, highly praised that taught by the Bhagavan.

The *Vajra Cutter: An Exalted Mahayana Sutra on the Wisdom Gone Beyond* is concluded.

Colophon for the English Translation

This translation is based on the Tibetan Lhasa Zhol text, having compared it with various other Tibetan printings as well as with Sanskrit versions, and having viewed several excellent earlier English translations.

It was completed on 22 March 2002 at Chandrakirti Tibetan Buddhist Meditation Centre, near Nelson, New Zealand, by Gelong Thubten Tsultrim (the American Buddhist monk George Churinoff).

PLAY RECORDINGS OR VIDEOS OF TEACHINGS [35]

See chapter 15.
See also other practices related to the guru: 1, 10, 18, 43, 47, 60, 72, and 85.

It is good for your loved one to receive the blessings of His Holiness the Dalai Lama's holy speech, so play recordings or watch videos of his teachings. Of course, you can play recordings of the teachings of other lamas as well, especially the person's own lama.

Hearing the subject matter, especially bodhichitta, reminds them to practice, inspires their mind, arouses devotion, and of course helps them avoid being born in the lower realms.

RECITE THE MEDICINE BUDDHA PRACTICE [36]

See chapters 16, 18, 20, 21, 22, 23, 27, and 29.
See also other practices related to the Medicine Buddha: 14, 22, 59, and 78.

The main practice to do before, during, and after death is Medicine Buddha. As I mentioned in practice 14, there is an entire sutra—the *Medicine Buddha Sutra*—that describes the unbelievable benefits of this practice and how the Medicine Buddha himself made a promise that whoever chants his name or mantra will have all their prayers and wishes fulfilled.

I translated a version of the practice, the second one below, many years ago in which you visualize the seven Medicine Buddhas—the main Medicine Buddha and six others—above your head. It's very powerful, and unique, with the prayer of the seven limbs, a mandala offering, and so on, then a strong requesting prayer to each buddha, recited seven times.

A simpler alternative, the first one below, is to visualize just the main Medicine Buddha above your head, and as you recite the mantra, imagine nectar flowing from the Medicine Buddha, purifying you.

When you are guiding your loved one in the meditation, you would recite the practices as written.

When you and your friends are doing the practices either before or after the death of your loved one, you would visualize the Medicine Buddhas above their head purifying them and so on, changing the words accordingly.

At the end dedicate for their future rebirth either in a pure land or in a perfect human existence where they meet the Dharma, meet the perfectly qualified Mahayana guru, practice, and become enlightened as quickly as possible.

THE SIMPLE VERSION

Request
Visualize Guru Medicine Buddha above the crown of your head and make the following prayer of request seven times.

[36] RECITE THE MEDICINE BUDDHA PRACTICE

The fully realized destroyer of all defilements,
fully completed buddha having fully realized the absolute truth of all phenomena,
Guru Medicine Buddha, King of Lapis Light,
to you I prostrate, go for refuge, and make offerings.
May your vow to benefit all sentient beings now ripen for myself and others.

Mantra Recitation
Then recite the Medicine Buddha mantra.

TADYATHA / OM BHAISHAJYE BHAISHAJYE MAHA BHAISHAJYE [BHAISHAJYE] / RAJA SAMUDGATE SVAHA

Or use the common pronunciation:

TAYATA OM BEKANZE BEKANZE MAHA BEKANZE [BEKANZE] RADZA SAMUNGATE SOHA

Visualization during Mantra Recitation
As you recite the mantra, visualize purifying rays of light pouring down from Guru Medicine Buddha's heart and holy body, entering into you and eliminating all your negative karma and their causes, and your mental obscurations.

Imagine your body is completely filled with light and becomes clean, clear like crystal. Then the light radiates out in all directions, purifying the sicknesses and delusions of all mother sentient beings.

Visualization after Mantra Recitation
Guru Medicine Buddha melts into light and dissolves into your heart. Your mind becomes completely one with the dharmakaya, the essence of all buddhas.

Dedication

Due to these merits, may I complete the ocean-like actions of the sons of the victorious ones.

> May I become the holy savior, refuge, and helper for
>   sentient beings,
> who have repeatedly been kind to me in past lives.
>
> By the virtues received from attempting this practice,
> may all living beings who see, hear, touch, or remember me—
> even those who merely say my name—
> in that very moment be released from their miseries
> and experience happiness forever.
>
> As all sentient beings, infinite as space, are encompassed by
> Guru Medicine Buddha's compassion,
> may I too become the guide for sentient beings existing
> throughout all ten directions of the universe.
> Because of these virtues, may I quickly become
> Guru Medicine Buddha
> and lead each and every sentient being into his enlightened
>   realm.

THE LONGER VERSION

About four inches above the crown of your head is a lotus flower. In the center of the lotus is a white moon disk, and seated on the moon disk is my root guru—the dharmakaya essence of all the buddhas—in the form of the Medicine Buddha.

He is blue in color, and his body radiates blue light. His right hand, in the mudra of granting sublime realizations, rests on his right knee and holds the stem of the *arura* (*Terminalia chebula*) plant between thumb and first finger. His left hand is in the mudra of concentration and holds a lapis lazuli bowl filled with nectar.

He is seated in the full vajra position and is wearing the three red-colored robes of a monk. He has all the signs and qualities of a buddha.

Refuge and Bodhichitta

> I go for refuge until I am enlightened
> to the Buddha, the Dharma, and the supreme assembly.

[36] RECITE THE MEDICINE BUDDHA PRACTICE

By my practice of giving and other perfections,
may I become a buddha in order to benefit all sentient
   beings. (3x)

The Four Immeasurable Thoughts

May all sentient beings have happiness and the causes of
   happiness.
May all sentient beings be free from suffering and the
   causes of suffering.
May all sentient beings never be separated from the
   happiness that is without suffering.
May all sentient beings abide in equanimity, free from both
   attachment and hatred, holding some close and others
   distant.

Special Bodhichitta

Especially for the benefit of all sentient beings,
I will quickly, very quickly, attain the precious state of
   perfect and complete buddhahood.
For this reason I will practice the yoga method of Guru
   Medicine Buddha.

The Seven-Limb Prayer

I prostrate to Guru Medicine Buddha.
Each and every offering, including those actually performed and
   those mentally transformed, I present to you.
I confess all nonvirtuous actions accumulated since
   beginningless time.
I rejoice in the virtues of both ordinary and noble beings.
As our guide I request you, O Buddha, please abide well and turn
   the wheel of Dharma until samsara ends.
All virtues, both my own and those of others,
I dedicate to the ripening of the two bodhichittas and the
   attainment of buddhahood for the sake of all sentient beings.

Short Mandala Offering

This ground, anointed with perfume, strewn with flowers,
adorned with Mount Meru, four continents, the sun, and
    the moon:
I imagine this as a buddhafield and offer it.
May all living beings enjoy this pure land!

Inner Mandala Offering

The objects of my attachment, aversion, and ignorance—
    friends, enemies, and strangers—
and my body, wealth, and enjoyments:
without any sense of loss, I offer this collection.
Please accept it with pleasure and bless me with freedom
    from the three poisons.

IDAM GURU RATNA MANDALAKAM NIRYATAYAMI

Prayers of Request

I beseech you, Bhagavan Medicine Guru—
whose sky-colored holy body of lapis lazuli
signifies omniscient wisdom and compassion as vast
    as limitless space—
please grant me your blessings.

I beseech you, compassionate Medicine Guru—
who hold in your right hand the king of medicines
symbolizing your vow to help all pitiful sentient beings
    plagued by the 424 diseases—
please grant me your blessings.

I beseech you, compassionate Medicine Guru—
who hold in your left hand a bowl of nectar
symbolizing your vow to give the glorious undying nectar of

[36] RECITE THE MEDICINE BUDDHA PRACTICE 251

the Dharma that eliminates the degenerations of sickness, old age, and death—
please grant me your blessings.

Visualization of the Medicine Buddhas
1. Above the crown of Guru Medicine Buddha is a wish-granting jewel, which is in essence my guru.
2. Above that is the Buddha Delightful King of Clear Knowing, whose body is coral red in color, his right hand in the mudra of bestowing sublime realizations and his left hand in the mudra of concentration.
3. Above him is the Buddha Melodious Ocean of Dharma Proclaimed, with a dark pink-colored body, his right hand in the mudra of bestowing sublime realizations and his left hand in the mudra of concentration.
4. Above him is the Buddha Supreme Glory Free from Sorrow, light pink in color with both hands in the mudra of concentration.
5. Above him is the Buddha Stainless Excellent Gold, gold in color, his right hand in the mudra of expounding the Dharma and his left hand in the mudra of concentration.
6. Above him is the Buddha King of Melodious Sound, Brilliant Radiance of Skill, Adorned with Jewels, Moon, and Lotus, yellow in color with his right hand in the mudra of expounding the Dharma and his left hand in the mudra of concentration.
7. Above him is the Buddha Renowned Glorious King of Excellent Signs, gold in color with his right hand in the mudra of expounding the Dharma and his left hand in the mudra of concentration.

Requests to the Medicine Buddhas
Repeat each verse seven times. After the seventh recitation, as you say "May your vow to benefit...," the Medicine Buddha whom you request dissolves into the one below.

(7) To you, Buddha Renowned Glorious King of Excellent Signs,
fully realized destroyer of all defilements, fully accomplished

buddha who has fully realized the absolute truth of all phenomena,
I prostrate, go for refuge, and make offerings.
May your vow to benefit all sentient beings now ripen for myself and others.

(6) To you, Buddha King of Melodious Sound, Brilliant Radiance of Skill, Adorned with Jewels, Moon, and Lotus,
fully realized destroyer of all defilements, fully accomplished buddha who has fully realized the absolute truth of all phenomena,
I prostrate, go for refuge, and make offerings.
May your vow to benefit all sentient beings now ripen for myself and others.

(5) To you, Buddha Stainless Excellent Gold,
fully realized destroyer of all defilements, fully accomplished buddha who has fully realized the absolute truth of all phenomena,
I prostrate, go for refuge, and make offerings.
May your vow to benefit all sentient beings now ripen for myself and others.

(4) To you, Buddha Supreme Glory Free from Sorrow,
fully realized destroyer of all defilements, fully accomplished buddha who has fully realized the absolute truth of all phenomena,
I prostrate, go for refuge, and make offerings.
May your vow to benefit all sentient beings now ripen for myself and others.

(3) To you, Buddha Melodious Ocean of Dharma Proclaimed,
fully realized destroyer of all defilements, fully accomplished buddha who has fully realized the absolute truth of all phenomena,
I prostrate, go for refuge, and make offerings.

May your vow to benefit all sentient beings now ripen for myself and others.

(2) To you, Buddha Delightful King of Clear Knowing,
fully realized destroyer of all defilements, fully accomplished buddha who has fully realized the absolute truth of all phenomena,
I prostrate, go for refuge, and make offerings.
May your vow to benefit all sentient beings now ripen for myself and others.

(1) To you, Buddha Medicine Guru, Great King with the Radiance of a Lapis Jewel,
fully realized destroyer of all defilements, fully accomplished buddha who has fully realized the absolute truth of all phenomena,
I prostrate, go for refuge, and make offerings.
May your vow to benefit all sentient beings now ripen for myself and others.

Guru Medicine Buddha Grants Our Request
Granting your request, King of Medicine, Guru Medicine Buddha, sends from his heart and holy body infinite rays of white light, which pour down and completely fill your body from head to toe. They purify all your diseases and afflictions due to spirits and their causes, all your negative karma and mental obscurations.

In the nature of light, your body becomes as clean and clear as crystal.

The light rays pour down twice more, each time filling your body with blissful clean-clear light, which you absorb.

You are thereby transformed into the holy body of Guru Medicine Buddha.

At your heart appears a lotus and moon disk. Standing at the center of the moon disk is the blue seed-syllable *hum* surrounded by the syllables of the mantra.

As you recite the mantra, visualize light radiating in all directions from the syllable at your heart. The light rays pervade the sentient beings of all six realms. Through your great love wishing them to have happiness, and through your great compassion wishing them to be free from all sufferings, they are purified of all diseases and afflictions due to spirits and their causes, all their negative karma and mental obscurations.

Long Mantra

> OM NAMO BHAGAVATE BHAISHAJYE / GURU VAIDURYA / PRABHA RAJAYA / TATHAGATAYA / ARHATE SAMYAKSAM BUDDHAYA / TADYATHA / OM BHAISHAJYE BHAISHAJYE MAHA BHAISHAJYE [BHAISHAJYE] / RAJA SAMUDGATE SVAHA

Short Mantra

> TADYATHA / OM BHAISHAJYE BHAISHAJYE MAHA BHAISHAJYE [BHAISHAJYE] / RAJA SAMUDGATE SVAHA

Or use the common pronunciation:

> TAYATA OM BEKANZE BEKANZE MAHA BEKANZE [BEKANZE] RADZA SAMUNGATE SOHA

Feel great joy and think: all sentient beings are transformed into the aspect of the Medicine Buddha Guru. How wonderful that I am now able to lead all sentient beings into the Medicine Buddha's enlightenment.

Dedication

> Due to these merits, may I complete the ocean-like actions
>   of the sons of the Victorious Ones.
> May I become the holy savior, refuge, and helper for
>   sentient beings,
> who have repeatedly been kind to me in past lives.
>
> By my virtues received from attempting this practice,
> may all living beings who see, hear, touch, or remember me—
> even those who merely say my name—

in that very moment be released from their miseries and
experience happiness forever.

As all sentient beings, infinite as space, are encompassed by
Guru Medicine Buddha's compassion,
may I too become the guide for sentient beings existing
throughout all ten directions of the universe.
Because of these virtues, may I quickly become
Guru Medicine Buddha
and lead each and every sentient being into his enlightened
realm.

MEDITATE USING STUPAS [37]

See chapters 16 and 18.
See also practices 6 and 87.

Stupas and other holy objects can be used for purifying or healing meditation. As I mentioned in practice 6, what makes a stupa powerful is the presence in it of the four dharmakaya relic mantras, usually written in gold on the "life tree," the central wooden pole within the stupa. (For the four mantras, see practice 87.)

Guide your loved one in the meditation.

The Meditation
First breathe in slowly, then breathe out. As you breathe out, visualize that all your disease, harm caused by spirits, negative actions and thoughts, and the imprints left by these on your consciousness are purified.

Imagine they all come out of your body as black smoke, or pollution, and disappear beyond this earth.

Now, as you breathe in, visualize that powerful light beams are emitted from the stupa, which symbolizes the perfect, pure mind of full enlightenment.

This white light illuminates your body, completely purifying you of all disease, harm caused by spirits, negative actions and thoughts, and the imprints of all these on your consciousness.

Feel that your whole body is in the nature of white light. You have no suffering or problems at all. Your mind and body are completely free. From the top of your head down to your toes, your entire body is filled with great joy, with great bliss.

After experiencing this great bliss, think that your positive energy, the cause of your happiness and success, has been increased. All your qualities of wisdom and compassion have also been developed. Everything is fully developed within you.

MEDITATE ON TONGLEN, GIVING AND TAKING [38]

See chapters 16 and 29.
See also other practices related to the Compassion Buddha: 13, 21, 42, and 73.

If your loved one has a compassionate nature, a brave mind, they will be able to do *tonglen*: giving and taking. It is a profound and powerful practice in which they can use their own suffering, in particular their death, to develop compassion for others. Rather than rejecting death as something to fear, they can use it to develop the ultimate good heart of bodhichitta.

Encourage them to think, "Even as I am dying, I will try to make my death beneficial for all other living beings. I prayed in the past to take upon myself the suffering of others. I am now experiencing my death on behalf of everyone who is dying now and who will have to die in the future. How wonderful it would be for all of them to be free from the suffering of death and for me alone to experience it! May they have this ultimate happiness!"

If they have faith in Jesus Christ, you can suggest that they think like this, like some saints do. In this way, as they have to experience death anyway, they make it most meaningful.

Guide your loved one in the meditation that follows.

TAKING SUFFERING

Generate Compassion

Generate compassion by thinking of how living beings constantly experience suffering even though they have no wish to do so, because they are ignorant of its causes, or because, although they know the causes of suffering, they are too lazy to abandon them.

Think: "How wonderful it would be if all living beings could be free from all suffering and the causes of suffering, karma and delusions."

Think: "I myself will free them from all their suffering and its causes."

Take in the Suffering of All Humans

As you breathe in, focus first on all the numberless other beings who are dying. Then think of all the other problems experienced by all living beings, as well as their causes.

As you slowly breathe in, imagine you take in all this suffering and its causes through your nostrils in the form of black smoke. Like plucking a thorn out of their flesh, you immediately free all the numberless living beings from all their suffering.

Take in the Subtle Obscurations of the Holy Beings

Next, take all the subtle obscurations from the arhats and higher bodhisattvas. (There is nothing to take from the gurus and buddhas; all you can do is make offerings to them.)

The black smoke comes in through your nostrils and dissolves into the self-cherishing in your heart, completely destroying it. Your self-cherishing, the creator of all your problems, becomes nonexistent. Like aiming a missile right on target, aim right at your self-cherishing thought.

Take in the Suffering Environments of Sentient Beings

Take from others all the undesirable environments that they experience. Breathe in through your nostrils in the form of black smoke all the undesirable places that sentient beings experience. For example, imagine that you are breathing in the red-hot burning ground of the hot hells, the ice of the cold hells, the inhospitable environments of the hungry ghosts and animals, and the dirty places of human beings. The black smoke comes in through your nostrils and down to your heart, where it sinks into your self-cherishing and completely destroys it. Your self-cherishing is now nonexistent.

Self-cherishing is based on the ignorance that holds to the concept of a truly-existent I. Even though no truly-existent I exists, we cherish this false I and regard it as the most precious and most important among all beings. At the same time as your self-cherishing becomes completely nonexistent, the false I that ignorance holds to be truly existent also becomes completely empty, as it is empty in reality.

Meditate for as long as possible on this emptiness, the ultimate nature of the self. This purifies the actual causes of suffering, the ignorance itself.

GIVING HAPPINESS

Generate Loving Kindness
Next, generate loving kindness by thinking that even though living beings want to be happy, they lack happiness because they are ignorant of its causes or lazy in creating them. And even if they achieve some temporary happiness, they still lack the ultimate happiness of full enlightenment.

Think: "How wonderful it would be if all living beings had happiness and the causes of happiness."

Think: "I myself will bring them happiness and its causes."

Give Everything You Have to Sentient Beings
Visualize your body as a wish-granting jewel, which can grant all the wishes of living beings. Then give everything you have to every living being.

Give all your good karma of the past, present, and future and all the happiness that results from it up to enlightenment.

Give your possessions, your family and friends, and your body, visualized as a wish-granting jewel.

Also make offerings to all the enlightened beings.

Human Beings Receive Everything They Need
Now imagine that all living beings receive everything that they want, including all the realizations of the path to enlightenment. Those who want a friend, find a friend; those who want a guru, find a perfect guru; those who want a job, find a job; those who want a doctor, find a qualified doctor; those who want medicine, find medicine. For those with incurable diseases, you become the medicine that cures them.

Since the main human problem is difficulty in finding the means of living, imagine that each human being is showered with millions of dollars from your body, which is a wish-granting jewel.

You can also think that the environment becomes a pure land—the pure land of Amitabha Buddha or of the Buddha of Compassion. You grant all human beings everything they want, including a pure land with perfect enjoyments. All these enjoyments cause them only to generate the path to enlightenment within their mind, and they all become enlightened.

Give the Gods Everything They Need

In a similar way, give the worldly gods everything they need, such as protective armor. And they too become enlightened.

Transform the Environments of Hell Beings and Hungry Ghosts into Pure Lands

Now imagine completely transforming the environment of the hell beings into a blissful pure land, with perfect enjoyments and no suffering at all. Visualize the hells as pure lands, as beautiful as possible. All the iron houses of the hell beings, which are one with fire, become jewel palaces and mandalas. All the hell beings receive everything they want and then become enlightened.

Do the same for the hungry ghosts. Transform their environment into a pure land and give them thousands of different foods that all taste like nectar. The hungry ghosts receive everything they need, but the ultimate point is that they all become enlightened.

Give the Animals Protection

Since animals mainly need protection, manifest as Vajrapani or another wrathful deity to protect them from being attacked by other animals. They receive everything they want, and everything they receive becomes the cause for them to actualize the path and become enlightened.

Give Realizations to the Holy Beings

Give also to the arhats and bodhisattvas: give them whatever realizations they need to complete the path to enlightenment.

Finally, Rejoice

After everyone has become enlightened in this way, rejoice by thinking, "How wonderful it is that I have enlightened every single living being."

MEDITATE ON THE DEATH PROCESS [39]

See chapter 16.
See also chapter 9, chapter 10, and practice 41.

Help your loved one become familiar with the death process by leading them through a meditation on the various stages: the dissolution of the elements, the senses, all the way to the extremely subtle consciousness. Help them learn to recognize the visions, and at each stage get them to think, with strong determination: "I must recognize the clear light and definitely meditate on bliss and voidness."

As I discussed in chapter 10, the death-process meditation is an important aspect of a highest-tantra deity practice, where the meditator visualizes going through the death process, then the intermediate state, and then being reborn as the deity. This is called taking death, intermediate state, and rebirth into the path as the three bodies of the buddha.

Your loved one can also practice this as they go to sleep; see practice 41.

THE MEDITATION

1. *The Vision of a Mirage*
Think: "Now the mirage appears. There is the appearance of the mirage happening, and on that I label 'vision of mirage.' My thought merely labels on that. Therefore the true existence of this vision is completely empty, completely empty. The wisdom that is aware of this emptiness is in the nature of great bliss." Concentrate on that for a little while.

Think: "I *must*, I must recognize the clear light. And definitely I'm going to meditate on bliss and emptiness." Make strong determination.

A part of the mind is focusing on the vision of the mirage sealed with bliss and emptiness while another part of your mind is expecting the next vision.

2. *The Vision of Smoke*
Think: "The vision of smoke is about to happen." Anticipate it. Then it happens. The vision of the mirage is gone, and now the vision of smoke

is there, because the earth element is dissolving into the water element. It's like a room filled with smoke or incense.

Think: "This looks unlabeled, existing from its own side, but actually it is not true. On this appearance my thought has merely labeled 'vision of smoke.' So the true existence of this vision of smoke is completely empty. The wisdom that is aware of the emptiness of the vision of smoke is in the nature of great bliss." Meditate on that for a while.

Then think: "This time I *must* recognize the clear light and definitely meditate on bliss and emptiness." Make a strong determination.

Concentrate more on the vision of smoke while a part of the mind anticipates the next appearance, the vision of sparks. As the water dissolves into the fire element, a part of the mind is preparing for this.

3. The Vision of Sparks

Think: "Now the sparks appear. There is the appearance of sparks, and on that I label 'vision of fire sparks'; my thought merely labels on that. Therefore the true existence of this vision is completely empty." The emptiness is stronger than before, the bliss is stronger. The wisdom that is aware of the emptiness of the vision of sparks is in the nature of great bliss. Meditate on that for a while.

Again think: "I *must* recognize the clear light and definitely meditate on bliss and emptiness."

Concentrate more on the vision of sparks while a part of the mind anticipates the next appearance, the vision of the flame. As the fire dissolves into the air element, a part of the mind is preparing for this.

4. The Vision of a Flame

Think: "Now there is the vision of the flame." Imagine the dim red-blue light around the flame as the breath is about to stop. Again, the emptiness is much greater, and because of that the bliss is much greater.

"I *must* recognize the clear light. And definitely I am going to meditate on bliss and emptiness."

Think: "This looks unlabeled, existing from its own side, but actually it is not true. On this appearance my thought has merely labeled 'vision of the flame.' So the true existence of this vision of the flame is completely empty. The wisdom that is aware of the emptiness of the vision of the flame is in the nature of great bliss."

A part of the mind is focusing on the vision of the flame sealed with bliss and emptiness, while another part of the mind is expecting the white vision.

5. The White Vision

Then comes the white vision as the white bodhichitta flows down the central channel. The wisdom that is aware of the emptiness of the white vision is in the nature of great bliss. Experience even greater emptiness and bliss.

Think: "The true existence of the white vision is completely empty." Meditate on this.

Concentrate on the white vision as part of the mind anticipates the red vision.

Think: "I *must* recognize the clear light and definitely meditate on bliss and emptiness."

6. The Red Vision

Think: "The red vision is about to happen." Anticipate it. Then it happens. The white vision has finished, and now the red vision appears as the red bodhichitta goes up the central channel.

Think: "This red vision is completely empty of existing from its own side. It appears unlabeled, but it's not: on this appearance my thought is merely labeling 'red vision.'"

Experience even greater emptiness, even greater bliss.

Think: "I *must* recognize the clear light and meditate on bliss and emptiness."

7. The Dark Vision

The red vision ceases, and now there is the dark vision.

Think: "It looks as if it's existing from its own side, unlabeled, but it's not true." Now there is even more bliss, even greater experience of emptiness.

Think: "I *must* recognize the clear light."

Concentrate part of the mind on the dark vision as you anticipate the clear light.

8. The Clear-Light Vision

Finally there is the clear light, like dawn in autumn. This is appearing, but there is also the wisdom understanding emptiness.

Think: "I, everything, is empty. This emptiness is the great emptiness."

And now there is even more bliss; the bliss is so great it almost doesn't fit in the sky. And it is unified with emptiness—emptiness is bliss and bliss is emptiness: oneness, same taste, like water mixed with water. Bliss is subject and emptiness is object but nondual. Now the emptiness is greatest, the bliss is greatest. The vision of clear light is totally empty of existing from its own side.

Now you can also check on this I. You're not seeing your body, not seeing anything else, just the clear-light vision. While you are holding the mind in this, have another tiny part of your mind look at how your I appears, like you're spying on yourself. Try to identify the feeling that this I brings.

Think, "How do I view the I? How does it feel? How does it appear to me?" There's a way that we usually believe in the I, the self; there's a certain feeling, a way that we view it.

If you just bring up the word *I*, if you're too intellectual about it, this will not help. Or if you try to grab it too strongly, you won't catch it: it'll be like one of those tiny goldfish that moves so quickly.

You have to be very skillful, very careful. So, slowly, within the state of the clear-light vision, try to check up on this I, this self.

Concentrate on that.

SLEEP IN THE LION POSITION [40]

See chapter 16.
See also practice 55.

You could have the person go to sleep in the lion position, the position that our compassionate Buddha lay in when he passed away. This position is recommended also for the time of death; see practice 55. Sleeping in this position makes it easier to adopt it at the time of death. It is better to do this than to lie in the position of a frog, with legs splayed!

Each time your loved one goes to sleep like this, they can think about the Buddha, how he passed into the sorrowless state and how they're following in his footsteps. Recollecting the Buddha before they become absorbed in sleep leaves a profoundly positive imprint on their mind. As many thoughts of the Buddha they have is as many seeds they plant to achieve enlightenment.

Then at the time of death, the thought of the Buddha will arise in their mind easily. There'll be no worries, and they'll be saved by this final thought.

Also, going to sleep like this protects us from nightmares. And it prevents spirits from harming us while we're asleep: say that we go to sleep one night not coughing, but we have a cough when we wake up in the morning. It can happen like this.

Your loved one doesn't need to spend the whole night in this position, just when they first go to sleep.

The Lion Position

The right hand should be under the right cheek with the ring finger blocking the right nostril, and the left arm should be stretched out along their left side.

The breath coming through the right nostril is the breath of attachment, so stopping it helps the mind not be controlled by attachment, to not die with attachment. It might not be so easy to block the right nostril in this way, so you could use cotton instead. And you could put pillows behind your loved one's back to support the body.

Ideally, they should be lying with their head pointing toward the north, which means they are facing the west, which is where Amitabha Buddha's pure land is.

MEDITATE ON THE PROCESS OF GOING TO SLEEP [41]

See chapters 9 and 16.
See also practice 39.

The stages of dissolution that occur at death also occur when we go to sleep. If your loved can practice going through the stages while they go to sleep, they will find it much easier to recognize the stages at the time of death.

This practice is the same as the meditation on the eight stages of death in practice 39.

Guide your loved one in the meditation as they go to sleep.

Here, however, when they reach the eighth stage, the clear light, tell them: "While you are holding the mind on the vision of clear light, with a tiny part of your mind look at how your I appears. Try to identify the feeling that this I brings. Then, concentrate on that as you fall asleep."

Tell them that holding for even a few seconds the feeling of the oneness of the clear-light vision and the emptiness of the self is a profound mind and a wonderful one to fall asleep with.

They can learn to extend the awareness to the whole duration of sleep, including dreaming. Remember, passing from sleep into a dream is similar to passing from this life to the intermediate state. Now while we are dreaming, we rarely recognize dreams as dreams, but it is possible to train our mind to do this.

SLEEP WITH BODHICHITTA [42]

See chapter 16.
See also practices 13, 21, and 38.

Encourage your loved one to go to sleep with the thought of bodhichitta.

Think: "The purpose of my life is to free the numberless sentient beings from the oceans of samsaric suffering and bring them to enlightenment: the numberless hell beings, the numberless hungry ghosts, the numberless animals, the numberless human beings, the numberless gods and demigods, the numberless intermediate state beings. Therefore I must achieve enlightenment. Therefore I am going to go to sleep."

SLEEP IN THE GURU'S LAP [43]

See chapter 16.
See also other practices related to the guru: 1, 10, 18, 35, 47, 60, 72, and 85.

Your loved one could go to sleep with guru devotion. With the virtuous thought of compassion, they imagine that their head is in the lap of their guru, visualized as the buddha they feel closest to. They should strongly take refuge. Visualize radiant white light coming from the guru buddha's holy body and pouring into theirs. All their negativities are purified, and they become oneness with the guru's holy qualities.

This protects them, and it makes it easier to remember the guru at the time of death.

SLEEP WITH EMPTINESS [44]

See chapter 16.
See also practice 41.

If your loved one has studied emptiness, you can talk to them about how all the fears and problems that everybody faces come from the wrong view of seeing everything, even life, as existing from its own side.

They could sleep while thinking about emptiness and dependent arising.

Or they could sleep with the thought that everything is a dream, is a mirage, is an illusion—actually, not *is* an illusion but *like* an illusion. Seeing everything *as if* it is an illusion cuts the grasping at the appearance of it as existing inherently, from its own side. In their heart they can understand that the I is empty, everything is empty.

Sleeping Yoga

If your loved one has received a highest tantra initiation, they could practice sleeping yoga, either with creativity or without creativity. "Without creativity" refers basically to meditating on emptiness while falling asleep—see practice 41. As discussed in chapters 10 and 24, the great tantric practitioners who can recognize the clear light at sleep are able to recognize the clear light of death, no question.

"With creativity" refers to going to sleep while meditating on the deity's mandala. When they wake up, they would arise from the clear light according to whichever deity they practice.

If your loved one practices a deity within the lower tantras, such as the Compassion Buddha as explained in the *nyungné* fasting practice (practice 73), they would visualize themselves as Compassion Buddha dissolving into the syllable HRIH, and then the HRIH gradually dissolving into emptiness or into the mandala.

MEDITATE ON THE EMPTINESS OF DEATH [45]

See chapter 16.

Remind your loved one that death is natural, that the mind that clings is what makes death terrifying. Death is merely the mind separating from the body, and this is labeled "death."

You can tell them that in emptiness, there is no such thing as birth and death. They can think: "Death appears to be real and existing from its own side, and I believe it to exist in this way, but actually this is a hallucination. There is no such thing. It is totally empty." Encourage them to keep their mind in that state.

You can remind them that they are striving to attain enlightenment for all sentient beings, and that even before then, when they reach the state of the arya-bodhisattva and perceive emptiness directly, they will have transcended disease, old age, and death. This is what awaits them, so there is no reason to fear death.

MEDITATE ON THE EMPTINESS OF THE MIND [46]

See chapter 16.

You can help your loved one think about how their mind is empty because it is a dependent arising, to meditate on the emptiness of the mind that appears to be not merely labeled by thought.

Tell them that the base of the label "mind" is that which is formless, that which is not obstructed, not obscured by substantial phenomena, and therefore is clear. This means that phenomena can appear to it, that it can perceive phenomena—just like a mirror, which, because it is not obscured by the substantial phenomenon of dust, is clear. Objects can be reflected in it; it can reflect objects.

That is the base. And "mind" is the label that is simply imputed by their own thought on the base. Mind is merely imputed by thought *because* there is this phenomenon that is formless, not obstructed by phenomena, clear, and that perceives objects.

So what is their mind? It is nothing *except* what is merely imputed by a thought. They can see now that there is no such thing as mind existing from its own side. There is a mind that exists in mere name, merely imputed by thought, but it is empty of existing from its own side. And while the mind is empty, it is existing. How is it existing? It exists in mere name, merely imputed by thought. It is unified with emptiness and dependent arising.

This is how all phenomena exist.

RECITE YOUR LOVED ONE'S DAILY PRACTICES [47]

See chapters 16, 18, 20, 21, 22, and 23.
See also other practices related to the guru: 1, 10, 18, 35, 43, 60, 72, and 85.

It is very good to recite your loved one's daily practices to them, especially their main sadhana if they have received initiations—the visualizations, prayers, and mantras. This helps them strengthen their connection with their particular deity and their guru.

They can meditate as you recite.

You can also recite these practices after your loved one has died.

HELP YOUR LOVED ONE PRACTICE PHOWA [48]

See chapter 16.
See also practices 62 and 81.

As I mentioned in chapter 6 and elsewhere, it is possible to be reborn in a pure land by practicing phowa, the transference of consciousness. This practice is one of the six yogas of Naropa. In fact, it is said that even someone who has led a very negative life, if they're careful at death and with the help of this practice, can be born in a pure land.

The practice can be done either by the dying person—they forcefully push their own consciousness from their body just before death and send it to a pure land—or by their guru or another lama, or even a close friend.

If Your Loved One Has Their Own Practice of Phowa
You can practice phowa up to six months before you die. Phowa should be practiced in advance, when the mind is clear.

If It Is to Be Performed by a Lama
It should happen as soon as the breath stops (practice 62), not before. It can also be done by a lama during the forty-nine days after the mind has left the body (practice 81).

If It Is to Be Performed by You and Your Dharma Friends
Recite the Amitabha phowa practice written by Lama Yeshe (practice 81) during the forty-nine days after the mind has left the body.

PURIFY WITH THE PRACTICE OF PROSTRATIONS TO THE THIRTY-FIVE BUDDHAS OF CONFESSION [49]

See chapters 17, 18, 20, 21, 22, and 23.
See also practice 15.

This practice contains the four opponent powers: reliance, regret, the remedy, and restraint (see practice 50 for details). Merely hearing the names of these thirty-five buddhas purifies many thousands of eons of negative karma and makes it impossible to be reborn in the lower realms.

Guide your loved one in the practice.

How to Meditate Before the Practice
Contemplate:

> The purpose of my life is to free the numberless sentient beings—who are the source of all my past, present, and future happiness, temporary as well as ultimate, including all the realizations of the path, liberation from samsara, and enlightenment—from all the oceans of samsaric suffering, including the causes: delusions and karma.
> To do this, I must achieve full enlightenment. Therefore I need to actualize the path. Therefore I need to purify negative karma and delusions.
> Samsara has no end.
> Not only that, karma increases: from even a small negative action huge suffering results can come. From just one negative karma, I have to experience the results over and over again for many hundreds of lifetimes.
> And karma is certain to be experienced, so every negative action I have created will definitely bring its result, no matter how long it takes, until it is purified.
> Understanding this, how can I stand to live life without purifying myself and getting rid of all these negative

karmas, just as I would try to get rid of a deadly poison in my body?
Not only that, I'm going to die, and death can come any moment, even today.
Therefore I must purify all my negative actions this second.
To do that, I am going to do these prostrations with the practice of confessing downfalls.
And I'm doing this to develop myself in order to work for the happiness of all sentient beings.

How to Meditate During the Practice

Visualize in the space in front of you your guru in the aspect of Shakyamuni Buddha, with Thousand-Armed Chenrezik, the Compassion Buddha, at his heart.

At the heart of Chenrezik is the syllable HRIH, and from this syllable thirty-four beams of light emanate, forming six rows in the space beneath Chenrezik.

At the end of each beam is a throne supported by elephants and adorned with pearls, and on each throne is seated one of the other thirty-four buddhas of confession.

In the *first row* are six buddhas, blue in color and in the aspect of Akshobhya, with the exception of the third buddha, King Lord of the Nagas, who has a blue body but a white head.

In the *second row*, there are seven buddhas, white in color, in the aspect of Vairochana.

In the *third row* are seven buddhas, yellow in color, in the aspect of Ratnasambhava.

In the *fourth row* are seven buddhas, red in color, in the aspect of Amitabha.

In the *fifth row* there are seven buddhas, green in color, in the aspect of Amoghasiddhi.

In the *sixth row* are the seven Medicine Buddhas.

Think that each one of these buddhas is the embodiment of the Three Rare Sublimes Ones of the three times and ten directions, as well as all statues, stupas, and scriptures. And think that in their essence, all of these are the guru.

[49] PURIFY WITH THE PRACTICE OF PROSTRATIONS

Have complete faith that each one has the power to purify all your negative karmas and imprints accumulated since beginningless time.

Increasing Mantras

Recite the following mantras as you imagine prostrating, thus increasing the merit of making prostrations one million times.

CHOMDENDÉ DEZHIN SHEKPA DRACHOMPA YANGDAKPAR DZOKPAI SANGYÉ RINCHEN GYALTSEN LA CHAK TSAL LO (7X)

OM NAMO BHAGAVATE RATNA KETU RAJAYA / TATHAGATAYA / ARHATE SAMYAK SAMBUDDHAYA / TADYATHA / OM RATNE RATNE MAHARATNE RATNA BIJAYE SVAHA (7X)

OM NAMO MANJUSHRIYE / NAMO SUSHRIYE / NAMA UTTAMA SHRIYE SVAHA (3X)

Refuge

Recite:

> I, [say your name], throughout all times, take refuge in the Guru,
> I take refuge in the Buddha,
> I take refuge in the Dharma,
> I take refuge in the Sangha. (3x)

Recite the Names of the Buddhas

Now imagine that you emanate numberless bodies in all directions, and, as you imagine prostrating, all these bodies prostrate along with you, covering every atom of the earth.

Recite each buddha's name several times. It is the recitation of the name of each buddha that brings the purification, so it makes a big difference whether you recite just a few times or many. You begin with this homage and then continue with the names:

> Homage to the confession of the bodhisattva's downfalls!

Shakyamuni Buddha
1. To the Founder, Bhagavan, Tathagata, Arhat, Perfectly Completed Buddha, Glorious Conqueror Shakyamuni Buddha, I prostrate.

First Row, Blue, in the Aspect of Akshobhya
2. To Tathagata Thoroughly Destroying with Vajra Essence, I prostrate.
3. To Tathagata Radiant Jewel, I prostrate.
4. To Tathagata King, Lord of the Nagas, I prostrate.
   [with a white face]
5. To Tathagata Army of Heroes, I prostrate.
6. To Tathagata Delighted Hero, I prostrate.
7. To Tathagata Jewel Fire, I prostrate.

Second Row, White, in the Aspect of Vairochana
8. To Tathagata Jewel Moonlight, I prostrate.
9. To Tathagata Meaningful to See, I prostrate.
10. To Tathagata Jewel Moon, I prostrate.
11. To Tathagata Stainless One, I prostrate.
12. To Tathagata Bestowed with Courage, I prostrate.
13. To Tathagata Pure One, I prostrate.
14. To Tathagata Bestowed with Purity, I prostrate.

Third Row, Yellow, in the Aspect of Ratnasambhava
15. To Tathagata Water God, I prostrate.
16. To Tathagata Deity of the Water God, I prostrate.
17. To Tathagata Glorious Goodness, I prostrate.
18. To Tathagata Glorious Sandalwood, I prostrate.
19. To Tathagata Infinite Splendor, I prostrate.
20. To Tathagata Glorious Light, I prostrate.
21. To Tathagata Sorrowless Glory, I prostrate.

Fourth Row, Red, in the Aspect of Amitabha
22. To Tathagata Son of Noncraving, I prostrate.
23. To Tathagata Glorious Flower, I prostrate.
24. To Tathagata Pure Light Rays Clearly Knowing by Play, I prostrate.

[49] PURIFY WITH THE PRACTICE OF PROSTRATIONS

25. To Tathagata Lotus Light Rays Clearly Knowing by Play, I prostrate.
26. To Tathagata Glorious Wealth, I prostrate.
27. To Tathagata Glorious Mindfulness, I prostrate.
28. To Tathagata Glorious Name Widely Renowned, I prostrate.

Fifth Row, Green, in the Aspect of Amoghasiddhi

29. To Tathagata King Holding the Victory Banner of Foremost Power, I prostrate.
30. To Tathagata Glorious One Totally Subduing, I prostrate.
31. To Tathagata Utterly Victorious in Battle, I prostrate.
32. To Tathagata Glorious Transcendence Through Subduing, I prostrate.
33. To Tathagata Glorious Manifestations Illuminating All, I prostrate.
34. To Tathagata All-Subduing Jewel Lotus, I prostrate.
35. To Tathagata, Arhat, Perfectly Completed Buddha, King, Lord of the Mountains Firmly Seated on Jewel and Lotus, I prostrate. (3x)

Now recite the names of the seven Medicine Buddhas while continuing to prostrate.

1. Buddha Renowned Glorious King of Excellent Signs
2. Buddha King of Melodious Sound, Brilliant Radiance of Skill, Adorned with Jewels, Moon, and Lotus
3. Buddha Stainless Excellent Gold
4. Buddha Supreme Glory Free from Sorrow
5. Buddha Melodious Ocean of Dharma Proclaimed
6. Buddha Delightful King of Clear Knowing
7. Buddha Medicine Guru, Great King with the Radiance of a Lapis Jewel

Confession Prayer
Recite:

All those [you thirty-five buddhas] and others, as many tathagatas, arhats, perfectly completed buddhas as there are existing, sustaining, and residing in all the world systems of the ten directions; all you buddha bhagavans, please pay attention to me.

In this life and in all the states of rebirth in which I have circled in samsara throughout beginningless lives, whatever negative actions I have created, made others create, or rejoiced in the creation of,

whatever possessions of stupas, possessions of the sangha, or possessions of the sangha of the ten directions that I have appropriated, made others appropriate, or rejoiced in the appropriation of,

whichever among the five actions of immediate [retribution] I have done, caused to be done, or rejoiced in the doing of,

whichever paths of the ten nonvirtuous actions I have engaged in, caused others to engage in, or rejoiced in the engaging in:

whatever I have created, being obscured by these karmas causes me and sentient beings to be born in the hell realms, in the animal realm, and in the hungry ghost realm; in irreligious countries, as barbarians, or as long-life gods; with imperfect faculties, holding wrong views, or not being pleased with Buddha's descent.

In the presence of the buddha bhagavans, who are transcendental wisdom, who are eyes, who are witnesses, who are valid, and who see with omniscient consciousness, I am admitting and confessing all these negativities. I will not conceal them nor hide them, and from now on in the future I will abstain and refrain from committing them again.

All buddha bhagavans, please pay attention to me. In this life and in all other states of rebirth in which I have circled in samsara throughout beginningless lives,

whatever roots of virtue I have created by generosity, even as little as giving just one mouthful of food to a being born in the animal realm,

whatever roots of virtue I have created by guarding
  morality,
whatever roots of virtue I have created by following pure
  conduct,
whatever roots of virtue I have created by fully ripening
  sentient beings,
whatever roots of virtue I have created by generating
  bodhichitta,
and whatever roots of virtue I have created by my
  unsurpassed transcendental wisdom:
all these assembled and gathered, combined together, I
  fully dedicate to the unsurpassed, the unexcelled, that
  higher than the high, that superior to the superior.

Thus I completely dedicate to the highest, perfectly
  complete enlightenment.
Just as the previous buddha bhagavans have fully dedicated,
  just as the future buddha bhagavans will fully dedicate,
  and just as the presently abiding buddha bhagavans are
  fully dedicating, like that I too dedicate fully.
I confess all negativities individually.
I rejoice in all the merits.
I urge and implore all buddhas to grant my request: may
  I receive the highest, most sublime transcendental
  wisdom.
To the conquerors, the best of humans—those who are
  living in the present time, those who have lived in the
  past, and those who will likewise come—to all those
  who have qualities as vast as an infinite ocean, with
  hands folded, I approach for refuge.

The General Confession Prayer

As you confess each of the negative actions contained in this prayer, think to yourself that you have created this negative action not just once but countless times in this and in beginningless lives, whether you remember it or not.

Generate very strong regret. The stronger the regret, the greater the purification. Then recite:

> U hu lak! (Woe is me!)
> O great Guru Vajradhara, all other buddhas and bodhisattvas who abide in the ten directions, and all the venerable sangha, please pay attention to me.
> I, who am named [say your name], circling in cyclic existence from beginningless time until the present, overpowered by mental afflictions such as attachment, aversion, and ignorance by means of body, speech, and mind, have created the ten nonvirtuous actions.
> I have engaged in the five uninterrupted negative karmas and the five nearing uninterrupted negative karmas.
> I have transgressed the vows of individual liberation, transgressed the vows of bodhisattvas, and transgressed the samaya of secret mantra.
> I have been disrespectful to my parents, have been disrespectful to my vajra masters, and to my abbot, and have been disrespectful to my spiritual friends living in ordination, have committed actions harmful to the Three Jewels, avoided the holy Dharma, criticized the arya Sangha, harmed sentient beings, and so on.
> These and many other nonvirtuous negative actions I have done, have caused others to do, have rejoiced in others' doing, and so forth.
> In the presence of the great Guru Vajradhara, all the buddhas and bodhisattvas who abide in the ten directions, and the venerable Sangha, I admit this entire collection of faults and transgressions that are obstacles to my own higher rebirth and liberation and are causes of cyclic existence and miserable lower rebirths.
> I will not conceal them, and I accept them as negative.
> I promise to refrain from doing these actions again in the future. By confessing and acknowledging them, I will attain and abide in happiness, while by not confessing and acknowledging them, true happiness will not come.

[49] PURIFY WITH THE PRACTICE OF PROSTRATIONS

Visualization at the End of the Practice

Think that through the force of reciting these names of the Thirty-Five Buddhas of Confession and Medicine Buddhas, through the power of their pure prayers and vows, through the power of generating regret and the other opponent powers, and through the power of having made these prostrations, nectars and light rays descend from the holy bodies of the buddhas, completely purifying all negative karmas, defilements, and imprints collected on your mental continuum since beginningless time.

Generate strong faith that your mind has become completely pure.

Determination to Change

At the end of the confession prayer, pause to make the determination not to commit these negative actions again in the future. Make this promise realistic, even if you are promising simply not to do the negative action for just the next five minutes or seconds. This is to make sure you that you do not tell a lie to the merit field.

Reflect on Emptiness

Then reflect on the emptiness of each of these negative actions, remembering that even negative actions do not truly exist from their own side. They arise in dependence on causes and conditions and are merely labeled by the mind. You can think either that they are completely nonexistent from their own side, or that they are merely labeled by mind, or that they are hallucinations.

Whichever method you use to understand emptiness, the conclusion that should come in your heart is that each of these negative actions is completely empty, not existing from its own side, even the slightest atom.

> In emptiness there is no I, the creator of negative actions.
> In emptiness there is no creating of negative actions.
> In emptiness there are no negative actions created.
> Even though there are infinite phenomena,
> in emptiness nothing exists at all.
> There is no this and that, no me and you, nothing.
> In emptiness everything is one taste.

From this emptiness, everything comes into existence.
Whatever exists is the manifestation of emptiness.

Colophon
The practice of the recitation of the names of the buddhas and the confession prayer is based on a translation by Lama Zopa Rinpoche. The motivation, visualizations, and meditations were compiled by Ven. Sarah Thresher according to Rinpoche's instructions. The general confession prayer is based on a translation by Glenn Mullin.

PURIFY WITH THE PRACTICE OF VAJRASATTVA AND THE FOUR OPPONENT POWERS [50]

See chapters 17, 18, 20, 21, 22, and 23.

The Vajrasattva recitation meditation, which also includes the four opponent powers, is an incredibly powerful method. Practicing it at the end of every day prevents negative karma from multiplying. It also helps purify that day's negative karma, as well as the negative karma created since the time we were born and in all our previous lives.

Guide your loved one in this practice composed by Lama Zopa Rinpoche.

Visualization
On your right side is your father; on your left side is your mother. Your enemies and those sentient beings who make you agitated are in front of you, and your friends and those to whom you are attached are seated behind you. All other universal living beings, in human form, are surrounding you, as far as you can imagine.

Visualize the object of refuge, the merit field, in the space in front of you, either the elaborate visualization of "one into many," where you visualize all the buddhas, thinking they are oneness with your guru, or the simple visualization of "the many into one," where you visualize just the guru, thinking he encompasses all the numberless buddhas.

(1a) The Power of Reliance: Taking Refuge
As you recite this verse, think that you and all sentient beings are together taking refuge in the Three Rare Sublime Ones.

> I forever take refuge in Buddha, Dharma, and Sangha
> and in all the three vehicles,
> in the dakinis of secret mantra yoga, in the heroes and
>   heroines,
> in the empowering goddesses and the bodhisattvas.
> But most of all, I take refuge in my holy guru forever. (3x)

(2) The Power of Regret

First recall the definition of negative karma—any action that results in suffering, usually an action motivated by ignorance, attachment, or aversion. Then contemplate:

> Almost every action I do, twenty-four hours a day, is motivated by worldly concern, attachment to the comfort of this life. It is like this from birth to death in this life and has been like that from beginningless rebirths. Nearly every action I have ever created has been nonvirtuous, the cause of suffering.
> Not only that, continuously I have also been breaking my individual liberation, bodhisattva, and tantric vows.
> Worst of all, I have created the heaviest of negative karmas in relation to my virtuous friends—getting angry at them, generating wrong views, having non-devotional thoughts toward them, harming their holy body, and disobeying their advice.
> Having these negative imprints on my mental continuum is unbearable. It's as if I've swallowed a lethal poison. I must practice the antidote right away and purify all this negative karma immediately, without a second's delay!

In this way, generate strong feelings of urgency and regret.

Remembering Impermanence and Death

Contemplate:

> Many people my age or younger have died. It's a miracle that I'm still alive and have this incredible opportunity to purify my negative karma. Death is certain, but its time is most uncertain.
> If I were to die right now, I would definitely be born in the lower realms. Because I could not practice Dharma there, I would remain in the lower realms for countless eons.
> Therefore, how unbelievably fortunate I am to be able to purify my negative karma right now, without even a second's delay, by practicing the Vajrasattva recitation meditation.

[50] PURIFY WITH THE PRACTICE OF VAJRASATTVA

(1b) The Power of Reliance: Generating Bodhichitta
Contemplate:

> But I am not practicing this Vajrasattva purification for myself alone. The purpose of my life is to release all hell beings, pretas, animals, humans, demigods, gods, and intermediate state beings from all their suffering and its causes and lead them to unsurpassed enlightenment.
> To do this, I must first reach enlightenment myself. Therefore I must purify all my negative karma immediately by practicing the Vajrasattva recitation meditation.

Visualization
Above the crown of your head, seated upon a lotus and moon seat, are Vajrasattva father and mother. Their bodies are white; each has one face and two arms. He holds a vajra and bell, she a curved knife and skull cup. They are embracing each other. The father is adorned with six mudras, the mother with five. He sits in the vajra posture, she in the lotus.
Think:

> Vajrasattva is my root guru, the holy mind of all the buddhas, the dharmakaya, who out of his unbearable compassion, which embraces me and all other sentient beings, appears in this form to purify me and all others.

In this way, your mind is transformed into guru devotion—the root of all blessings and realizations of the path to enlightenment.

(3) The Power of the Remedy: Mantra Recitation
On a moon disk at Vajrasattva's heart stands a HUM encircled by a garland of the hundred-syllable mantra. A powerful stream of white nectar flows from the HUM and mantra garland, and you are cleansed of all sickness, spirit harm, negative karma, and obscurations.

Recite the mantra seven or twenty-one times or as many times as possible, practicing the three techniques of downward cleansing, upward cleansing, and instantaneous cleansing.

OM VAJRASATTVA SAMAYA MANUPALAYA / VAJRASATTVA
TVENOPATISHTHA / DRIDHO ME BHAVA / SUTOSHYO ME BHAVA /
SUPOSHYO ME BHAVA / ANURAKTO ME BHAVA / SARVA SIDDHIM ME
PRAYACCHA / SARVA KARMA SUCHAME / CHITTAM SHRIYAM KURU
HUM / HA HA HA HO / BHAGAVAN SARVA TATHAGATA / VAJRA MAME
MUNCHA / VAJRA BHAVA MAHA SAMAYA SATTVA AH HUM PHAT

Generating Faith in Having Been Purified

From the crown of your head, Guru Vajrasattva says, "Child of the race [lineage], your negativities, obscurations, and broken and damaged pledges have been completely purified."

Generate strong faith that all is completely purified, just as Guru Vajrasattva has said.

(4) The Power of Restraint: Refraining from Creating Negativities Again

Resolve:

> Before Guru Vajrasattva, I vow never again to commit those negative actions from which I can easily abstain and not to commit for a day, an hour, or at least a few seconds those negative actions from which I find it difficult to abstain.

Absorption

Guru Vajrasattva is extremely pleased with your pledge. Vajrasattva father and mother melt into light and dissolve into you. Your body, speech, and mind become inseparably one with Guru Vajrasattva's holy body, holy speech, and holy mind.

Meditate on Emptiness

Recite:

> In emptiness, there is no I, no creator of negative karma;
> there is no action of creating negative karma;
> there is no negative karma created.

Place your mind in that emptiness for a little while. In this way, look at all phenomena as empty—they do not exist from their own side.

Dedication

With this awareness of emptiness, dedicate the merits:

> Due to all these merits of the three times collected by all the buddhas, bodhisattvas, myself, and all other sentient beings (which appear to be real, from their own side, but which are empty),
> may I (who appears to be real but is empty) achieve Guru Vajrasattva's enlightenment (which appears to be real but is empty)
> and lead all sentient beings (who appear to be real but are totally empty) to that enlightenment (which appears to be real but is empty)
> by myself alone (who appears to be real but is also totally empty, nonexistent from my own side).

> May the precious bodhichitta, the source of all happiness and success for myself and all other sentient beings,
> be generated within my own mind and in the minds of all sentient beings
> without even a second's delay;
> and may that which has been generated be increased.

> May I and all other sentient beings have Lama Tsongkhapa as our direct guru in all our lifetimes,
> never be separated for even a second from the pure path that is greatly praised by the conqueror buddhas,
> and actualize the complete path—the three principal aspects of the path and the two stages of highest tantra— the root of which is guru devotion,
> within our minds as quickly as possible.

> Just as the brave Manjushri and Samantabhadra realized things as they are,
> I dedicate all these virtues in the best way, that I may follow after them.
> Whatever dedication the three-time victorious ones gone to bliss admire as best,

in the same way, I also perfectly dedicate all these roots of virtue
so that I may perform good works.

The Meaning of the Mantra
Here is a rough translation of the hundred-syllable mantra of Vajrasattva that appears above:

> You, Vajrasattva, have generated the holy mind (bodhichitta) according to your pledge (samaya). Your holy mind is enriched with the simultaneous holy actions of releasing transmigratory beings from samsara (the circling, suffering aggregates). Whatever happens in my life—happiness or suffering, good or bad—with a pleased, holy mind, never give up but please guide me. Please stabilize all happiness, including the happiness of the upper realms, actualize all actions and sublime and common realizations, and please make the glory of the five wisdoms abide in my heart.

PURIFY WITH THE PRACTICE OF SAMAYAVAJRA [51]

See chapters 17, 18, 20, 21, 22, and 23.

The practice of Samayavajra (Tibetan: Damtsik Dorje) is a powerful practice that purifies in particular the negative karmas accumulated in the relationship with the guru. Those of us who have taken all three levels of vows have continually broken and degenerated our commitments—our pledges to our gurus—especially the tantric commitments. Because of their compassion all our gurus have manifested as Samayavajra so that we can purify all these negative karmas.

You can guide your loved one in the practice.

Visualization
At the heart of myself clearly visualized as my guru yidam is a variegated lotus and moon mandala. Above it is a green HA (ཧ), which transforms into a sword adorned with a HA inside the handle.

This then transforms into Samayavajra, who has a green holy body with three faces (central face green, right black, and left white) and six arms, which embrace the mother who is in similar aspect. Both father and mother are marked with the three syllables (OM at the crown, AH at the throat, and HUM at the heart). The first two hands of both are embracing. The second right hand holds a vajra, the third right hand, a sword. The second left hand holds a bell, and the third left hand carries a flower. The mother's right and left hands hold the same implements.

At the heart of Samayavajra is a flat variegated vajra with HA in the center surrounded by the mantra.

Recitation of the Mantra
As you recite the mantra, visualize nectar flowing down, filling and blessing your whole body, and purifying all samayas degenerated due to carelessness, and all obscurations and negative karmas accumulated with your three doors:

OM AH PRAJÑA DHRIK HA HUM

At the end of your recitation, imagine Guru Samayavajra says: "All your negative karmas, obscurations, and degenerated samayas are completely purified."

Generate strong faith that exactly what Samayavajra says has happened in reality: your mental continuum has become completely pure. Not the slightest obscuration is left. Even the heaviest negative karmas accumulated in the relationship with the guru have been purified.

Absorption

Guru Samayavajra is very pleased and dissolves into the indestructible seed at your heart, your own subtle mind-wind. Your own body, speech, and mind become oneness with Samayavajra's holy body, holy speech, and holy mind.

Meditate on Emptiness

Meditate on the emptiness of the three circles: yourself as the creator of the negative karma, the action of creating negative karma, and the negative karma accumulated are all empty of existing by their own nature.

Dedicate in Emptiness

With this same awareness of emptiness and dependent arising, dedicate the merits: yourself as the dedicator, the action of dedicating, and the merits that are dedicated are all merely imputed by thought.

> Due to all these merits of the three times collected by all the buddhas, bodhisattvas, myself, and all other sentient beings (which appear to be real, from their own side, but which are empty),
> may I (who appears to be real but is empty) achieve Guru Vajrasattva's enlightenment (which appears to be real but is empty)
> and lead all sentient beings (who appear to be real but are totally empty) to that enlightenment (which appears to be real but is empty)
> by myself alone (who appears to be real but is also totally empty, nonexistent from my own side).

[51] Purify with the Practice of Samayavajra

May the precious bodhichitta, the source of all happiness
 and success for myself and all other sentient beings,
be generated within my own mind and in the minds of all
 sentient beings
without even a second's delay;
and may that which has been generated be increased.

May I and all other sentient beings have Lama Tsongkhapa
 as our direct guru in all our lifetimes,
never be separated for even a second from the pure path
 that is greatly praised by the conqueror buddhas,
and actualize the complete path—the three principal
 aspects of the path and the two stages of highest tantra—
 the root of which is guru devotion,
within our minds as quickly as possible.

Just as the brave Manjushri and Samantabhadra realized
 things as they are,
I dedicate all these virtues in the best way, that I may follow
 after them.
Whatever dedication the three-times victorious ones gone
 to bliss admire as best,
in the same way, I also perfectly dedicate all these roots of
 virtue
so that I may perform good works.

PURIFY WITH AN ABBREVIATED OFFERING OF TSOK [52]

See chapters 17, 18, 20, 21, 22, and 23.
See also practice 53.

Another very powerful way to help your loved one purify broken vows of individual liberation, bodhisattva vows, and tantric vows and commitments, as well as to collect merits, is to offer tsok. It is one of the main causes to achieve the Heruka and Vajrayogini pure lands, to be born there.

Guide your loved one in the practice.

The Practice

This abbreviated tsok offering practice should be preceded by self-generation into any highest-tantra deity on the basis of refuge and bodhichitta, or Six-Session Guru Yoga, the sadhana of the deity, the *Guru Puja*, and so on.

Then the requisite substances, as well as an offering of food, should be blessed as you would bless the inner offering. For convenience, an abbreviated blessing by Kirti Tsenshab Rinpoche has been included here, which should be performed on the basis of having generated oneself as the deity.

After this, the tsok may be offered as indicated.

Blessing the Tsok

E MA HO!
Food, drink, five meats, five nectars—that which is in the
    skull—is in the nature of bliss and voidness.
Purified, actualized, and increased by the three vajras,
it becomes an ocean of uncontaminated nectar.

OM AH HUM (3X)

[52] PURIFY WITH AN ABBREVIATED OFFERING OF TSOK

Offering the Tsok

> HO! In order to please this assembly of the root and lineage gurus,
> the yidams Vajrayogini and so forth,
> the Three Jewels, and the ocean of dakinis and oath-bound protectors,
> together with the beings of the six realms who have been my mothers,
> I present this blessed offering of inseparable bliss and void.
> OM AH HUM
> Having joyfully received this,
> may all degenerated vows be renewed.
> Please lead us quickly to the pure land of the dakinis,
> and having quickly caused a great rain of supreme and common accomplishments to fall,
> may all the obscuring false appearances of all motherly beings
> be effortlessly purified this very moment.

Recite once, three times, or any number of times.

Colophon

In these degenerate times, there are those who are like Mount Meru when it comes to taking commitments but like the smallest atoms when it comes to practicing. So, in order to heal degenerated commitments of all sorts and in order to please the glorious, holy guru, I, Thubten Zopa, a so-called incarnation, with great delight have written this at the time of the wood-tiger New Year. Also, by this, may the teachings of the victorious Losang (Drakpa) remain for a long time.

PURIFY WITH AN OFFERING OF TSOK TO VAJRASATTVA BY LAMA YESHE [53]

See chapters 17, 18, 20, 21, 22, 23, and 29.
See also practice 52.

When Lama Yeshe wrote the Vajrasattva tsok offering, in 1982, he said he composed it "in case students were getting bored with the older pujas. It's shorter, too, and therefore suits our busy lifestyles!"

This tsok offering can be made to other highest-tantra deities by substituting that deity's name for Vajrasattva's and by blessing the offerings in accordance with the yoga method of that deity and reciting that deity's mantra.

Guide your loved one in the practice.

A BANQUET OF THE GREATLY BLISSFUL CIRCLE OF PURE OFFERINGS: AN ANTIDOTE TO THE VAJRA HELLS

Preliminaries
After completing either the abbreviated or elaborate meditation on the generation of oneself in the form of Vajrasattva, visualize as follows.

Meditation on the Mandala of Guru Vajrasattva:
Field for the Collection of Merit

> HUM
> In the space before me,
> from the enjoyment of indivisible great bliss and emptiness,
> appear the complete supporting and supported mandalas of
>   Vajrasattva.
> Clouds of Samantabhadra's offerings fill all of space.
> In the sphere of great nondual bliss,
> all beings miraculously appear as gods and goddesses
> embodying thoroughly developed method and wisdom
> as skillful dancers manifesting peace, expansion, power,
>   and wrath.

[53] PURIFY WITH AN OFFERING OF TSOK TO VAJRASATTVA

Blessing the Offerings

OM KHANDAROHI HUM HUM PHAT

All those who create obstacles are dispelled,
and by reciting they are purified of ordinary appearances.

OM SVABHAVA SHUDDHA SARVA DHARMA SVABHAVA SHUDDHO HAM

All becomes empty.
From the sphere of emptiness
appears the letter AH (ཨཱཿ), which transforms
into a very large and spacious skull cup
containing the five meats and five nectars.
Melting, they all transform
into a great ocean of wisdom nectar.

OM AH HUM HA HO HRIH (3X)

Presenting the Offerings and Reciting the Mantra

This pure offering is the yogi's commitment (samaya)
and, as the pure vision of their great bliss,
transcends being an object of ordinary senses.
It is the basis of all attainments and the most supreme
  nectar.
Therefore, O Guru, with your non-superstitious
simultaneously born great bliss, please enjoy it.

(1) HUM O miraculous rainbow cloud
appearing in the space of dharmakaya,
holy body of Vajrasattva—
having purified the hallucinated vision
and dualistic conception that fails to recognize
that the guru, in essence, is the deity,
the dakini, and the Dharma protector—

298   PURIFY WITH AN OFFERING OF TSOK TO VAJRASATTVA [53]

in order to please you, Guru Vajrasattva,
I am presenting these sacred ingredients
as pure offerings to be enjoyed by your five senses.
Please bless me to generate simultaneously born great bliss.

OM VAJRA HERUKA SAMAYA MANUPALAYA / HERUKA TVENOPATISHTHA /
DRIDHO ME BHAVA / SUTOSHYO ME BHAVA / SUPOSHYO ME BHAVA /
ANURAKTO ME BHAVA / SARVA SIDDHIM ME PRAYACCHA / SARVA KARMA
SUCHAME / CHITTAM SHRIYAM KURU HUM / HA HA HA HA HO /
BHAGAVAN VAJRA HERUKA MAME MUNCHA / HERUKA BHAVA MAHA
SAMAYA SATTVA AH HUM PHAT

(2) HUM O miraculous rainbow cloud
appearing in the space of dharmakaya,
holy body of Vajrasattva—
having purified the hallucinated vision
of the five sense consciousnesses' clinging
to the pleasure of desirable objects,
thereby depriving this perfect human birth of all
    meaning—
in order to please you, Guru Vajrasattva,
I am presenting these sacred ingredients
as pure offerings to be enjoyed by your five senses.
Please bless me to abandon clinging
to the ordinary concepts and appearances of this life.

OM VAJRA HERUKA SAMAYA MANUPALAYA / HERUKA TVENOPATISHTHA /
DRIDHO ME BHAVA / SUTOSHYO ME BHAVA / SUPOSHYO ME BHAVA /
ANURAKTO ME BHAVA / SARVA SIDDHIM ME PRAYACCHA / SARVA
KARMA SUCHAME / CHITTAM SHRIYAM KURU HUM / HA HA HA HA HO /
BHAGAVAN VAJRA HERUKA MAME MUNCHA / HERUKA BHAVA MAHA
SAMAYA SATTVA AH HUM PHAT

(3) HUM O miraculous rainbow cloud
appearing in the space of dharmakaya,
holy body of Vajrasattva—

[53] PURIFY WITH AN OFFERING OF TSOK TO VAJRASATTVA

having purified the hallucinated vision:
the demon dualistic conception and veiling obscurations
of improper attention, superstition, karma, and delusions—
in order to please you, Guru Vajrasattva,
I am presenting these sacred ingredients
as pure offerings to be enjoyed by your five senses.
Please bless me to generate immaculate renunciation.

OM VAJRA HERUKA SAMAYA MANUPALAYA / HERUKA TVENOPATISHTHA /
DRIDHO ME BHAVA / SUTOSHYO ME BHAVA / SUPOSHYO ME BHAVA /
ANURAKTO ME BHAVA / SARVA SIDDHIM ME PRAYACCHA / SARVA
KARMA SUCHAME / CHITTAM SHRIYAM KURU HUM / HA HA HA HA HO /
BHAGAVAN VAJRA HERUKA MAME MUNCHA /
HERUKA BHAVA MAHA SAMAYA SATTVA AH HUM PHAT

(4) HUM O miraculous rainbow cloud
appearing in the space of dharmakaya,
holy body of Vajrasattva—
having purified the hallucinated vision
of holding oneself more dear than others:
the door to all suffering and the dualistic conception
that is the chief of all evils—
in order to please you, Guru Vajrasattva,
I am presenting these sacred ingredients
as pure offerings to be enjoyed by your five senses.
Please bless me to generate immaculate bodhichitta.

OM VAJRA HERUKA SAMAYA MANUPALAYA / HERUKA TVENOPATISHTHA /
DRIDHO ME BHAVA / SUTOSHYO ME BHAVA / SUPOSHYO ME BHAVA /
ANURAKTO ME BHAVA / SARVA SIDDHIM ME PRAYACCHA / SARVA KARMA
SUCHAME / CHITTAM SHRIYAM KURU HUM / HA HA HA HA HO /
BHAGAVAN VAJRA HERUKA MAME MUNCHA / HERUKA BHAVA MAHA
SAMAYA SATTVA AH HUM PHAT

(5) HUM O miraculous rainbow cloud
appearing in the space of dharmakaya,
holy body of Vajrasattva—

having purified the hallucinated vision:
the stain of dualistic conception holding
what is merely imputed by superstition as true—
in order to please you, Guru Vajrasattva,
I am presenting these sacred ingredients
as pure offerings to be enjoyed by your five senses.
Please bless me to realize the great seal of emptiness.

OM VAJRA HERUKA SAMAYA MANUPALAYA / HERUKA TVENOPATISHTHA / DRIDHO ME BHAVA / SUTOSHYO ME BHAVA / SUPOSHYO ME BHAVA / ANURAKTO ME BHAVA / SARVA SIDDHIM ME PRAYACCHA / SARVA KARMA SUCHAME / CHITTAM SHRIYAM KURU HUM / HA HA HA HA HO / BHAGAVAN VAJRA HERUKA MAME MUNCHA / HERUKA BHAVA MAHA SAMAYA SATTVA AH HUM PHAT

(6) HUM O miraculous rainbow cloud
appearing in the space of dharmakaya,
holy body of Vajrasattva—
having purified the hallucinated vision
of ordinary appearance and conception:
the eighty superstitions both gross and subtle,
the violent, uncontrollable wind of the dualistic mind—
in order to please you, Guru Vajrasattva,
I am presenting these sacred ingredients
as pure offerings to be enjoyed by your five senses.
Please bless me to receive the four actual empowerments.

OM VAJRA HERUKA SAMAYA MANUPALAYA / HERUKA TVENOPATISHTHA / DRIDHO ME BHAVA / SUTOSHYO ME BHAVA / SUPOSHYO ME BHAVA / ANURAKTO ME BHAVA / SARVA SIDDHIM ME PRAYACCHA / SARVA KARMA SUCHAME / CHITTAM SHRIYAM KURU HUM / HA HA HA HA HO / BHAGAVAN VAJRA HERUKA MAME MUNCHA / HERUKA BHAVA MAHA SAMAYA SATTVA AH HUM PHAT

(7) HUM O miraculous rainbow cloud
appearing in the space of dharmakaya,
holy body of Vajrasattva—

[53] PURIFY WITH AN OFFERING OF TSOK TO VAJRASATTVA

having purified the hallucinated vision
of experiencing the vajra hells
resulting from the uncontrollable downpour
of negative actions and broken samaya—
in order to please you, Guru Vajrasattva,
I am presenting these sacred ingredients
as pure offerings to be enjoyed by your five senses.
May infinite purity alone arise.

OM VAJRA HERUKA SAMAYA MANUPALAYA / HERUKA TVENOPATISHTHA / DRIDHO ME BHAVA / SUTOSHYO ME BHAVA / SUPOSHYO ME BHAVA / ANURAKTO ME BHAVA / SARVA SIDDHIM ME PRAYACCHA / SARVA KARMA SUCHAME / CHITTAM SHRIYAM KURU HUM / HA HA HA HA HO / BHAGAVAN VAJRA HERUKA MAME MUNCHA / HERUKA BHAVA MAHA SAMAYA SATTVA AH HUM PHAT

Offering to the Vajra Master

The offering of tsok to the vajra master should now be made while reciting:

O holder of the vajra, please pay attention to me.
This pure offering presented by the assembled circle of
    dakas and dakinis,
this nectar free of all divisions of subject and object,
transcendentally blissful, please enjoy it eternally.

AH LA LA HOH

The vajra master then replies:

O hail, great blissful wisdom! The great collected offering,
the seed that causes the *tumo* heat to explode,
this joyful, blissful experience beyond concepts, beyond
    words—
welcome, great eternal bliss!

AH HO MAHA SUKHA HO

Distribute the tsok offerings to the assembly.

Verses of Praise
Praise is offered by reciting the following:

> Merely thinking of just your name
> eradicates all obstacles
> and immediately purifies all negative karma.
> Thus to you, unsurpassed Vajrasattva,
> I pay homage and make prostration.

Eight-Limb Praise

> OM to you whose brilliance equals the fire that ends a great eon HUM HUM PHAT
> OM to you who have an inexhaustible crowning top knot HUM HUM PHAT
> OM to you with bared fangs and a wrathful face HUM HUM PHAT
> OM to you whose thousand arms blaze with light HUM HUM PHAT
> OM to you who hold an axe, a noose, a spear, and a skull staff HUM HUM PHAT
> OM to you who wear a tiger-skin cloth HUM HUM PHAT
> OM I bow to you whose great smoke-colored body ends all obstructions HUM HUM PHAT
> OM I prostrate to Bhagavati Vajravarahi HUM HUM PHAT
> OM to the queen of the female arya practitioners, invincible in the three realms HUM HUM PHAT
> OM to you who destroy all fears of evil spirits with your great diamond-like means HUM HUM PHAT
> OM to you whose eyes empower those who sit on the diamond throne not to be conquered by anyone HUM HUM PHAT
> OM to you whose wrathful body of psychic heat can desiccate Brahma HUM HUM PHAT
> OM to you who terrify and dry up the demons and thus can vanquish all other forces HUM HUM PHAT

OM to you who triumph over all that can make you ill-tempered,
  excited, or stupefied HUM HUM PHAT
OM I bow to Vajravarahi, the consort who overpowers lust HUM
HUM PHAT

Offering the Remaining Tsok

OM AH HUM (3x)
To the assembly of the eight classes of wrathful governing
  protectors
I present all the remaining pure offerings—
the nectar of the five wisdoms contained in this skull cup—
an illusory appearance of indivisible bliss and emptiness.
Do your duty, the four rites for Dharma practitioners.

Concluding Prayer of Auspiciousness

May all be auspicious for me to see my mind as the lama:
who understands perfectly all beings' thoughts,
whose speech fulfills countless beings' wishes,
and whose pure body arises from an infinite collection of merit.
May all be auspicious for realizing the unity of dharmakaya
  and rupakaya
by discovering my own subtle, continually residing
  consciousness
through the power of taking the three bodies as the path:
the antidote to imminent death, bardo, and rebirth.
May all be auspicious for everything within samsara and nirvana
to be synthesized with great emptiness and great bliss
through the unusual embrace of the mother—the sphere of space
  beyond all puzzling divisions—
and the father—the great blissful wisdom, the appearance of all
  existent phenomena.

Postscript

The following poem in jest came uncontrollably and without premeditation to the mind of the author while he was composing this work.

All of samsara appears
as a foe to one who fears
he might be gored and torn
by the proverbial rabbit's horn
of tantric ordinations:
the golden ground foundation,
in the common path untrained,
in tantra unordained,
he has no initiation;
what a situation!
How strange! What a joke!
He's a sky-flower yogi!
Through the blessings of all the root and lineage lamas,
the great accomplishments of the mind-bound deity
  Vajrasattva
and the divine actions of the dakinis and protectors of the
  three places,
may auspiciousness allow all beings to be satisfied by
  ultimate peace.

Original Colophon and Dedications
On the special day of the dakas and dakinis—the twenty-fifth day of the eleventh month of the Iron-Bird year (January 19, 1982)—Ven. Lama Thubten Yeshe wrote this tsok offering of Heruka Vajrasattva for a puja performed at Bodhgaya, India under the bodhi tree by an international gathering of sangha and lay students who together made hundreds and thousands of offerings. This puja was offered by the Italian gelong Thubten Dönyö, a disciple having unsurpassed understanding of the sutra and tantra path to enlightenment and indestructible devotion to Shakyamuni Buddha's teachings, and who was adorned outwardly with saffron robes and inwardly with the three sets of vows.

This tsok offering was written with the prayer that all the sangha of the ten directions enjoy harmonious relationships with one another, guard the precepts of pure moral conduct, and accomplish the practice of the three higher trainings, thereby becoming skillful guides providing great help to all beings. It is dedicated to the speedy return of our great guru of unmatched and inexpressible kindness, Kyabje Trijang

Dorje Chang. For the benefit of all sentient beings, our mothers, may we remain inseparable from this great guru during our entire path to enlightenment.

Furthermore, it has been noted that in many countries today—Tibet, for example—those whose lives are not opposed to the three ordinations of the pratimoksha, bodhichitta, and tantric vows are not considered to be human beings! Yet even in such extremely degenerate times there are still many fortunate practitioners, and it is very important that these yogis and yoginis have a method, such as this Vajrasattva practice, powerful enough for achieving the exalted realization of simultaneously born great bliss and emptiness.

This profound method is easy and simple to practice, accumulates a great store of meritorious potential, and is capable of destroying all the negativities resulting from breaking one's pledged commitments. In fact, it is such a powerful method that many lamas of the Geluk tradition have stated that even transgressions of root tantric vows can be purified by reciting the Vajrasattva mantra. Therefore, one should understand that there is no negativity so strong that it cannot be purified through the practice of Vajrasattva.

For all these reasons, then, this tsok offering has been composed by Vajrasattva yogi and follower of Guru Shakyamuni Buddha's teachings, the bhikshu Muni Jñana.

Colophon for the English Translation
The text was translated with the kind assistance of Lama Thubten Zopa Rinpoche and Ven. Könchog Yeshe, and edited by Jonathan Landaw.

PURIFY WITH THE SELF-INITIATION OF YOUR LOVED ONE'S MAIN DEITY [54]

See chapters 17, 18, 20, 21, 22, 23, and 29.

Chöden Rinpoche says that if the person who is passing away is qualified to take the self-initiation—that is, they have received a highest tantra initiation and have completed the retreat and burning offering puja—and cannot themselves do it, they can invite someone else to recite the prayers for them while they meditate on the meaning.

Of course, if there is a lama nearby, according to Rinpoche, it is good to take the initiation again.

As I mentioned, performing a self-initiation purifies not only degenerations of tantric vows, such as root downfalls, but also broken bodhisattva and individual-liberation root and secondary vows. All these negative karmas get completely purified, making it impossible to be born in the lower realms.

With this practice you plant the seeds to achieve the bodies of a buddha (as discussed in chapter 10). This leaves such strong imprints of the tantric path on your mind, which causes you to quickly gain realizations of the path to enlightenment.

HAVE YOUR LOVED ONE LIE IN THE LION POSITION [55]

See chapters 5 and 18.
See also practice 40.

As the moment of death approaches, it's good to have your loved one follow the example of our kind, compassionate Buddha when he passed away into the sorrowless state and have them lie in the lion position. If they've practiced sleeping in this position (practice 40), it will be easier now.

Lying in this position naturally makes it easy to transfer the consciousness from the crown to a pure land—especially, remember, as we discussed in chapter 12, if your loved one is facing west, which is where Amitabha Buddha's pure land is.

Lying in this position also helps virtuous thoughts arise in the person's mind at the time of death; it makes it easy for this to happen. And it reminds them of the Buddha, that they're following in his footsteps. At the time of death, there will be no worries, they'll be saved by this last thought of reflecting on the Buddha.

If they are a practitioner, they may choose to die sitting in the meditation posture; it's up to the individual.

The Lion Position
The right hand should be under the right cheek with the ring finger blocking the right nostril, and the left arm should be stretched out along their left side.

The breath coming through the right nostril is the breath of attachment, so stopping it helps the mind not be controlled by attachment, to not die with attachment. It might not be so easy to block the right nostril in this way, so you could use cotton instead. And you could put pillows behind your loved one's back to support the body.

Ideally, as I mention above, they should be lying with their head pointing north, which means they are facing west, which is where Amitabha Buddha's pure land is.

OFFER A MANI PILL FROM HIS HOLINESS THE DALAI LAMA [56]

See chapter 18.

As advised in *Tibetan Ceremonies of the Dead*, it is good to give the person who is dying a mani pill when the time of death is close. This blesses and purifies your loved one's mind, helping them generate virtuous thoughts.

You can give the pills to children and people who don't have the ability to understand, as well as to animals.

These pills contain many blessed substances and relics of enlightened beings, bodhisattvas, and great yogis. They have been blessed with the prayers of His Holiness the Dalai Lama, the actual Compassion Buddha, for the benefit of sentient beings; and many great lamas, meditators, and sangha have also prayed day and night for many days, continuously blessing them.

How to Give the Mani Pill

Crush the pill, mix it with water, and put a little into your loved one's mouth, making sure they swallow it. Chöden Rinpoche says it's important to do this before the outer breath has stopped, because after that you should not touch the body.

OFFER A RELIC OF THE BUDDHA [57]

See chapter 18.
See also practice 56.

As death approaches, you could give your loved one a relic of the Buddha: another method to help the dying person avoid being reborn in the lower realms.

As with the blessed pills (practice 56), the relic can be given to children and animals.

How to Give the Relic

You put it into their mouth before the breath has stopped—otherwise, as it says in *Tibetan Ceremonies of the Dead*, it will just sit there and not go down the throat. Also, offering the relic after the breath has stopped could delay the death.

BLESS THE BODY WITH WRITTEN MANTRAS [58]

See chapters 18, 20, 21, 22, 23, and 26.
See also practices 21–30 and 31.

It is beneficial to place written mantras on the body of your loved one, before death, after the breath has stopped but before the mind has left the body, and after the mind has left. It helps purify negative karma and cause a good rebirth.

In all scenarios, it is good to leave the mantras on the body until it is buried or cremated.

You can do this for animals as well.

I have written out eleven mantras, a small version of which is included in the Liberation Box; included are some of the five great mantras (practice 31) and ten powerful mantras (practices 21–30), as well as the mantra of Vajra Armor.

You could also use any of the five great mantras or the ten powerful mantras.

Namgyalma (practice 25), which is included in both groups (and is also in the Liberation Box), is one of the best for the dying; or Kunrik (practice 27), Mitrukpa (practice 24), Stainless Pinnacle (practice 31)—any mantras you like can be used.

Before Death (Chapter 18)
Place a sheet of paper or card with mantras written on it face down on the person's body so that the words touch the skin; any part of the body will do.

After the Breath Has Stopped but Before the Mind Has Left (Chapters 20–23)
If you haven't done so already, you can place a sheet of paper or card with mantras written on it face down on the person's body so that the words touch the skin, as above.

Be careful not to disturb the body.

[58] BLESS THE BODY WITH WRITTEN MANTRAS

After the Mind Has Left (Chapter 26)
If you have not already put written mantras on the body of your loved one, you could do so now. You can put the sheets of mantras on any part of the body so that the words are touching the skin, as above. Or you can rub the body with them.

Or you can put rolls of mantras on the body—on the head, for example.

Or you can wrap mantras around the body—the chest, for example, as Kirti Tsenshab explained they do in Amdo in Tibet; they use Mitrukpa mantras.

A Liberation Box Is Available From
Website fpmt.org/death/
Email shopfpmt@fpmt.org

SPONSOR MONASTERIES, DHARMA CENTERS, OR FRIENDS TO PERFORM PRACTICES SUCH AS MEDICINE BUDDHA [59]

See chapters 18, 20–23, and 29.
See also other practices related to the Medicine Buddha: 14, 22, 36, and 78.

At various stages it is excellent to make offerings to other people—monks and nuns in monasteries or Dharma centers, such as Kopan Monastery near Kathmandu, or friends—and request them to perform Medicine Buddha or other practices for your loved one.

- During the hours before death (chapter 18)
- During the hours and days after the breath has stopped (chapters 20–23)
- During the forty-nine days after the mind has left the body (chapter 29)

You could also request prayers to be recited for your loved one by His Holiness the Dalai Lama, Lama Zopa Rinpoche, and FPMT sangha communities.

Kopan Monastery
Website kopanmonastery.com/index.php/prayers-pujas/order-a-puja
Email puja@kopanmonastery.org

Prayers for the Dead by His Holiness the Dalai Lama, etc.
Website fpmt.org/death/

SHOUT IN YOUR LOVED ONE'S EAR THE NAME OF THEIR GURU OR THE BUDDHA [60]

See chapter 19.
See also other practices related to the guru: 1, 10, 18, 35, 43, 47, 72, and 85.

As soon as your loved one's breath stops, before you do anything else, shout loudly close to their ear the name of their lama, or of His Holiness the Dalai Lama, or the name of the buddha they usually pray to, or any buddha, and remind them to take refuge.

As I mentioned in practice 10, hearing the name of their guru is considered a very effective kind of transference of consciousness. Chöden Rinpoche refers to a quotation from the *Kalachakra Tantra*: "To recall the name of your guru for even one second is the best phowa."

This is true even for someone who has created the five heavy negative actions: if they have devotion in their guru, merely hearing the name of their lama can help their consciousness take a good rebirth.

PUT BLESSED SUBSTANCES ON YOUR LOVED ONE'S CROWN [61]

See chapter 19.

Once your loved one has stopped breathing and you have shouted the name of their guru or any buddha in their ear, put one of the following blessed substances on their crown—at the chakra, which is toward the back of the head. Doing this helps your loved one's consciousness go to the crown chakra so that it leaves from there, causing it to go to a pure land.

- A phowa pill
- An inner-offering pill
- A mani pill
- Sand from a Kalachakra mandala

You can use butter and honey to help them stick. Be sure not to touch any other part of the body, as discussed in chapter 19.

The phowa pills consist of the ashes of the great yogis and bodhisattvas, also relics of buddhas. There is a phowa pill in the Liberation Box.

If you don't have phowa pills you can use an inner-offering pill made by high lamas. The mani pills are from His Holiness the Dalai Lama. The sand is from a Kalachakra mandala, also blessed by His Holiness.

When the body is taken out, you can keep the pill or sand and use it for others who die.

A Liberation Box Is Available From
Website fpmt.org/death/
Email shopfpmt@fpmt.org

REQUEST A LAMA TO PERFORM PHOWA [62]

See chapter 19.
See also practices 48 and 81.

If your loved one has requested this, invite a lama to perform phowa immediately after the breath has stopped and, except for putting the blessed substances on the crown, before you touch the body.

The lama can either come to where the body is or, as advised in *Tibetan Ceremonies of the Death,* "do the practice from a distance." If the latter, tell them in what direction your loved one's head is pointing; this helps the phowa be more precise.

It is said that phowa should not be done before the breath has stopped, unless the dying person is doing it themselves. In that case, see practice 48.

If phowa is to be practiced during the forty-nine days after the mind has left the body, see practice 81.

OFFER LIGHTS IN FRONT OF THE BODY [63]

See chapter 20.

Chöden Rinpoche said that as long as the body of your loved one is in the house, you must always offer a light nearby. In Tibet, of course, they would offer a butter lamp; you could use any kind of lights: electric, candles, and so on.

This is not an offering to the body but to the Three Rare Sublime Ones. It is mentioned in the Heruka root tantra that one will achieve realizations if one offers lights—hundreds, thousands of lights. There are many statements like this in the teachings.

Another reason to have lights on—you could keep the room lights on—is that it helps prevent a spirit from entering the body, which is a danger. You should have the lights lit all the time, day and night.

RECITE THE "KING OF PRAYERS" [64]

See chapters 20, 21, 22, 23, 27, and 29.
See also chapter 6 and other practices related to Amitabha: 11, 20, 66, and 81.

The First of the Eight Prayers to Benefit the Dead

> I bow down to the youthful Arya Manjushri!
>
> You lions among humans,
> gone to freedom in the present, past, and future
> in the worlds throughout ten directions,
> to all of you, with body, speech, and sincere mind,
>   I bow down.
>
> With the energy of aspiration for the bodhisattva way,
> with a sense of deep respect,
> and with as many bodies as there are atoms of the world,
> to all you buddhas visualized as real, I bow down.
>
> On every atom are buddhas numberless as atoms,
> each amid a host of bodhisattvas,
> and I am confident the sphere of all phenomena
> is entirely filled with buddhas in this way.
>
> With infinite oceans of praise for you,
> and oceans of sound from the aspects of my voice,
> I sing the breathtaking excellence of buddhas
> and celebrate all of you gone to bliss.
>
> Beautiful flowers and regal garlands,
> sweet music, scented oils, and parasols,
> sparkling lights and sublime incense,
>   I offer to you victorious ones.

Fine dress and fragrant perfumes,
sandalwood powder heaped high as Mount Meru,
all wondrous offerings in spectacular array,
I offer to you victorious ones.

With transcendent offerings peerless and vast,
with profound admiration for all the buddhas,
with strength of conviction in the bodhisattva way,
I offer and bow down to all victorious ones.

Every harmful action I have done
with my body, speech, and mind
overwhelmed by attachment, anger, and ignorance,
all these I openly lay bare before you.

I lift up my heart and rejoice in all the merit
of the buddhas and bodhisattvas in ten directions,
of pratyekabuddhas, shravakas still training, and those
    beyond,
and of all ordinary beings.

You who are the bright lights of worlds in ten directions,
who have attained a buddha's omniscience through the
    stages of awakening,
all you who are my guides,
please turn the supreme wheel of Dharma.

With palms together I earnestly request:
you who may actualize parinirvana,
please stay with us for eons numberless as atoms of the world,
for the happiness and well-being of all wanderers in samsara.

Whatever slight merit I may have created
by paying homage, offering, acknowledging my faults,
rejoicing, and requesting that the buddhas stay and teach,
I now dedicate all this for full awakening.

May you buddhas now living in the worlds of ten directions
and all you gone to freedom in the past accept my offerings.
May those not yet arisen quickly perfect their minds,
awakening as fully enlightened ones.

May all worlds in ten directions
be entirely pure and vast.
May they be filled with bodhisattvas
surrounding buddhas gathered beneath a bodhi tree.

May as many beings as exist in ten directions
be always well and happy.
May all samsaric beings live in accord with the Dharma,
and may their every Dharma wish be fulfilled.

Remembering my past lives in all varieties of existence,
may I practice the bodhisattva way,
and thus, in each cycle of death, migration, and birth,
may I always abandon the householder's life.

Then, following in the footsteps of all the buddhas
and perfecting the practice of a bodhisattva,
may I always act without error or compromise,
with ethical discipline faultless and pure.

May I teach the Dharma in the language of gods,
in every language of spirits and nagas,
of humans and of demons,
and in the voice of every form of being.

May I be gentle-minded, cultivating the six perfections,
and never forget bodhichitta.
May I completely cleanse without omission
every negativity and all that obscures this awakening mind.

May I traverse all my lives in the world,
free of karma, afflictions, and interfering forces,

just as the lotus blossom is undisturbed by the water's wave,
just as the sun and moon move unhindered through the sky.

May I ease the suffering in the lower realms
and in the many directions and dimensions of the universe.
May I guide all wanderers in samsara to the pure bliss of awakening
and be of worldly benefit to them as well.

May I practice constantly for eons to come,
perfecting the activities of awakening,
acting in harmony with the various dispositions of beings,
showing the ways of a bodhisattva.

May I always have the friendship
of those whose path is like mine,
and with body, words, and also mind,
may we practice together the same aspirations and activities.

May I always meet a spiritual mentor
and never displease that excellent friend,
who deeply wishes to help me
and expertly teaches the bodhisattva way.

May I always directly see the buddhas,
masters encircled by bodhisattvas,
and without pause or discouragement for eons to come,
may I make extensive offerings to them.

May I hold within me the Buddha's genuine Dharma,
illuminate everywhere the teachings that awaken,
embody the realizations of a bodhisattva,
and practice ardently in all future eons.

While circling through all states of existence,
may I become an endless treasure of good qualities—

skillful means, wisdom, samadhi, and liberating
   stabilizations—
gathering limitless pristine wisdom and merit.

On one atom I shall see
buddhafields numberless as atoms,
inconceivable buddhas among bodhisattvas in every field,
practicing the activities of awakening.

Perceiving this in all directions,
I dive into an ocean of buddhafields,
each an ocean of three times' buddhas in the space of
   a wisp of hair,
so I, too, shall practice for an ocean of eons.

Thus I am continually immersed in the speech of the buddhas,
expression that reveals an ocean of qualities in one word,
the completely pure eloquence of all the buddhas,
communication suited to the varied tendencies of beings.

With strength of understanding I plunge
into the infinite enlightened speech of the Dharma
of all buddhas in three times gone to freedom,
who continually turn the wheel of Dharma methods.

I shall experience in one moment
such vast activity of all future eons,
and I shall enter into all eons of the three times
in but a fraction of a second.

In one instant I shall see all those awakened beings,
past, present, and future lions among humans,
and with the power of the illusion-like stabilization
I shall constantly engage in their inconceivable activity.

I shall manifest upon one single atom
the array of pure lands present, past, and future.

Likewise, I shall enter the array of pure buddhafields
in every direction without exception.

I shall enter the very presence of all my guides,
those lights of this world who are yet to appear,
those sequentially turning the wheels of complete awakening,
those who reveal nirvana—final, perfect peace.

May I achieve the power of swift, magical emanation,
the power to lead to the Great Vehicle through every approach,
the power of always beneficial activity,
the power of love pervading all realms,
the power of all-surpassing merit,
the power of supreme knowledge unobstructed by discrimination,
and through the powers of wisdom, skillful means, and
    samadhi,
may I achieve the perfect power of awakening.

Purifying the power of all contaminated actions,
crushing the power of disturbing emotions at their root,
defusing the power of interfering forces,
I shall perfect the power of the bodhisattva practice.

May I purify an ocean of worlds,
may I free an ocean of beings,
may I clearly see an ocean of Dharma,
may I realize an ocean of pristine wisdom.

May I purify an ocean of activities,
may I fulfill an ocean of aspirations,
may I make offerings to an ocean of buddhas,
may I practice without discouragement for an ocean of eons.

To awaken fully through this bodhisattva way,
I shall fulfill without exception
all the diverse aspirations of the awakening practice
of all buddhas gone to freedom in the three times everywhere.

In order to practice exactly as the wise one
called Samantabhadra, All-Embracing Good,
the elder brother of the sons and daughters of the buddhas,
I completely dedicate all this goodness.

Likewise may I dedicate
just as the skillful Samantabhadra,
with pure body, speech, and mind,
pure actions and pure buddhafields.

I shall give rise to the aspirations of Manjushri
for this bodhisattva practice of all-embracing good,
to perfect these practices
without discouragement or pause in all future eons.

May my pure activities be endless,
my good qualities boundless,
and through abiding in immeasurable activity,
may I actualize infinite emanations.

Limitless is the end of space.
Likewise, limitless are living beings.
Thus limitless are karma and afflictions.
May my aspiration's reach be limitless as well.

One may offer to the buddhas
all wealth and adornments of infinite worlds in ten directions,
and one may offer during eons numberless as atoms of the world
even the greatest happiness of gods and humans.

But whoever hears this extraordinary aspiration
and, longing for highest awakening,
gives rise to faith just once
creates far more precious merit.

Those who make this heartfelt aspiration for the bodhisattva way
will be free of all lower rebirths,

free of harmful companions,
and will quickly see Amitabha, Infinite Light.

And even in this very human life,
they will be nourished by happiness and have all conducive circumstances.
Without waiting long,
they will become like Samantabhadra himself.

Those who give voice to this extraordinary aspiration
will quickly and completely purify
the five boundless harmful actions
created under the power of ignorance.

Blessed with supreme knowledge,
excellent body, family, attributes, and appearance,
they will be invincible to vast interfering forces and misleading teachers,
and all the three worlds will make offerings.

Going quickly to the noble Bodhi Tree,
and sitting there to benefit sentient beings,
subduing all interfering forces,
they will fully awaken and turn the great wheel of Dharma.

Have no doubt that complete awakening
is the fully ripened result—comprehended only by a buddha—
of holding in mind by teaching, reading, or reciting
this aspiration of the bodhisattva practice.

In order to train just like
the hero Manjushri who knows reality as it is
and just like Samantabhadra as well,
I completely dedicate all this goodness, just as they did.

[64] THE KING OF PRAYERS

With that dedication, which is praised as greatest
by all the buddhas gone to freedom in the three times,
I, too, dedicate all my roots of goodness
for the attainments of the bodhisattva practice.

When the moment of my death arrives,
by eliminating all obscurations
and directly perceiving Amitabha,
may I go immediately to Sukhavati, Pure Land of Great Joy.

Having gone to Sukhavati,
may I actualize the meaning of these aspirations,
fulfilling them all without exception
for the benefit of beings for as long as this world endures.

Born from an extremely beautiful, superlative lotus
in this joyful land, the Buddha's magnificent mandala,
may I receive a prediction of my awakening
directly from Buddha Amitabha.

Having received a prediction there,
may I create vast benefit
for beings throughout the ten directions,
with a billion emanations by the power of wisdom.

Through even the small virtue I have accumulated
by offering this prayer of the bodhisattva practice,
may all the positive aspirations of beings
be fulfilled in an instant.

Through creating limitless merit
by dedicating this prayer of Samantabhadra's deeds,
may all beings drowning in this torrent of suffering
enter the presence of Amitabha.

Through this king of aspirations, which is the greatest of
   the sublime,
helping infinite wanderers in samsara
through the accomplishment of this scripture dazzling
   with Samantabhadra's practice,
may suffering realms be utterly emptied of all beings.

Colophon for the English Translation
Thus, "The Extraordinary Aspiration of the Practice of Samantabhadra," also known as the "King of Prayers," from the Gandavyuha chapter of *The Avatamsaka Sutra* (translated by Jinamitra, Surendrabodhi, and Yeshe-de, circa 900 C.E.), is complete. The Tibetan was compared with the Sanskrit and revised by Lotsawa Vairochana.

   Translated by Jesse Fenton in Seattle, Washington in 2002 by request of her teacher, Ven. Thubten Chodron, relying on the commentary *Ornament Clarifying the Exalted Intention* of Samantabhadra ('phags pa bzang po spyod pa'i smon lam gyi rnam par bshad pa kun tu bzang po'i dgongs pa gsal bar byed pa'i rgyan) by Jangkya Rolpäi Dorje, and on clarification of many difficult points by the very kind Khensur Rinpoche Konchog Tsering of Ganden Monastery.

RECITE THE "DEDICATION" CHAPTER FROM SHANTIDEVA'S *GUIDE TO THE BODHISATTVA WAY OF LIFE* [65]

See chapters 20, 21, 22, 23, and 29.

The Second of the Eight Prayers to Benefit the Dead

> May all sentient beings be graced with the bodhisattva way of life
> by the virtue I have obtained while reflecting on *A Guide to the Bodhisattva Way of Life*.
>
> Through my merit, may all those in all directions who are afflicted by bodily and mental sufferings
> obtain oceans of joy and contentment.
>
> As long as the cycle of existence lasts, may their happiness never decline.
> May the world attain the constant joy of the bodhisattvas.
>
> As many hells as there are in the worlds,
> may beings in them delight in the joys of contentment in Sukhavati.
>
> May those afflicted with cold find warmth.
> May those oppressed with heat be cooled by oceans of water springing from the great clouds of the bodhisattvas.
>
> May the forest of sword-leaves become for them the splendor of a pleasure grove,
> and may the swordlike *shalmali* trees grow as wish-fulfilling trees.

May the regions of hell become vast ponds of delight, fragrant
    with lotuses,
beautiful and pleasing with the cries of white geese, wild ducks,
    ruddy geese, and swans.

May the heap of burning coal become a mound of jewels.
    May the burning ground become a crystal marble floor.
And may the mountains of the Crushing Hell become temples
    of worship filled with ones gone to bliss.

May the rain of burning coal, lava, and daggers from now
    on become a rain of flowers,
and may mutual battling with weapons now become a playful
    flower fight.

By the power of my virtue, may those whose flesh has
    completely fallen off, whose skeletons are the color of a white
    jasmine flower,
and who are immersed in the river Vaitarani, whose water is
    like fire, attain celestial bodies and dwell with goddesses
    by the river Mandakini.

May the horrifying agents of Yama, crows, and vultures suddenly
    watch here in fear. Those looking upward behold blazing
    Vajrapani in the sky and wonder:
"Whose is this brilliant light that dispels darkness all around
    and generates the joy of contentment?" May they depart
    together with him, freed of vice through the power of their
    joy.

A rain of lotuses falls mixed with fragrant waters. It is seen to
    extinguish the unceasing fires of the hells.
May the beings of the hells, suddenly refreshed with joy, wonder,
    "What is this?" and may they see Padmapani.

[65] THE DEDICATION CHAPTER FROM SHANTIDEVA

Friends, come, come quickly! Cast away fear! We are alive!
A fragrant radiant vanquisher of fear, a certain prince in a monastic robe, has come to us.
By his power every adversity is removed, streams of delight flow, the spirit of awakening is born, as is compassion, the mother of protection of all beings.

Behold him whose lotus feet are worshipped with tiaras of hundreds of gods, whose eyes are moist with compassion, on whose head a stream of diverse flowers rains down, with his delightful summer palaces celebrated by thousands of goddesses singing hymns of praise.
Upon seeing Manjughosha before them, may the beings of the hells immediately cheer.

Through my virtues, may the beings of the hells rejoice upon seeing the unobscured clouds of bodhisattvas,
headed by Samantabhadra and bearing pleasant, cool, and fragrant rains and breezes.

May the intense pains and fears of the beings of the hells be pacified.
May the inhabitants of all miserable states of existence be liberated from their woeful states.

May the animals' risk of being eaten by each other disappear.
May the pretas be as happy as the people in Uttarakuru.

May the pretas always be satiated, bathed, and refreshed
by the streams of milk pouring from the hand of noble Avalokiteshvara.

May the blind always see forms, and may the deaf hear.
May pregnant women give birth without pains, as did Mayadevi.

May they acquire everything that is beneficial and desired by
  the mind:
clothing, food, drink, flower garlands, sandal paste, and
  ornaments.

May the fearful become fearless and those struck by grief
  find joy.
May the despondent become resolute and free of trepidation.

May the ill have good health. May they be freed from every
  bondage.
May the weak become strong and have affectionate hearts for
  one another.

May all regions be advantageous to all those who travel on
  roads.
May the purpose for which they set out be expediently
  accomplished.

May those who journey by boat succeed as they desire.
May they safely reach the shore and rejoice with their
  relatives.

May those who find themselves on wrong paths in dreary
  forests come upon the company of fellow travelers,
and without fatigue, may they journey without fear of
  bandits, tigers, and the like.

May deities protect the dull, the insane, the deranged, the
  helpless, the young, and the elderly,
and those in danger from sickness, the wilderness, and so on.

May they be free from all lack of leisure; may they be endowed
  with faith, wisdom, and compassion;
may they be possessed of stature and good conduct; and may
  they always remember their former lives.

May they be inexhaustible treasuries just like Gaganagañja.
Free of conflict or irritation, may they have an independent way of life.

May beings who have little splendor be endowed with great magnificence.
May unattractive wretches be endowed with beauty.

May the women in the world become men.
May the lowly obtain grandeur and yet be free of arrogance.

Through this merit of mine, may all beings without exception
abstain from every vice and always engage in virtue.

Not lacking the spirit of awakening, devoted to the bodhisattva way of life,
embraced by the buddhas, and free of the deeds of maras,
may all beings have immeasurable life spans.
May they always live happily, and may even the word "death" disappear.

May all quarters of the world be delightful with gardens of wish-fulfilling trees,
filled with the buddhas and the children of the buddhas,
and be enchanting with the sounds of Dharma.

May the ground everywhere be free from stones and rocks,
smooth like the palm of the hand, soft and made of lapis lazuli.

May the great assemblies of bodhisattvas sit on all sides.
May they beautify the earth with their own resplendence.

May all beings unceasingly hear the sound of Dharma
from the birds, from every tree, from the rays of light, and from the sky.

May they always encounter the buddhas and the heirs of the buddhas.
May they worship the spiritual mentor of the world with endless clouds of offerings.

May a god send rain in time, and may there be an abundance of crops.
May the populace be prosperous, and may the king be righteous.

May medicines be effective, and may the mantras of those who recite them be successful.
May dakinis, rakshasas, and other ghouls be filled with compassion.

May no sentient being be unhappy, sinful, ill, neglected, or despised;
and may no one be despondent.

May monasteries be well established, full of chanting and study.
May there always be harmony among the Sangha, and may the purpose of the Sangha be accomplished.

May monks who wish to practice find solitude.
May they meditate with their minds agile and free of all distractions.

May nuns receive provisions and be free of quarrels and troubles.
May all renunciates be of untarnished ethical discipline.

May those who are of poor ethical discipline be disgusted and become constantly intent on the extinction of their vices.
May they reach a fortunate state of existence, and may their vows remain unbroken there.

May they be learned and cultured, receive alms, and have provisions.

[65] THE DEDICATION CHAPTER FROM SHANTIDEVA

May their mindstreams be pure and their fame be proclaimed in every direction.

Without experiencing the suffering of the miserable states of existence and without arduous practice,
may the world attain buddhahood in a single divine body.

May all sentient beings worship all the buddhas in many ways.
May they be exceedingly joyful with the inconceivable bliss of the buddhas.

May the bodhisattvas' wishes for the welfare of the world be fulfilled;
and whatever the protectors intend for sentient beings, may that be accomplished.

May the pratyekabuddhas and shravakas be happy,
always worshipped by the lofty gods, demigods, and humans.

Through the grace of Manjughosha, may I always achieve ordination
and the recollection of past lives until I reach the Joyous Ground.

May I live endowed with strength in whatever posture I am.
In all my lives, may I find plentiful places of solitude.

When I wish to see or ask something, may I see the protector,
Manjunatha himself, without any impediment.

May my way of life be like that of Manjushri, who lives to accomplish
the benefit of all sentient beings throughout the ten directions.

For as long as space endures and for as long as the world lasts,
may I live dispelling the miseries of the world.

Whatever suffering there is for the world, may it all ripen
 upon me.
May the world find happiness through all the virtues of the
 bodhisattvas.

May the teaching that is the sole medicine for the suffering of
 the world and the source of all prosperity and joy
remain for a long time, accompanied by riches and honor.

I bow to Manjughosha, through whose grace my mind turns
 to virtue.
I salute my spiritual friend, through whose kindness it
 becomes stronger.

Colophon
Reprinted, with permission, from *A Guide to the Bodhisattva Way of Life*, translated by Vesna A. Wallace and B. Alan Wallace (Ithaca: Snow Lion Publications, 1997), 137–44.

RECITE "THE PRAYER TO BE REBORN IN THE BLISSFUL REALM OF AMITABHA BUDDHA" BY LAMA TSONGKHAPA [66]

See chapters 20, 21, 22, 23, and 29.
See also chapter 6 and other practices related to Amitabha: 11, 20, 64, and 81.

The Third of the Eight Prayers to Benefit the Dead

Namah Shri Guru Manjugoshaya

I prostrate to Amitabha, leader of humans and gods.
Through compassion you always see each transmigrator as your own child;
remembering you just once leaves the fear of the Lord of Death far behind;
may your eminent activities for transmigrators be glorious and without end.

The Buddha praised the supreme buddhafield
many times in an excellent manner.
Moved by compassion, various prayers were composed
mentioning the potential to be born in Sukhavati.

Being obscured by thick ignorance, [not knowing what to] adopt and [what to] discard,
the weapon of anger deprives me of the life of a higher rebirth.
Through the rope of attachment and craving, I am bound to samsara's prison.

Carried about in the ocean of samsara due to karma,
wandering around through the waves of suffering of sickness and old age,
entering the mouth of the terrifying sea monster, the Lord of Death,

buried under loads of unwanted suffering,
helplessly tormented, with an anguished voice
I make this prayer from my heart.

As witness to my yearning mind,
My guide and sole friend, Amitabha, draw me out of this
    miserable [state]!
With respect, I also make requests to your retinue,
and to the bodhisattvas Avalokiteshvara and Vajrapani:
please don't forget the commitment of your supreme mind
made over immeasurable eons for our benefit.
And just as the king of birds flies through the sky, the path
    of the gods,
please come here by your miraculous power and
    compassion.

By the power of combining oceans of the two accumulations created in the three times by myself and others, may I, at the time of death, directly see the guide Amitabha together with his retinue, his two chief disciples, and so forth. At that time, may I generate intense strong faith by focusing on the Victorious One and his retinue.

May I not experience the suffering of death and may I remember the object of faith when death draws near. As soon as my consciousness has left [this body], may the eight bodhisattvas come in a magical way and show me the path to Sukhavati. May I be reborn with great intelligence in a precious lotus in the lineage of the Great Vehicle.

Directly after birth, may I hold up a collection of immeasurable qualities such as retention, meditative stabilization, bodhichitta of nonapprehension, and inextinguishable courage. Having pleased the unsurpassed teachers such as Amitabha, the victorious ones, and the bodhisattvas of the ten directions, may I receive the pure teachings and transmissions of the Great Vehicle.

Realizing the true meaning of these [teachings], may I be able to go, during every moment, to boundless buddhafields using magical powers without obstruction and complete all the great deeds of the bodhisattvas.

After birth in the pure land, may I also be motivated by resilient compassion, and, with magical powers without obstruction, mainly go to impure worlds and establish the pure paths praised by the victorious ones through teaching the Dharma to all sentient beings in accordance with their dispositions.

May I, for the purpose of all limitless transmigrators, quickly obtain the state of the victorious one by completing all these marvelous deeds without delay.

> When the activities of this life are spent,
> May I clearly behold in my path of vision
> Amitabha and his ocean of retinues,
> And may my mind be filled with faith and compassion.
>
> As soon as the appearance of the intermediate state arrives,
> May the eight bodhisattvas show me the unmistaken path,
> And may I be reborn in Sukhavati
> To guide the transmigrators of impure worlds with my emanations.

Even if I do not achieve such a supreme state, may I, through all my lives, always obtain the perfect basis for hearing, contemplation, and meditation upon the victorious one's teachings of scriptures and realizations.

May I never be separated from this basis, ornamented with the seven qualities of the higher realms. May I, in all those circumstances, achieve the recollection of remembering all previous states [of rebirth].

Throughout all future lives, may I see samsara as being completely without essence and be attracted to nirvana's qualities. With this state of mind, and through the Bhagavan's excellent teachings on vinaya, may I go forth for ordination. When ordained, may I not even commit the smallest downfall or misdeed and, just as Bhikshu Mitrukpa did, achieve great enlightenment by completing the collection of morality.

Furthermore, throughout all future lives, may I realize the correct ways of knowing how afflictions arise and how to purify them, and obtain the marvelous recollection of the apprehension of never forgetting all the words and meanings of the Dharma, the branch of perfection. May I obtain the perfect courage of teaching others that which I apprehend, without obstruction.

Furthermore, throughout all future lives, may I obtain and never be parted from the doors of meditative stabilizations, such as the brave-like one, the supernatural eyes, the fleshy eye, clairvoyance, and the ability to perform miraculous deeds.

Furthermore, throughout all future lives, may I obtain great wisdom, the ability to self-reliantly differentiate between what to adopt and what to discard. May I obtain clear wisdom, the ability to differentiate between the diversity of the most subtle points without joining them, of the way afflictions arise and how to purify them. May I obtain quick wisdom, the ability to stop as soon as they arise all incomprehension, wrong views, and doubts. May I obtain profound wisdom, which penetrates inexhaustibly the words and meaning of scripture unfathomable to others.

In short, may I become like the foremost Manjushri, reaching the perfection of all the bodhisattvas' deeds with skillful wisdom differentiating the words and meanings of the scriptures, without the fault of imperfect knowledge. Having easily gained great, clear, quick, and profound wisdom, may I, in order to gather the fortunate, crush false expounders and, to please the wise, may I perfect the skill of teaching, debating, and composition that focuses upon all the scriptures of the victorious one.

Furthermore, throughout all future lives, may I stop all apprehension that is primarily concerned with self and all laziness of inadequacy and weaknesses regarding the great deeds of the bodhisattvas. May I become like the foremost Avalokiteshvara, reaching the perfection of all the bodhisattvas' deeds with skillful bodhichitta, perfecting supreme courage and taking responsibility for others.

Furthermore, throughout all future lives, whenever engaging in the welfare of self and others, may I become like the foremost Vajrapani, reaching the perfection of all the bodhisattvas' deeds with the skillful abilities to destroy maras, those with extreme views, and opponents having wrong views.

Throughout all future lives, may I become like the unequalled King of the Shakyas, reaching great enlightenment. And in order to complete the bodhisattvas' deeds with effort lacking laziness, may I, after generating bodhichitta without being distracted for even an instant, work with great fervor.

Throughout all future lives, may I become like the one gone to bliss, the King of Medicine Buddhas, and in order to destroy all illnesses of body and mind, the obstacles to the achievement of enlightenment, may I have the ability to pacify all suffering of body, speech, and mind by merely mentioning his name.

Furthermore, throughout all future lives, may I, by merely mentioning his name, become like the victorious Amitayus in having the ability to destroy untimely death and complete my life span as I wish. When life-threatening obstacles approach, by seeing the appearance of the body of the protector Amitayus that subdues through the four activities, may all life obstacles be completely pacified.

Throughout all future lives, may I, through the power of having generated uncontrived stable faith in recognizing teachers as being the protector Amitayus himself, whose body appears in accordance with whoever needs to be subdued, never be separated from the victorious Amitayus, who directly acts as spiritual teachers.

Furthermore, throughout all future lives, may I be fostered by spiritual teachers of the Mahayana, the root of all mundane and supramundane qualities. During this care, may I only please them with all my [three] doors through stable, unshakable faith and never, even for an instant, displease them.

May spiritual teachers instruct me with all teaching in its entirety, and may I have the ability to realize the complete meaning as intended and bring my practice to perfection. May I never, even for an instant, fall under [the influence of] misleading teachers and harmful friends.

Throughout all future lives, may I have faith in the law of cause and effect, and enter a continuous, effortless experience of the realizations of renunciation, bodhichitta, and the complete pure view. Throughout all future lives, may all my virtuous activities of body, speech, and mind be causes solely for the benefit of others and perfect enlightenment.

Colophon for the English Translation
Translated by Geshe Tenzin Namdak, Sera Je Monastery, Sakadawa, June, 2014. The most compassionate and kind lama, Kyabje Thubten Zopa Rinpoche, asked me to translate this text.

By any merit created through this translation, may His Holiness the Dalai Lama, Kyabje Lama Zopa Rinpoche, and all of our other precious gurus have long and healthy lives. May their holy wishes be spontaneously fulfilled, may they, at the time of our deaths, lead us to the pure land of Sukhavati and may we quickly obtain the state of full enlightenment for the benefit of all mother sentient beings.

With many thanks to Ven. Gyalten Lekden for proofreading this text.

> Being unrealized, low in acquired knowledge and learning,
> Saturated with wrong views and defilements,
> Taking the lamas and deities as my witness,
> I confess my mistakes to the wise.

RECITE "THE PRAYER FOR THE BEGINNING, MIDDLE, AND END OF PRACTICE" BY LAMA TSONGKHAPA [67]

See chapters 20, 21, 22, 23, and 29.

The Fourth of the Eight Prayers to Benefit the Dead

> I bow before the conquering buddhas, bodhisattvas, and arhats of all directions and of all times.
>
> I offer this boundless prayer with the purest of minds
> to free countless beings from cycles of existence.
> By the power of the unfailing Three Jewels and of great
>   rishis possessed of the force of truth,
> may these sincere words bear fruit.
>
> Life after life, may I never be born into realms
> of great suffering or unfavorable circumstance
> but gain always a precious human form
> blessed with every conducive provision.
>
> From the moment of birth may I never
> be lured by the pleasures of existence,
> but, guided by renunciation intent on freedom,
> be resolute in seeking the pure life.
>
> May there be no hindrance to becoming a monk
> from friends, family, or possessions,
> and for every conducive circumstance,
> by mere thought may it appear.
>
> Once a monk, may I be
> untainted as long as I live
> by breech of vow or natural fault,
> as promised in the presence of my preceptor.

I pray that on such pure foundation,
and for every mother sentient being,
I devote myself with hardship for countless eons
to every aspect, profound and vast, of the Mahayana.

May I be cared for by true spiritual friends,
filled with knowledge and insight,
senses stilled, minds controlled, loving, compassionate,
and with courage untiring in working for others.

As Sadaprarudita devoted himself to Dharmodgata,
may I sincerely please my spiritual master
with body, life, and wealth,
never disappointing him for an instant.

I pray that the Perfection of Wisdom, forever profound,
a bringer of peace, unbound by fabrication,
be taught to me as taught to Sadaprarudita,
unsullied by the muddy waters of false views.

May I never fall under the sway
of false teachers and misleading friends,
their flawed views of existence and nonexistence
well outside the Buddha's intention.

With sail hoisted of the sincerest of intentions,
driven by winds of unflagging effort,
on this well-built ship of study, thought, and meditation,
may I bring living beings from samsara's ocean.

As much as I excel in learning,
as much as I give to others,
as pure as my morality grows,
as much as I become wise,
by as much may I be empty of pride.

[67] THE BEGINNING, MIDDLE, AND END OF PRACTICE

I pray that I listen insatiably
to countless teachings at the feet of a master,
single-handedly with logic unflawed,
prizing open scriptures' meanings.

Having examined day and night
with fourfold logic all that I have heard,
may I banish every doubt with the discerning
    understanding
that arises from such contemplation.

With conviction on dharmas profound
gained from understanding born of contemplation,
I pray that I retreat to solitude with a perseverance severing
    life's attachments
to devote myself to proper practice.

When the Buddha's thoughts dawn upon me
through study, thought, and meditation,
I pray that things of this life forever bonded to samsara
and thoughts of my happiness alone never arise in
    my mind.

Unattached to my possessions
I pray that I destroy parsimony,
gathering disciples around me by giving first
of material wealth to satisfy them with Dharma.

With a mind renounced may I never transgress
on the road to enlightenment even the smallest precept,
though it may cost my life,
flying forever therefore the flag of freedom.

When I see, hear, or think of those
who struck, beat, or maligned me,
may I be without anger, speak of their virtues,
and meditate upon patience.

I pray I will apply myself to enthusiasm,
achieving virtues unachieved, improving those attained,
banishing utterly the threefold laziness
that weakens such attainments.

I pray to abandon the meditative absorption
that lacks the power of insight to quell samsara,
that is divorced from the moist compassion to quash
  nirvana's passivity, and that mostly throws one back to
  cycles of existence
but develop instead the meditative absorption that unites
  compassion and insight.

I pray that I banish false views of emptiness,
mentally fabricated and partially known,
born from fear of the most profound truth, cherished
  as supreme,
and that I realize all phenomena to have been forever
  empty.

May I bring to faultless morality
those so-called practitioners with their wayward ethics,
their minds shamelessly empty of pure precepts,
rashly pursuing paths shunned by the wise.

May I easily bring to the path praised by buddhas
those lost and fallen onto wrong paths,
Swayed by deluded teachers
and misleading friends.

I pray that my lion-like roar of teaching, argument,
  and composition
flattens the pride of fox-like false orators,
and caring for them by all skillful means necessary,
I fly the banner of the teachings forever.

[67] THE BEGINNING, MIDDLE, AND END OF PRACTICE

In whatever life I may drink the nectar of Buddha's
  teachings,
I pray to be born into a good family
and be of handsome build, wealthy, powerful, and wise,
blessed with long life and sound health.

May I develop the unique love of a mother
for those who malign me
and harbor ill designs upon my life,
my body, or my possessions.

By growing within myself
the pure and extraordinary bodhi mind
that meditates on cherishing others more than self,
may I soon give them unsurpassable enlightenment.

Whoever hears, sees,
or calls these verses to mind,
may they be undaunted in fulfilling
the powerful prayers of the bodhisattvas.

By the power of these vast prayers
made with the purest intention,
may I attain the perfection of prayer
and fulfill the hopes of every living being.

Colophon

Reprinted from Tsongkhapa, *The Splendor of an Autumn Moon: The Devotional Verse of Tsongkhapa*, translated by Gavin Kilty (Boston: Wisdom Publications, 2001), 193–208.

RECITE "UNTIL BUDDHAHOOD" [68]

See chapters 20, 21, 22, 23, and 29.

The Fifth of the Eight Prayers to Benefit the Dead

> Until I manifest
> the holy state of a supreme subduer,
> may I obtain a basis for accomplishing the pure noble path,
> take ordination, and remember all my lives.
>
> May I uphold the treasury of many infinite qualities—
>   dharani, confidence,
> meditative stabilization, clairvoyance, magical emanation,
>   and more.
> Having attained peerless knowledge, mercy, and ability,
> may I swiftly perfect the conduct of enlightenment.
>
> When I see signs of untimely death,
> in that very moment may I clearly see the body
> of Protector Amitayus and destroy the Lord of Death;
> may I quickly become an immortal knowledge-holder.
>
> In all my lives by the force of Amitayus
> directly acting as a virtuous friend of the Supreme Vehicle,
> may I never turn away, even for an instant,
> from this noble path admired by the conquerors.
>
> May I never generate a mind that,
> neglecting sentient beings, hopes for my welfare alone.
> May I strive for the welfare of others with skill in means,
> unobscured regarding the way to accomplish their welfare.
>
> Also by merely expressing and remembering my name,
> may all those tormented by the result of their negative
>   actions

become rich with the glory of sublime happiness, and
may they climb the stairway leading to the Supreme
   Vehicle.

By illustrating a mere fragment of the biographies of
the conquerors' heirs, may all the interferences
to the conduct of the conquerors' heirs be pacified without
   exception,
and may helpful necessities be achieved by just calling
   them to mind.

By the truth of the ruler of the Shakyas,
the guides Amitabha, Maitreya, Manjushri, the Lord of the
   Secret,
Avalokiteshvara, and the ones gone to bliss and their
   retinues,
may all these prayers be quickly fulfilled.

Colophon
Translated by Geshe Thubten Sherab, Taos, New Mexico.

RECITE "A DAILY PRAYER TO MAITREYA BODHISATTVA" TAUGHT BY BUDDHA SHAKYAMUNI [69]

See chapters 20, 21, 22, 23, and 29.
See also other practices related to Maitreya: 30, 70, and 71.

The Sixth of the Eight Prayers to Benefit the Dead

> To the awakened ones I prostrate,
> as well as to all the bodhisattvas,
> to the yogis with the power of the divine eye,
> and to the shravakas and so forth.
>
> I prostrate to bodhichitta,
> which bars the way to unfortunate destinies
> and shows the path that leads to the highest realms
> and even to the state beyond old age and death.
>
> Controlled by negative habits,
> I have often given harm to others.
> I now confess those actions
> in the sight of the Buddha.
>
> From the beneficial actions
> of my body, speech, and mind,
> I pray that the seeds for generating omniscience
> may never be exhausted.
>
> All that has been offered to the buddhas
> in all lands throughout the ten directions,
> all that the buddhas see and rejoice in,
> in those virtues I also rejoice.
>
> In short, I confess all harmful actions,
> I rejoice in all acts of virtue,

[69] A DAILY PRAYER TO MAITREYA BODHISATTVA

and I make prostration to all the buddhas.
May I myself obtain supreme wisdom!

May all you bodhisattvas
of all ten levels
abiding in all the ten directions
work for highest enlightenment.

May you obtain buddhahood, supreme enlightenment,
joining those who have subdued the demon of
 self-cherishing.
May you turn the Dharma wheel
in order to benefit all sentient beings.

I pray that you may liberate sentient beings without
 exception
by the sound of the great Dharma drum.
Please stay in the world and teach the path to
 enlightenment
for inconceivable millions of eons.

O supreme beings, best of bipeds,
please watch over those stuck hard
in the mud of desire,
tightly bound by the rope of samsara.

O buddhas, your love is not obscured
like that between sentient beings.
With your loving kindness and compassion,
lead them across the ocean of samsara.

May I follow with care
the path of the buddhas
of the past, present, and future,
and may I perform the deeds of bodhisattvas.

Having accomplished the six perfections,
may I liberate all beings of the six realms.
Having manifested the six supramundane powers,
may I reach great enlightenment.

Not born and not arising,
with no self-nature, no location,
no awareness, and no true existence,
may I realize the emptiness of phenomena.

Just like the Buddha, the great lord,
may I understand the teaching of non-self,
that sentient beings do not exist, life does not exist,
a person does not exist, no being at all is there that exists.

Not grasping at anything existing,
no ego nor what is mine,
in order to benefit all sentient beings,
may I develop generosity without limit.

Since material resources do not exist,
may my prosperity be unhindered.
Since all things are transient,
may I accomplish the perfection of generosity.

Never transgressing the discipline of morality,
with morality perfectly purified of appearances,
and thus morality without pride,
may I accomplish the perfection of morality.

With patience as steady as earth or water,
not changeable like the wind,
knowing both patience and anger do not exist,
may I accomplish the perfection of patience.

With diligence may I practice effort
with enjoyment free of laziness.
By the power of mind and body,
may I accomplish the perfection of effort.

With the magical samadhi,
the heroic samadhi,
and the vajra-like samadhi,
may I accomplish the perfection of samadhi.

Realizing the practices of all three vehicles,
the three doors to liberation,
and the three knowledges,
may I gain the perfection of wisdom.

Having followed a complete practice like this,
may I, like he who is named Maitreya,
accomplish well the six perfections
and quickly reach beyond the ten levels.

Mantra of Maitreya Buddha's Promise

NAMO RATNA TRAYAYA / NAMO BHAGAVATE SHAKYAMUNAYE / TATHAGATAYA / ARHATE SAMYAK SAMBUDDHAYA / TADYATHA / OM AJITE AJITE / APARAJITE / AJITAÑCHAYA HARA HARA MAITRI / AVALOKITE KARA KARA MAHASAMAYA SIDDHE / BHARA BHARA / MAHABODHI MANDA VIJE SMARA SMARA ASMAKAM / SAMAYA BODHI BODHI MAHABODHI SVAHA

Heart Mantra of Maitreya

OM MOHI MOHI MAHA MOHI SVAHA

Near Heart Mantra of Maitreya

OM MUNI MUNI SMARA SVAHA

When my death comes to me in this place,
may I pass with ease to the pure land of Ganden.
May I quickly please the bodhisattva Maitreya
and learn from him the time and place of my awakening.

Colophon

Translator unknown. This prayer is found in the *Questions of Maitreya Sutra*.

RECITE "THE PRAYER FOR A STATUE OF MAITREYA" BY THE FIRST DALAI LAMA GENDUN DRUP [70]

See chapters 20, 21, 22, 23, and 29.
See also other practices related to Maitreya: 30, 69, and 71.

The Seventh of the Eight Prayers to Benefit the Dead

May the embodied beings who have fulfilled all requirements
for building an excellent statue of Maitreya
be in the presence of the savior, perfect, pure Maitreya,
and enjoy the splendor of the Mahayana Dharma.

When the mighty sun, the savior Maitreya,
shines above the hills of Bodhgaya,
may the lotus bloom of my wisdom be opened,
so that I may satisfy a swarm of bees of fortunate ones.

At that time Buddha Maitreya is extremely pleased,
and as he lays his right hand upon my head
and my supreme incomparable enlightenment is prophesied,
may I then quickly attain buddhahood for the sake of all sentient beings.

Even in all future lifetimes while I am completing enlightenment,
after gathering as one all the great waves of deeds, whatever there are,
of all the buddhas and bodhisattvas of the three times,
may I properly give teachings.

Draped in delicate drawing-like scriptures of good explanation,
supported by a golden staff of discernment,

and adorned with a jeweled tip of the three trainings,
may the victory banner of Buddha's teachings be planted everywhere.

May the teachings, the source of all well-being, spread and flourish,
and may all holy beings, the repository of the teachings, enjoy good health.
May the source of happiness for all embodied beings,
the teachings of the Buddha, always spread.

By the continual force of cultivating the three aspects of love [immeasurable love, affectionate love, and superior-thought love],
may there be the auspiciousness of the savior, Buddha Maitreya,
who destroys the hosts of maras with the power of his love
and nurtures all sentient beings with the strength of his love.

Colophon

Composed by the omniscient master, Gendun Drub. The translator is unknown.

RECITE "THE PRAYER FOR SPONTANEOUS BLISS" BY THE SECOND DALAI LAMA GENDUN GYATSO [71]

See chapters 20, 21, 22, 23, and 29.
See also other practices related to Maitreya: 30, 69, and 70.

The Eighth of the Eight Prayers to Benefit the Dead

> Respectfully I prostrate to the mighty protector Maitreya,
> who pervades the world with clouds of love and
>   compassion
> from the space of dharmakaya, which spontaneously
>   completes
>   great bliss,
> and who rains down deeds in a continuous shower.
>
> From your wisdom manifestation that sees, just as they are,
> the minds and natural elements of countless disciples,
> please come down here by the power of faith unimpeded in
>   all places,
> like the reflected image of the moon in water.
>
> Like jeweled inlay of many kinds of precious gemstones
> set into a Mount Meru of exquisite refined gold,
> your supreme form, which satisfies on sight,
> I request to remain firmly for as long as cyclic existence
>   lasts.
>
> You, savior, hold closely with your compassionate hands
> all sentient beings who have provided the requirements
> for constructing a statue of affectionate love [Maitreya],
> and please lead them definitely to the land of Tushita.
>
> Inseparable from your face, nectar for their eyes,
> nurtured by your speech, the Mahayana scriptures,

and having perfected all the bodhisattva's practices,
please bestow your blessings for them to quickly attain
  buddhahood.

In the meantime, may all wishes be fulfilled,
may all sentient beings have a loving attitude,
may the teachings of the Buddha spread and extend in all
  directions,
and may all sentient beings enjoy wonderful well-being.

May this place be filled by an assembly of ordained monks
  and nuns
clad in saffron robes and upholding the three trainings,
and may deeds of explanation and practice bring good
  fortune
  of extending
the Buddha's teachings everywhere for as long as cyclic
  existence lasts.

By the truth of the infallible Three Precious Jewels,
the blessings of the power of Buddha Maitreya,
and the enlightened deeds of the mighty Dharma
  protectors,
may the complete essence of this pure prayer be fulfilled.

Colophon
This aspirational prayer of truthful words for achieving excellence was composed at Chokhor Gyäl monastery by Gendun Gyatso [the Second Dalai Lama], a monk who expounds the Dharma, at the request of the great woman leader, Nyima Päl, an incarnation of Bishwakarma [the legendary King of Artistry who designed the main temple in central Lhasa].

Translated by Geshe Lhundub Sopa for members of the Maitreya Project, Singapore, February 1998.

RECITE THE GURU PUJA [72]

See chapters 20, 21, 22, 23, and 29.
See also other practices related to the guru: 1, 10, 18, 35, 43, 47, 60, and 85.

The *Guru Puja* by Panchen Lama Losang Chökyi Gyaltsen is an incredible practice to do. It's got everything in it, including phowa.

If you like, you can recite just the refuge section. Whatever practices you do—jangwa, phowa, self-initiation—the foundation is refuge, relying on Buddha, Dharma, Sangha. So take strong refuge in the Guru Buddha while visualizing him above the head of the your loved one—you can visualize the entire merit field or just Shakyamuni Buddha. Then, as you recite a few hundred of each of the refuge mantras, pray that your loved one purifies all their negative karma immediately and is born in the pure lands of the buddhas or receives a perfect human rebirth.

Refuge Mantras from the Guru Puja

NAMO GURUBHYA
To the Guru I go for refuge.
NAMO BUDDHAYA
To the Buddha I go for refuge.
NAMO DHARMAYA
To the Dharma I go for refuge.
NAMO SANGHAYA
To the Sangha I go for refuge.

LAMA YIDAM KONCHOK SUMLA KYABSU CHIWO
To the Guru, the Deity, and the Three Rare Sublime Ones
I go for refuge.

The Guru Puja *Is Available From*
(Published as *Lama Chöpa Jorchö*)
Website fpmt.org/death/
Email shopfpmt@fpmt.org

DO A NYUNGNÉ FASTING RETREAT [73]

See chapters 20 and 29.
See also other practices related to the Compassion Buddha: 21 and 38.

It is excellent to do a three-day nyungné fasting retreat. It is an unbelievable way to create merit, skies of merit.

On the first day you take only lunch, and on the second day you fast completely, including no drinks. You can think that you are fasting for the sake of your loved one and all sentient beings.

The practice combines many powerful practices such as reciting mantras, the Eight Mahayana Precepts, meditation on the Compassion Buddha, and bodhichitta. When you meditate, you can either visualize yourself as the Compassion Buddha or see him in front of you, and as you recite his mantra, the long one or short one (practice 21), imagine nectar flowing from his heart, purifying your loved one.

The practice also includes quite a lot of prostrations, which you perform while you recite a praise to the Compassion Buddha as well as the names of the Thirty-Five Buddhas of Confession (practice 15).

The Nyungné Practice and Commentary Is Available From
Website fpmt.org/death/
Email shopfpmt@fpmt.org

CHECK THAT THE MIND HAS LEFT THE BODY [74]

See chapters 20, 21, 22, 23, and 25.

Before you move the body of your loved one, check that the consciousness has already left. There are various signs that indicate that the mind is no longer there. These signs are visible in both ordinary people and meditators.

No Longer Warm at the Heart
The easiest, most common way to check if the mind has left the body is to put your hand just above the heart chakra, without touching the body. If you feel warmth there, even if every other part of the body is cold, your loved one's consciousness is still present.

The White and Red Drops Have Left the Body
As described in the presentation of the death process in chapter 9, the consciousness has left the body when, in the male, the white drop (a whitish liquid) leaves through the lower chakra and the red drop (a pinkish liquid) leaves through the nose; for the female it's the opposite. Both will not necessarily come out of the body; sometimes it may be just one. And sometimes, perhaps because of chronic disease or long-time illness, nothing comes out.

The Body Smells
If the body starts to smell like rotten meat, this is another indication that the consciousness has left.

The Flesh Does Not Respond
Another indication that the mind has left the body is if, when you press with your fingers on part of the body, the flesh doesn't respond—the impression of your fingers remains.

The Head Moves
For meditators, whether they're sitting up or lying down, another sign is that the head shifts when the consciousness leaves.

TUG AT THE HAIR AT THE CROWN CHAKRA [75]

See chapters 20, 21, 22, 23, and 25.

If the indication is that the mind has not yet left the body, tug the hair at the crown chakra a few times—toward the back of the head—or firmly tap on the crown there. If the consciousness is still there, this can encourage it to go to the crown chakra and leave from there, which means your loved one would go to a pure land, as I discussed in chapter 9. Anyway, it is auspicious to do this the first time you touch the body.

CONSULT A TIBETAN ASTROLOGER [76]

See chapters 20, 21, 22, and 23.

Typically, a Tibetan would consult an astrologer immediately after the mind of their loved one has left the body. Astrology can indicate what practices should be done to prevent your loved one from being born in the lower realms or to help them to take a good rebirth. For instance, it can indicate which statue or thangka painting should be made on their behalf or whether, if you do this or that practice, they will have a good rebirth or be reborn as a monk or a nun or even as a great lama. It can even predict where the good rebirth will be taken. However, it is said that this usually only works for ordinary people; astrology cannot predict the future of either great holy beings or very evil people.

Tell the astrologer which of the twelve animal signs your loved one was born under as well as the date and time they passed away, even perhaps the hour or whether it was in the morning, the afternoon, and so on. It's important to be accurate.

There is astrology in the West, of course, but I'm not sure if it predicts future lives and so forth.

Consult a Tibetan Astrologer
Men-Tsee-Khang
The Tibetan Medical and Astro-Science Institute
Dharamsala, India
Website men-tsee-khang.org

SPRINKLE BLESSED SEEDS, WATER, AND SO FORTH ON YOUR LOVED ONE'S BODY [77]

See chapter 26.

Get some sesame or mustard seeds, say, or talcum powder, water, perfume, or something you can easily sprinkle. Now recite the Namgyalma mantra twenty-one times (practice 25)—the long mantra is better, but the short mantra is okay—or any other mantras that you know, such as the Compassion Buddha mantra (practice 21).

Having blessed your breath with the recitation, now blow on the seeds or water or whatever, blessing them. Now sprinkle them over the body.

Every day, after I have chanted thousands of various mantras, I blow on the powder or seeds to bless them. I use them whenever I see dead insects or animals, or for people who have died.

BLESS THE ASHES, HAIR, NAILS, AND SO FORTH OF YOUR LOVED ONE WITH JANGWA [78]

See chapter 28.
See also other practices related to the Medicine Buddha: 14, 22, 36, and 59.

Originally jangwa was done in conjunction with Buddha Kunrik, who, as mentioned in practice 27, is known as the king of deities for purifying the lower realms.

Eventually other buddhas were used as well, such as Medicine Buddha, Vajrayogini, and Maitreya. The practice I recommend is in association with the Medicine Buddha. At the end there is phowa, shooting the consciousness into a pure land.

As soon after the funeral service as possible, organize a jangwa practice, during which the buddhas' wisdom is invoked into the remains. You will need a small amount of the ashes or bones, hair, nails, or the like.

Keeping the ashes of your loved one that haven't been blessed has no benefit for the dead or the living. Whereas, as Kirti Tsenshab Rinpoche said, when the ashes are purified and blessed with jangwa, they are actual relics or holy objects.

Best is to request the lama at your nearest Tibetan Buddhist center to perform the ceremony, or you can request monks or nuns to do it. If you cannot get anyone to do the practice, you and your Dharma friends can do it.

You dedicate all the merits created by doing jangwa to your loved one, praying that their negative karma is purified and that they receive a perfect human rebirth or rebirth in a pure land, meet the perfectly qualified virtuous friend, hear the holy Dharma, and quickly achieve full enlightenment.

For addresses of centers that will bless the ashes of your loved ones with jangwa, see practice 79.

The Practice of Jangwa Is Available From
Website fpmt.org/death/
Email shopfpmt@fpmt.org

MAKE TSA-TSAS, STATUES, OR STUPAS USING THE BLESSED ASHES [79]

See chapter 28.
See also practice 87.

Having blessed the ashes with jangwa (practice 78), you can now include them in holy objects such as tsa-tsas, stupas, or statues, which brings so much benefit, both to your loved one and to you. As I mention in practice 87, it is said that if a person is destined to be reborn in the lower realms, making a holy object—even simply on their behalf—can change the situation and help them get a good rebirth.

You can decide which buddha to use for the tsa-tsa or statue—Medicine Buddha, Amitabha, or the Compassion Buddha, for example—or you could ask a lama or a Tibetan astrologer which buddha would have the strongest effect in liberating your loved one. Or, as I mentioned, you could make a stupa.

There are FPMT centers where the ashes of your loved ones can be blessed in a jangwa ceremony and then kept in a specially-made stupa in a memorial shrine, where you can visit and make offerings.

Australia
Garden of Enlightenment
Chenrezig Institute
Website chenrezig.com.au/stupa-information/#page-content
Email arts@chenrezig.com.au

The Great Stupa
Website stupa.org.au/memorials/
Email info@stupa.org.au

New Zealand
Dorje Chang Institute
Website dci.org.nz/memorial/
Email dci@dci.org.nz

United States
Land of Medicine Buddha
Website landofmedicinebuddha.org
Email office@medicinebuddha.org

For a list of centers worldwide who perform jangwa: fpmt.org/death/.

THROW BLESSED ASHES INTO THE WIND OR WATER [80]

See chapter 28.
See also practices 78 and 79.

Once the ashes of your loved one have been blessed with jangwa (practice 78), you could throw them into the wind from a high mountain or into the sea, a lake, a river, and so on. All the sentient beings touched by the ashes in the air or by the water are purified of their obscurations and negative karma.

REQUEST A LAMA TO PRACTICE PHOWA, OR YOU AND YOUR DHARMA FRIENDS PRACTICE AMITABHA PHOWA BY LAMA YESHE [81]

See chapter 29. See also chapter 6.
See also practices 48 and 62 and other practices related to Amitabha: 11, 20, 64, and 66.

If a Lama Does the Practice
If phowa has not been performed by your loved one (practice 48) or by a lama when the breath stopped (practice 62), it can be performed by a lama after the mind has left the body.

If You and Your Friends Do the Practice
If you cannot request a lama, you and your Dharma friends can do the Amitabha phowa composed by Lama Yeshe below.

I once asked Kirti Tsenshab Rinpoche how to make a phowa practice effective. Rinpoche said that during our daily Vajrasattva practice we should visualize sentient beings at our heart on a moon disc and then, when we do the purifying meditation, imagine the nectar beams emitting from Vajrasattva and entering the hearts of the sentient beings, purifying them.

Rinpoche said that the practice becomes more effective, more powerful, when you do Medicine Buddha meditation beforehand. You recite the names of the seven Medicine Buddhas and the mantra—both included below.

Normally it is necessary to have received an empowerment into this Amitabha Buddha phowa practice before practicing it, but if you have faith in the Dharma you can practice it, especially with the motivation of helping your loved one.

THE TECHNICAL METHOD FOR TRANSFERRING THE CONSCIOUSNESS TO GURU BUDDHA AMITABHA'S PURE LAND

Recite the Names of the Seven Medicine Buddhas

1. Buddha Renowned Glorious King of Excellent Signs

2. Buddha King of Melodious Sound, Brilliant Radiance of Skill, Adorned with Jewels, Moon, and Lotus
3. Buddha Stainless Excellent Gold
4. Buddha Supreme Glory Free from Sorrow
5. Buddha Melodious Ocean of Dharma Proclaimed
6. Buddha Delightful King of Clear Knowing
7. Buddha Medicine Guru, Great King with the Radiance of a Lapis Jewel (7x)

Recite the Medicine Buddha Mantra

Short Mantra
TADYATHA / OM BHAISHAJYE BHAISHAJYE MAHA BHAISHAJYE [BHAISHAJYE] / RAJA SAMUDGATE SVAHA

Common Pronunciation
TAYATA OM BEKANZE BEKANZE MAHA BEKANZE [BEKANZE] RADZA SAMUNGATE SOHA

[Preparation]
[Clean the place of meditation, set up an image of Amitabha, make many offerings, and face west (or visualize that you are doing so).]

Refuge and Bodhichitta Motivation
Take refuge in the Triple Gem and generate a bodhichitta motivation while reciting the following prayer with single-pointed concentration and devotion.

I go for refuge until I am enlightened
to the Buddha, the Dharma, and the Supreme Assembly.
By my merit of giving and other perfections,
may I become a buddha to benefit all sentient beings. (3x)

The Four Immeasurable Thoughts

May all sentient beings have happiness and its cause.
May all sentient beings be free of suffering and its cause.

May all sentient beings attain that happiness without
   limits.
May all sentient beings be free of attachment and aversion,
   holding some close and others distant.

Visualize Guru Buddha Amitabha

Visualize the following with single-pointed clarity.

Above my crown on a lotus and a moon and sun throne sits Guru Buddha Amitabha in the vajra pose. His holy body is radiant and ruby red. He has one face and two hands that rest in the gesture of single-pointed contemplation. He holds a nectar bowl filled with the elixir of immortality and wears the saffron robes of moral purity. His crown is marked by a shining white OM, his throat by a radiant red AH, and his heart by a deep blue HUM.

From the HUM in his heart boundless light shines forth filling all of space. This light penetrates especially Amitabha's western pure land, invoking Buddha Amitabha, the eight great lion-like bodhisattvas, and the vast assembly of male and female bodhisattvas who reside in the western pure land. These all enter into Guru Amitabha's crown chakra, descend his central channel, and mingle with his heart. He and they are unified and of one essence.

Hold this thought with single-pointed concentration.

Seven-Limb Prayer (optional)

This practice purifies the mind of poisonous imprints and their suffering results and empowers the mind with wholesome energy by cultivating extensive virtuous imprints and the dedication of their good results to the ultimate aim, the supreme happiness of enlightenment for all sentient beings.

I prostrate with body, speech, and mind in heartfelt faith and
   admiration.
I make material offerings and fill the boundless sky with
   billions of exquisite offerings mentally transformed.
Every evil or deluded action done by me since beginningless
   time is declared and offered for purification.
I rejoice in all the countless virtuous actions done by ordinary

beings and the inconceivable virtuous actions done by superior ones.

[Visualize a jeweled throne marked by a crossed vajra.] Please, Guru Buddha, remain within your present vajra form until samsara is utterly emptied.

[Visualize a golden thousand-spoked wheel.] And turn the wheel of the perfect Dharma for the sake of sentient beings.

I dedicate all past, present, and future merits to the full enlightenment of all sentient beings.

Offering the Universal Mandala (optional)

This ground, anointed with perfume, strewn with flowers,
adorned with Mount Meru, four continents, the sun, and the moon:
I imagine this as a buddhafield and offer it.
May all living beings enjoy this pure land!

[Requests]

[May I be able to practice phowa at the time of death and be able to do this for others,
may all sentient beings be liberated from the suffering of the lower realms and be lifted up to higher realms,
and with your hook, please bring me to your blissful realm.]

IDAM GURU RATNA MANDALAKAM NIRYATAYAMI

Prostrations (optional)

Guru, invincible one beyond all evil, endowed with all virtues,
tathagata, foe destroyer, fully complete and perfect buddha magnificent king, Guru Amitabha of boundless light,
I prostrate, make offerings, and take refuge in you.
Please bestow upon me your countless blessings. [21x]

Purification Meditation

Then in heartfelt devotion I concentrate single-pointedly on Guru Amitabha. From his holy body five-colored nectar light streams down through my central channel. From here it flows through all the other channels of my body, completely filling it with blissful nectar-light.

All hindrances, such as illness and an untimely death, are completely purified.

All negative forces utterly disappear, especially the grasping at mundane existence.

The power to be successful in transferring consciousness and taking rebirth in the western pure land is granted.

My body becomes crystal clear and translucent like a rainbow.

Prayer of Bodhichitta Motivation and Dedication

> All past, present, and future gurus, buddhas, and bodhisattvas
>   dwelling in the ten directions of space,
> especially Buddha Amitabha and the eight great lion-like
>   bodhisattvas, please pay attention to me.
> Wishing to liberate all mother sentient beings from the vast
>   ocean of samsaric suffering and to lead them all to the
>   supreme joy of full enlightenment,
> I realize that I myself must become a buddha.
>
> Thus I determine to take rebirth in the western pure land
>   and to hear teachings directly from Buddha Amitabha
>   himself.
> Therefore, by the force of all my past, present, and future merits
>   collected together and the immutable promise of all the
>   tathagatas, and by the power of wisdom and absolute truth,
> may I, at the very moment of death, take immediate and
>   spontaneous rebirth upon a fully opened lotus flower,
> face to face with Buddha Amitabha's shining form.
>
> May I obtain without difficulty the ability to hear teachings
>   directly from the mouth of Buddha Amitabha.
> May I develop the six transcending perfections to their ultimate

completion, and may I accomplish the ten stages of the bodhisattva's path.

May I attain all the wisdom, love, and power of myriad buddhas in countless buddhafields more numerous than all the atoms of the boundless universe.

With clarity, visualize the following.

The consciousness principle (the very subtle mind of clear light) is seen as a brilliantly bright white-red energy drop in the center of my heart channel-wheel inside the central channel. From here I can look upward into Guru Amitabha's heart, the wisdom of nonduality, which is vividly clear like the surface of a mirror yet having a five-colored radiance.

Guru Amitabha, looking down and seeing the radiant energy-drop in my heart, says, "Please, my son or daughter, arise." With joyful expectation, I look forward to going.

Then recite:

> Since time without beginning I have been in constant confusion and have been circling in samsaric existence.
> Bound by grasping and longing attachment, I have experienced continuing misery.
> Unless I give up this deluded and grasping mind, no buddhas or bodhisattvas can be of ultimate benefit to me.
> Nothing in samsara is certain except that all mundane pleasures die away.
> This grasping and ignorant mind is the noose that binds me to the relentless turning of the wheel of conditioned existence.
> I yearn to go to Amitabha's pure land, where even the word "suffering" does not exist and from where I can never fall again into samsara's misery.
> With the power of perfect conviction, I prepare to go and dwell in Amitabha's enlightened realm.

The Prayer of Praise

> You are like the sun dispelling all darkness
> and the panacea curing all illness and disease.

You are the perfect guide that leads all beings to blissful
   freedom
by the radiant red hook emanating from your heart.

The Prayer for the Time of Death (optional)

The moment the messenger of death arrives,
please come instantaneously from your pure land,
advise me to give up grasping at mundane existence,
and invite me to come to your pure land.

When earth sinks into water
and the mirage-like appearance is perceived
and my mouth becomes dry and foul tasting,
please come and tell me to not be afraid and inspire me with
   true courage.

When water sinks into fire
and the smoke-like appearance is perceived
and my tongue gets thick and my speech is lost.
please reveal to me your shining face and give me solace and
   peaceful joy.

When fire sinks into air
and the firefly-like appearance is perceived
and my body heat and the light of my eyes rapidly fade away,
please come and fill my mind with the sound of Dharma
   wisdom.

When air sinks into consciousness
and the burning like a butter lamp appearance is perceived
and my body becomes like the earth and my breathing ceases,
please draw me to your pure land with the radiant light of your
   shining face.

And then may the radiant red hook
emanating from your pristine heart
enter my crown, then descend my central channel,

hook my very subtle clear-light mind, and bring it to your pure
land.

Yet if I must enter the intermediate state by the force of my
negative karma,
may all the buddhas and bodhisattvas rescue me with the
power of Dharma
and inspire me with the pure view that sees all beings as
utterly pure,
hears all sounds as Dharma teaching, and sees all places
as your pure land.

Then with clarity visualize the following:

From Guru Amitabha's heart a reed of radiant white light descends to my crown and forms there an indestructible and cohesive bond. There is now an unobstructed passageway between my very subtle mind, the white-red clear light energy-drop in the center of my heart, and the clear mirror-like heart of Guru Amitabha.

Then suddenly a radiant hook of red light emanates from Guru Amitabha's heart, descends through the passageway, and securely hooks the delicate and pure clear-light energy drop in my heart.

[Or you can visualize that Guru Amitabha's heart draws the energy-drop upward just as a magnet attracts iron filings.]

Contemplate this with single-pointed concentration.

The Prayer for Accomplishment

Guru Buddha Amitabha, essence of the perfect truth of the
Triple Gem,
courageous one who liberates all sentient beings from the
bondage of mundane existence
and delivers them to the supremely blissful realm of
buddhahood,
please release me and all others from the difficulties and
fears of the death process and the intermediate state
of the after-death plane.
Easily guide me to your wisdom heart by inspiring me to

thoroughly renounce the grasping at mundane existence and to achieve success in transferring my consciousness.
You are my only liberator.
Please with great compassion take me to your pure land.

The Meditation of Transferring Your Consciousness

Now with crystal clarity and vivid concentration, visualize your very subtle mind of clear light in the form of the very blissful and radiant white-red energy-drop in your heart, the reed of radiant white light, and Guru Amitabha's clear and radiant heart. See the energy-drop as the traveler, the white light reed as the path, and Guru Amitabha's heart as the destination.

Then reverse the flow of the downward-moving energy-winds and bring the other energy-winds into and up through the central channel by means of holding the vase breath.

As you hold the breath, focus your concentration single-pointedly upon the very blissful white-red energy-drop in your heart.

When you feel that it is time to go, the very subtle mind, which is lighter than a feather, determines to go to Guru Amitabha's heart. As you exhale, recite the mantra HIC.

Your consciousness as the blissful energy-drop, by the force of concentration and the upward-flowing energy-winds, flies like an arrow to meet and mingle with the clear, nondual, and radiant wisdom of Guru Amitabha's heart. Remain there in single-pointed concentration for as long as you like.

When you feel that it is time to return the consciousness principle to the body, visualize the white-red energy-drop in the center of the clear and radiant space of Guru Amitabha's heart. As you bring the energy-drop back to your heart, recite the mantra KAH.

[For the first three repetitions, visualize the drop going to Amitabha's heart, then twenty-one times to your crown only, then three more times to Amitabha's heart.

Amitabha then transforms into Amitayus.

Recite the mantra of Amitayus as you visualize what follows:]

OM AMARANI JIVAN TIYE SVAHA

From Guru Amitayus's nectar bowl flows inexhaustible clear and blissful elixir of immortality that streams down my central channel and completely fills my vajra body. It renews the life force and bestows the power of longevity.

Then the reed, lotus, moon, sun, and Guru Amitayus all melt into light and dissolve into my central channel. Guru Amitayus and my heart essence become indestructibly one. My crown is sealed by a vajra seal.

[Think: I have received the undying life realization.]

Bodhichitta Motivation and Dedication

Then, if there is time, again recite the prayer of bodhichitta motivation and dedication:

> All past, present, and future gurus, buddhas, and
>   bodhisattvas dwelling in the ten directions of space,
> especially Buddha Amitabha and the eight great lion-like
>   bodhisattvas, please pay attention to me.
> Wishing to liberate all mother sentient beings from the vast
>   ocean of samsaric suffering and to lead them all to the
>   supreme joy of full enlightenment,
> I realize that I myself must become a buddha.
>
> Thus I determine to take rebirth in the western pure land
>   and to hear teachings directly from Buddha Amitabha
>   himself.
> Therefore, by the force of all my past, present, and future
>   merits collected together and the immutable promise
>   of all the tathagatas, and by the power of wisdom and
>   absolute truth,
> may I, at the very moment of death, take immediate and
>   spontaneous rebirth upon a fully opened lotus flower,
>   face to face with Buddha Amitabha's shining form.
>
> May I obtain without difficulty the ability to hear teachings
>   directly from the mouth of Buddha Amitabha.
> May I develop the six transcending perfections to their

ultimate completion, and may I accomplish the ten
stages of the bodhisattva's path.
May I attain all the wisdom, love, and power of myriad
buddhas in countless buddhafields more numerous than
all the atoms of the boundless universe.

Dedication

Through the merits of these virtuous actions
may I quickly attain the enlightened state of Amitabha
and lead all living beings, without exception,
into that enlightened state.

[May I and all the sentient beings,
due to our merits of the three times,
be born from a beautiful lotus in the joyful pure mandala
of the conqueror,
and may we receive the prediction directly from the
conqueror Infinite Light.]

[Or you can recite this alternative translation by Gelong Jampa Gendun.]
[May I be reborn from a beautiful, sacred lotus
In the joyous and wondrous mandala of the Conqueror
Through the direct prophecy of the Conqueror of Infinite
Light.]

Colophon
This technical method for accomplishment was composed on February 3, 1981 at Tushita Retreat Centre, McLeod Ganj, Dharamsala, India, by Lama Yeshe in accordance with the scriptures and oral transmission. It arises in response to a request by Gelong Stefano Piovella, and was edited by Ngawang Chotok.

The words in brackets were added by Gelong Pende Hawter, from an oral commentary by Lama Zopa Rinpoche.

Edited by FPMT Education Office.

MAKE THE OFFERING OF SUR [82]

See chapter 29.

After they die, all beings except those destined for the formless realm have to go through the intermediate state. Because the body of beings in the intermediate state is subtle, as discussed in chapter 9, their only food is smells—this is all they can consume. Thus they are sometimes called "smell eaters."

It is excellent to make the offering of the smell of food to them with the practice called *sur*. The Tibetan word *sur* refers to the smell of roasted barley flour. Chöden Rinpoche advised that the practice can be done three times each day: in the morning, in the afternoon, and in the evening.

This practice has many benefits. It pacifies obstacles. It's an offering to the Guru, Buddha, Dharma, and Sangha. It's a practice of charity to all beings of the six realms, in particular the intermediate-state beings, those who have passed away from the human and other realms and have not yet been reborn. You finish your karmic debts. It's a method for helping you be reborn in the pure lands. It's a cause of success of whatever wishes you have.

By doing it you collect so much merit, purify obstacles, and all your wishes are achieved according to the holy Dharma; you complete the two types of merit and, ultimately, achieve enlightenment.

The Practice of Sur Is Available From
Website fpmt.org/death/
Email shopfpmt@fpmt.org

PRACTICE DORJE KHADRO BURNING OFFERING [83]

See chapter 29.

The practice of Dorje Khadro has many benefits. It is very powerful for purifying defilements and negative karma, it restores degenerated samaya and vows, and it dispels obstacles.

I received the lineage of this practice from Lama Yeshe at Kopan. It is highly admired and has great blessings as an instruction for success taught by Vajradhara.

THE PRACTICE

Take Refuge and Generate Bodhichitta

> I go for refuge until I am enlightened
> to the Buddha, the Dharma, and the Supreme Assembly.
> By my merit from giving and the other perfections,
> may I become a buddha to benefit all sentient beings. (3x)

Special Bodhichitta Prayer

> Especially to benefit all mother sentient beings,
> I shall attain the fully accomplished stage of buddhahood,
> quickly and more quickly.
> For this reason, I shall make the Dorje Khadro burning
>   offering. (3x)

Meditate on Emptiness

Now say the mantra that purifies hindrances:

> OM VAJRA AMRITA KUNDALI HANA HANA HUM PHAT

Now say the mantra that purifies the wrong conception and its view of the fire as self-existent:

[83] DORJE KHADRO BURNING OFFERING

OM SVABHAVA SHUDDHA SARVA DHARMA SVABHAVA SHUDDHO HAM

Visualization

The fire becomes void: that is, the wrong, ordinary view of fire as self-existent becomes empty. While you maintain this view of voidness, a blazing wisdom-fire appears, and at its center are the seed syllable HUM and a vajra.

These transform into the wrathful deity Dorje Khadro. He is deep blue in color, has one face and two arms, and holds a vajra and a bell. He exhibits the mudra of divine wisdom, HUM. Wearing a crown of five skulls, he snarls into space, showing four great fangs. He is also adorned by a necklace of fifty bleeding heads and a scanty, tiger skin loin cloth. He is seated with his legs forming a circle, and his whole aspect is that of a powerful, magnificent destroyer of all negativities and obstructions.

He has a white OM at his crown chakra, a red AH at his throat chakra, and a blue HUM at his heart chakra. From the HUM at his heart, rays of light are emitted, inviting Dorje Khadro's transcendental wisdom and the initiating deities from their abode in absolute nature.

JAH HUM BAM HOH

They merge and never part, becoming nondual. Thus initiated by these deities, he is crowned by Akshobhya.

Offerings

OM VAJRA DAKA SAPARIVARA ARGHAM PRATICCHA HUM SVAHA
OM VAJRA DAKA SAPARIVARA PADYAM PRATICCHA HUM SVAHA
OM VAJRA DAKA SAPARIVARA PUSHPE PRATICCHA HUM SVAHA
OM VAJRA DAKA SAPARIVARA DHUPE PRATICCHA HUM SVAHA
OM VAJRA DAKA SAPARIVARA ALOKE PRATICCHA HUM SVAHA
OM VAJRA DAKA SAPARIVARA GANDHE PRATICCHA HUM SVAHA
OM VAJRA DAKA SAPARIVARA NAIVIDYA PRATICCHA HUM SVAHA
OM VAJRA DAKA SAPARIVARA SHAPTA PRATICCHA HUM SVAHA

Praise

To you, Vajra Akshobhya:
great wisdom, the vajra sphere so very wise;

your three vajras of body, speech, and mind are the three
    mandalas;
to you who has this knowledge, I prostrate.

Visualization

While seeing yourself in ordinary human form, a black PAM, seed syllable of all your negativities, appears at your heart. At your navel, from a red RAM, a red fire mandala appears, and beneath your feet appears a blue YAM, which transforms into a blue air mandala.

Light rays emanate from the PAM, bringing forth all negativities and obscurations of your three doors, which appear as black rays and dissolve into the PAM.

From below, a blue wind blows, and blue air rises up your legs, fanning the fire that blazes at your navel. Flaming rays pursue the PAM, chasing it out through the door of your nose. The PAM takes the form of a large black scorpion and dissolves into the sesame seeds.

These seeds are then offered to the mouth of Dorje Khadro.

Offering Mantra

> OM VAJRA DAKA KHA KHA KHAHI KHAHI SARVA PAPAM DAHANA BAKMI KURU SVAHA

As you recite the mantra, say the following prayer:

> All negativities and obscurations that I have created
> and all pledges that I have broken since beginningless
>   samsaric lifetimes,
> SHIN TING KURU SVAHA (all are completely purified).

Each time you say the mantra and make the prayer, also visualize clearly and strongly that you are continuously making offerings.

Offerings

> OM VAJRA DAKA SAPARIVARA ARGHAM PRATICCHA HUM SVAHA
> OM VAJRA DAKA SAPARIVARA PADYAM PRATICCHA HUM SVAHA
> OM VAJRA DAKA SAPARIVARA PUSHPE PRATICCHA HUM SVAHA

[83] DORJE KHADRO BURNING OFFERING

OM VAJRA DAKA SAPARIVARA DHUPE PRATICCHA HUM SVAHA
OM VAJRA DAKA SAPARIVARA ALOKE PRATICCHA HUM SVAHA
OM VAJRA DAKA SAPARIVARA GANDHE PRATICCHA HUM SVAHA
OM VAJRA DAKA SAPARIVARA NAIVIDYA PRATICCHA HUM SVAHA
OM VAJRA DAKA SAPARIVARA SHAPTA PRATICCHA HUM SVAHA

Praise

> In the center of the blazing wisdom-fire stands the dark blue, wrathful cannibal, Dorje Khadro.
> Just by remembering him, all demons and delusions are destroyed completely.
> To you, Dorje Khadro, I prostrate!

Ask for Forgiveness

> Please forgive all my wrong actions,
> done while powerless through not understanding
> and through not having found the materials to offer.

The transcendental wisdom returns to the absolute nature, from where it came, and the commitment deity, Dorje Khadro, is transformed into a blazing fire.

Dedication

> Because of these merits,
> may I be taken care of by and not be separated from the Mahayana guru,
> who shows the infallible path,
> and drink the nectar of his speech,
> not being satisfied with just a few words.

> Through the power received by completing the practices of renunciation, bodhichitta, the right view of shunyata (emptiness),
> the six perfections, and the two tantric stages,

may I quickly attain the stage of buddhahood, possessed of
   the ten faculties.

May this benefit me so that I quickly reach buddhahood,
   omniscient mind,
my prayers fulfilled through the power of the blessings of
   the guru,
who never betrays the Three Supreme Jewels,
of the unchangeable, absolute sphere and of unbetraying
   interdependence.

Colophon

Translated in 1975 by Lama Thubten Zopa Rinpoche, Ven. Jampa Zangpo, and Ven. Thubten Donyo (Nick Ribush) under the guidance of Lama Thubten Yeshe.

OFFER LIGHTS, FLOWERS, AND SO FORTH ON BEHALF OF YOUR LOVED ONE [84]

See chapters 27 and 29.

It is good to make light offerings to the Three Rare Sublime Ones on behalf of the person who has passed away, especially at the end of each of the seven weeks; you can use candles, butter lamps, or electric lights. You can also offer water bowls or flowers.

It is very common for Tibetans to offer hundreds, even thousands, of light offerings; for them this is a very important practice. They make offerings at home, where the person is, but they also go to the monasteries, where there are many precious holy objects.

OFFER MONEY ON BEHALF OF YOUR LOVED ONE [85]

See chapter 29.

Offering money to organizations that help, such as charities, collects inconceivable merit, which you can dedicate for your loved one. As well as making these offerings during the forty-nine days after your loved one's passing, you can also do so on the holy days in the Tibetan lunar calendar, such as the buddha days when the merit is multiplied by one hundred million.

Here are some possible charities:

Sponsor Pujas
The FPMT Puja Fund
Website fpmt.org/projects/fpmt/puja/

Your Loved One's Guru or Your Own Guru
For example, the author's **Bodhichitta Fund**
Website fpmt.org/projects/fpmt/lzrbf/

The Ordained Sangha
The FPMT's **International Mahayana Institute**
Website imisangha.org

Places that Take Care of Animals
Animal Liberation Fund
Website fpmt.org/projects/fpmt/alf/

A Dharma Center
A place where people can meditate on the path, learn Dharma, purify their minds, and collect merit
Website fpmt.org/centers/

The Sick, the Poor, or the Homeless
For instance, the **Tibet Health Services Project**
Website fpmt.org/projects/fpmt/tibet-health-services-project/

It is also meritorious to make offerings to students who have the same guru as your loved one. Or you could make offerings in the ways suggested in practice 86.

SPONSOR DHARMA ACTIVITIES WITH YOUR LOVED ONE'S MONEY [86]

See chapter 29.

There are many ways you can use your loved one's money in order to help them. For example:

Sponsor Someone to Do Retreat
Sponsor someone to do a retreat—a monk or nun or a layperson—who can't afford it themselves and request them to dedicate all the merits to the person who passed away, the sponsor.

Make an Offering to a Dharma Center
Use the money to make a contribution to a Dharma center, or in any of the ways suggested in practice 85.

Publish or Sponsor the Publishing of Dharma Books
For example:

FPMT Education Fund
Website fpmt.org/projects/office/education/

FPMT Education Scholarship and Development Fund
Website fpmt.org/projects/fpmt/edufund/

The FPMT Translation Fund
Website fpmt.org/projects/fpmt/translations/

Lama Yeshe Wisdom Archive
Website lamayeshe.com

Wisdom Publications
Website wisdomexperience.org/support-wisdom/

MAKE HOLY OBJECTS ON BEHALF OF YOUR LOVED ONES [87]

See chapter 29.
See also practice 79.

You could make, or have made, holy objects and dedicate them for your loved one. It is said that if a person is destined to be reborn in the lower realms, doing this can change the situation and help them get a good rebirth.

Tsa-Tsas

You can make tsa-tsas of whichever deity you wish, unless you have particular advice from an astrologer or a lama. It's common to choose Mitrukpa, Medicine Buddha, the Compassion Buddha, and the Thirty-Five Buddhas—and, of course, the more the better.

Stupas

If you make a stupa, as you insert the four dharmakaya relic mantras—Ornament of Enlightenment, Secret Relic, Beam of Completely Pure Stainless Light, and Stainless Pinnacle—say the name of your loved one and dedicate for their future rebirth.

The Ornament of Enlightenment Mantra

NAMASTRAIYA DHVIKANAM / SARVA TATHAGATANAM / OM BHUV BHAVAN VARE VACATAU / CHULA CHULA DHARA DHARA / SARVATATHAGATA DHATU DHARE / PADMA GARBHE JAYA VARE ACHALE SMARA / TATHAGATA DHARMACHAKRA PRAVARTTANE / VAJRA BODHI MANDALAMKARA ALAMKRITE / SARVA TATHAGATA ADHISHTHITE / BODHAYA BODHAYA / BODHANI BODHANI / BUDDHYA BUDDHYA / SAMBODHANI SAMBODHANI / CHAL CHALA CHALANTU / SARVA AVARANANI SARVA PAPA VIGATE / SARVA TATHAGATA HRIDAYA / VAJRINI SAMBHAVA SAMBHAVA / TATHAGATA GUHYADHARANI MUDRE / BUDDHE SUBUDDHE SARVA TATHAGATA / ADISHTHITE DHATUGARBHE SVAHA / SAMAYA ADHISHTHITE

[87] MAKE HOLY OBJECTS 387

SVAHA / SARVA TATHAGATA HRIDAYA DHATUMUDRE SVAHA /
SUPRATISHTHITA STUPE / TATHAGATA ADHISHTHITE HUM HUM
SVAHA / OM SARVA TATHAGATA USHNISHA DHATU MUDRANI / SARVA
TATHAGATA DHARMADHATU VIBHUSHITE HURU HURU HUM HUM
SVAHA

The Secret Relic Mantra

OM NAMO BHAGAVATE VIPULA VADANA KANCHAN OTKSHIPTA
PRABHASA KETU MURDHNE TATHAGATAYA / NAMO BHAGAVATE
SHAKYAMUNAYE TATHAGATAYA ARHATE SAMYAK SAMBUDDHAYA /
TADYATHA / BODHI BODHI BODHINI BODHINI / SARVA TATHAGATA
GOCHARE / DHARA DHARA HARA HARA PRAHARA PRAHARA
MAHABODHI CHITTA DHARE / CHULU CHULU / SHATARASHMISAN
CHODITE / SARVA TATHAGATA ABHISHIKTE GUNE GUNAVATE /
SARVA BUDDHA GUNA AVABHASE / MILI MILI GAGANATALE /
SARVA TATHAGATA ADHISHTHITE NABHASTALE / SHAME SHAME
PRASHAME PRASHAME SARVA PAPAM PRASHAMANA /
SARVA PAPA VISHODHANE / HULU HULU / MAHABODHI MARGA
SAMPRATISHTHITE / SARVA TATHAGATA SUPRATISHTHITE
SHUDDHE SVAHA

The Mantra of Beam of Completely Pure Stainless Light

NAMA NAVATINAM TATHAGATA GANGANAM DIVA LUKANAM / KOTI
NIYUTA SHATA SAHASRANAM / OM VOVORI / CHARI NI* CHARI /
MORI GOLI CHALA VARI SVAHA

[*indicates a high tone]

The Heart Mantra of Stainless Pinnacle

OM NAMASTRAIYA DHVIKANAM / SARVA TATHAGATA HRIDAYA
GARBHE JVALA JVALA / DHARMADHATU GARBHE / SAMBHARA MAMA
AYU / SAMSHODHAYA MAMA SARVA PAPAM / SARVA TATHAGATA
SAMANTOSHNISHA VIMALE VISHUDDHE / HUM HUM HUM HUM / AM
VAM SAM JA SVAHA

You could also have statues made or thangkas painted.

Holy Objects Are Available From

Australia
Chenrezig Institute Arts Studio
Email arts@chenrezig.com.au

France
Nalanda Monastery
Website nalanda-monastery.eu
Email workshop@nalanda-monastery.eu

Nalanda Monastery specialises in tsa-tsa molds.

Hospice Services

Australia
Cittamani Hospice Service
Website cittamanihospice.com.au

Karuna Hospice Service
Website karuna.org.au

Pure Land of Amitabha Buddhist Hospice
Website buddhahouse.org/amitabha-buddha-hospice/

Denmark
Medicin Buddhas Lysende Klare Land
Website besøgs-vågetjeneste.dk

Malaysia
Kasih Hospice
Website kasihhospice.org

New Zealand
Amitabha Hospice Service
Website amitabhahospice.org

Singapore
Hospice Under the Care of Amitabha Buddha
Website fpmtabc.org/outreach_hospice.php

Spain
Potala Hospice
Website potalahospiceluzclara.org

United States
Tara Home
Website tarahome.org

Picture Credits

Frontispiece: Photo of Lama Zopa Rinpoche by Piero Sirianni.

Page 2: Painting of Shakyamuni Buddha by Jane Seidlitz.

Page 18: Painting of the Compassion Buddha: Artist unknown.

Page 32: Buddha Amitabha with the Compassion Buddha, left, and a peaceful aspect of Buddha Vajrapani. Artist unknown.

Page 46: Painting of Buddha Vajrasattva: Artist unknown; photo by Robert Beer.

Page 62: A card designed by Lama Zopa Rinpoche; published as "Liberation Card for a Dying Person" and available from fpmt.org/death/.

Page 80: The Seven Medicine Buddhas, with, at the top, Lama Tsongkhapa; left, Buddha Amitabha and, right, Buddha Shakyamuni. Artist unknown; photo by Bob Cayton.

Page 98: The Thirty-Five Buddhas of Confession with, top left and right, Buddha Vajrasattva and Buddha Mitrukpa; below them, left and right, Buddha Kunrik and Buddha Namgyalma; below the Thirty-Five Buddhas, Buddha Shakyamuni and the Seven Medicine Buddhas; and, finally, eight offering goddesses. Painted by Peter Iseli.

Page 110: Statue of Shakyamuni Buddha in the courtyard of Jamyang Buddhist Centre, London, sculpted by Nick Durnan; photo by Natascha Sturny.

Page 124: Buddha Amitayus with, above, Lama Tsongkhgapa; below, left and right, Buddha Namgyalma and Buddha White Tara. Painted by Peter Iseli.

Page 126: Painting of Buddha Amitayus by Peter Iseli.

Page 134: Photo of Lama Thubten Yeshe in Mussoorie, India, in 1973 courtesy of Lama Yeshe Wisdom Archive; lamayeshe.com.

Page 144: Buddha Namgyalma with, at the top, left to right, Jetsun Milarepa, Buddha Shakyamuni, and unknown yogi; and at the bottom, left and right, Buddha Amitayus and Buddha White Tara. Artist unknown.

Page 150: Buddha Mitrukpa with the Thirty-five Buddhas of Confession; at the top, Buddha Amitabha in the Blissful Realm; below, from left, Buddha Samayavajra, Buddha Vajrsattva, and Buddha Namgyalma; and, below them, the Seven Medicine Buddhas; and, finally, eight offering goddesses. Painted by Peter Iseli.

Page 152: Painting of Buddha Mitrukpa by Peter Iseli.

Page 162: Painting of Buddha Samayavajra: Artist unknown.

Glossary

afflictions. *See* delusions.

aggregates. *See* five aggregates.

Amitabha's pure land. The Blissful Realm (Tibetan: Dewachen; Sanskrit: Sukhavati). *See also* pure land.

anger. Aversion. A *delusion* that exaggerates the unpleasant qualities of a person, object, event, etc., which arises when *attachment* doesn't get what it wants. *See also* motivation; nonvirtuous thought.

arhat (Sanskrit). Here referring to a practitioner of the *Lower Vehicle* who, having ended their *suffering* and its causes, has achieved *liberation* from *samsara*. *See also* emptiness.

arranged fields. The *bodhisattvas'* activity of creating the causes of their future *pure land*.

arya bodhisattva (Sanskrit; superior awakening person). A *bodhisattva* who has achieved a nonconceptual *realization* of *emptiness*. *See* meditation.

attachment. Desire, craving, clinging, grasping. On the basis of the root delusion, *ignorance,* the main cause of *samsara*, a *delusion* that exaggerates the pleasant qualities of a person, event, action, object, etc., including the self and one's own body, based on the assumption that the having or doing of it causes *happiness*, thus giving rise to expectation, possessiveness, and fear of losing it; one of the main causes of *suffering* at the time of death. *See also* negative karma; nonvirtuous thought.

aversion. *See* anger.

beginningless. All minds as well as the four elements that constitute the physical world, being governed by the law of cause and effect—this moment of *mind* or matter being the product of a previous moment of that mind or matter—necessarily cannot have a causeless first moment, a beginning. *See also* karma; mental continuum.

Bodhgaya. The town in the state of Bihar in northern India that is built around the site where *Shakyamuni Buddha* achieved *enlightenment*; a pilgrimage site for Buddhists worldwide.

bodhichitta (Sanskrit; awakening mind or attitude). Of the two bodhichittas, aspirational and engaged, the engaged is the effortless and continuously present wish in the *minds* of *bodhisattvas* to (1) only benefit others and (2) never give up perfecting themselves and becoming a *buddha* solely for the sake of others. In *tantra*, also refers to *drops*. *See also* compassion; Mahayana.

bodhisattva (Sanskrit; awakening person). One who has accomplished *bodhichitta*. *See also* arya bodhisattva; Mahayana.

bodhisattva vows. *See* three sets of vows.

buddha (Sanskrit). Enlightened being. A person who has achieved *enlightenment*; when capitalized, refers to *Shakyamuni Buddha*. *See also* bodhichitta; deity; Mahayana.

buddhahood. *See* enlightenment.

chakras (Sanskrit; wheels). According to *Vajrayana*, formed by the branching of *channels* at various points along the central channel—crown, brow, throat, heart, navel, and secret—that constrict the central channel and prevent the *winds*—and thus the *minds* that ride on them—from entering into and abiding there. *See also* death process.

channels. According to *Vajrayana*, the 72,000 channels of the body, the main one of which is the central channel, which, with the *winds* and the red and white *drops*, constitute the *subtle body*. *See also* chakras; death process; subtle mind.

clear light. Extremely subtle mind, very subtle mind. According to *Vajrayana*, the subtlest level of *mind*, linked inextricably with the extremely subtle *wind*, which occurs naturally at the eighth stage of the *death process*, then leaves the body and goes to another life. Accomplished *yogis and yoginis* can meditate on *emptiness* with this mind at the time of death, even becoming enlightened then. *See also* extremely subtle body and extremely subtle mind; gross body and gross mind; subtle body; subtle mind.

compassion. Empathy with the *suffering* of others, and the wish that they be free from it and its causes, which gives rise to the wish, "I myself will free them from suffering," known as great compassion, the unique characteristic of the compassion of the *bodhisattva*; this, in turn, gives rise to *bodhichitta*.

completion stage. The more advanced of the two stages of practice of *highest tantra*, the first being the *generation stage*. See also tantra; Vajrayana.

concentration (Sanskrit: *samadhi*). When accomplished in *meditation*, a deep state of focus at a level of *mind* far subtler than the level of consciousness of the day-to-day mind, a level of cognition not posited in contemporary psychology. The fifth of the *six perfections* of a *bodhisattva*. See also form and formless realms.

consciousness. See mind.

daka and **dakini** (Sanskrit). In tantra, realized male and female beings, respectively.

damaru (Sanskrit). A small, hand-held drum used by *Vajrayana* practitioners.

death process. As explained in *Vajrayana*, the gradual breakdown of the physical and mental components of a person, listed as *twenty-five components* and described in eight stages, from the gross to the subtle to the extremely subtle, which culminates in the *extremely subtle mind* and *wind* leaving the body, going to the *intermediate state*, and then to another life determined by the karmic *seeds* triggered during the process. See also clear light; gross body and gross mind; reincarnation; subtle body; subtle mind.

defilements. See delusions.

deity. A term used in *Vajrayana* for an enlightened being such as Vajrasattva, the Compassion Buddha, and Amitabha.

delusions. Afflictions, defilements, disturbing thoughts, negative thoughts, nonvirtuous thoughts. Within the categories of positive, negative, and neutral states of mind that constitute the *mental consciousness*, negative states that necessarily distort or exaggerate or embellish whatever they cognize, which are adventitious and therefore can be removed. With *karma*, the cause of *samsara*. See also anger; attachment; ignorance; liberation; suffering.

dependent arising. Every phenomenon exists—"arises"—in dependence upon (1) causes and conditions (impermanent phenomena only), (2) its parts, and, most subtly, (3) the *mind* labeling it, and therefore is empty of *existing from its own side*; the way things exist conventionally. *See also* emptiness; karma.

desire. *See* attachment.

desire realm. A realm of *rebirth* within *samsara*, which, in turn, includes six realms: those of *gods and demigods*, humans, animals, spirits (often referred to as *hungry ghosts*, one category of spirit), and hell beings. *See also* form and formless realms; lower realms; samsara.

deva. *See* gods and demigods.

Dewachen. *See* Amitabha's pure land.

Dharma (Sanskrit). Refers here to Buddha's teachings; the second of the *Three Rare Sublime Ones*. *See also* refuge.

dharmakaya (Sanskrit; truth body). *See* three bodies of a buddha.

disturbing thoughts. *See* delusions.

drops. According to *Vajrayana*, red and white subtle liquid energy, the essence of which abides in the heart *chakra* as the *indestructible drop* and part of which abides at the crown and navel chakras, and which, with the *channels* and the *winds*, constitute the *subtle body*; also referred to as red and white *bodhichitta*. *See also* death process; subtle mind.

eight bodhisattvas. The close entourage of *Shakyamuni Buddha*: Manjushri, Vajrapani, Avalokiteshvara, Kshitigarbha, Sarvanivarana Vishkambhin, Akashagarbha, Maitreya, and Samantabhadra.

eighty superstitions. The conceptual states of *subtle mind* that dissolve during the fifth through seventh of the eight stages of the *death process*.

emptiness. Because everything that exists—a self, the *aggregates*, a thing, an event, an action, etc.—is a *dependent arising*, it is therefore empty of *existing from its own side*; the absence in everything that exists of this impossible way of existing. *See also* arya bodhisattva; ignorance; illusion; liberation; meditation.

enlightened being. *See* buddha.

enlightenment. Full enlightenment, buddhahood. In the *Mahayana*, the enlightenment of a *buddha*, the state of having removed all *delusions* and their *imprints* from the *mind* and having accomplished all virtues, forever; characterized by three essential qualities: (1) omniscience, (2) *compassion* for all *sentient beings*, and (3) the power to do whatever needs to be done to benefit them; according to the Mahayana, the potential of every *sentient being*.

existing from its own side. Existing inherently, truly existent. The way every phenomenon appears to exist, that is, without depending upon (1) causes and conditions (impermanent phenomena only), (2) parts, and, most subtly, (3) the mind labeling it; an impossible way of being that the root *delusion, ignorance,* grasps at as real, which gives rise to *attachment* and the other delusions and causes the *sufferings* of *samsara*. *See also* dependent arising; emptiness; liberation; meditation.

extremely subtle body and extremely subtle mind. Very subtle body and very subtle mind. The extremely subtle *wind* inextricably conjoined with the subtlest level of *mind*, which at conception mixes with the white *drop* from the father and the red drop from the mother in the *indestructible drop* at the heart *chakra*, where it resides throughout life until it leaves the body at the time of death and continues to another life, propelled by past *karma*. *See also* clear light; death process; gross body and gross mind; subtle body; subtle mind.

five aggregates. All impermanent phenomena can be divided into these; here used to refer to the impermanent phenomena that make up a sentient being. (1) Form: the body. (2) Feeling: either pleasant, unpleasant, or indifferent; one of the fifty-one *mental factors*. (3) Recognition or discrimination: another of the mental factors; distinguishes one thing from another. (4) Compounding aggregates or compositional factors: all impermanent phenomena other than the above four aggregates, including the remaining forty-nine mental factors. (5) Consciousness: the primary or main consciousness—*mental consciousness*—and the *five sense consciousnesses*.

five degenerations, time of. A period in history—measured in terms of eons—said to be now, during which there is a radical degeneration of (1) delusions, (2) lifespan, (3) the quality of things (or time) and (4) view, and (5) experiences (or sentient beings).

five heavy negative actions. Five *negative karmas*: (1) killing one's mother, (2) killing one's father, (3) killing an *arhat*, (4) maliciously drawing blood from a *buddha*, and (5) creating a schism in the *Sangha*.

five inner sense objects. Five of the *twenty-five components* that dissolve during the *death process*: inner form, sound, smell, taste, and touch.

five sense consciousnesses. The gross consciousness, or *mind*, that functions through the medium of the five sense bases, which are subtle physical energy, of the (1) eyes, (2) ears, (3) nose, (4) tongue, and (5) touch. In some contexts, *mental consciousness* is included as a sixth "sense," which also has its own, non-physical, "sense base." *See also* gross body and gross mind; twenty-five components.

five wisdoms. Five of the *twenty-five components* that gradually cease to function throughout the *death process*: mirror-like wisdom, wisdom of equanimity, wisdom of discriminating awareness, all-accomplishing wisdom, and wisdom of the sphere of phenomena. The "base-time" wisdoms are the natural states of mind that dissolve during the death process; the "result-time" wisdoms are actual realizations in the minds of *yogis and yoginis*.

form and formless realms. Two realms of existence within *samsara*, achieved as a result of deep meditative absorption. The third of the three realms is the *desire realm*. *See also* concentration; meditation.

four opponent powers. *See* purification.

FPMT. Foundation for the Preservation of the Mahayana Tradition. The name given by *Lama Yeshe* in 1975, at *Kopan Monastery*, to his growing network of Tibetan Buddhist centers worldwide. The international office of the FPMT is a nonprofit in Portland, Oregon, with which some 160 centers and projects worldwide are affiliated, and of which the author is the spiritual director.

full enlightenment. *See* enlightenment.

Ganden Throneholder. The title of the head of the *Geluk* tradition of Tibetan Buddhism, Ganden being the name of the first monastery established by *Lama Tsongkhapa*.

Geluk (Tibetan). One of the four main traditions of Tibetan Buddhism, founded by *Lama Tsongkhapa* in the early fifteenth century; the others are Nyingma, Kagyü, and Sakya.

Gen Jampa Wangdu. One of the author's *gurus*, who remained in *meditation* after passing away in Dharamsala, India, in 1984. *See also* yogi and yogini.

generation stage. The first of the two stages of practice within *highest tantra*—the second being the *completion stage*—during which the meditator visualizes themselves as a *deity*, a cause for becoming that *buddha*. *See also* tantra; Vajrayana.

geshe (Tibetan; spiritual friend). The title conferred on graduates of the ten-to-twenty-year program of philosophical and psychological studies at *Geluk* Tibetan monastic universities. *See also* Lama Tsongkhapa.

Geshe Lhundup Sopa (1923–2014). One of the author's *gurus*, who in 1967 joined the faculty of the Buddhist Studies program at the University of Wisconsin at Madison in the USA, and in 1975 founded Deer Park Buddhist Center in Oregon, Wisconsin.

gods and demigods. Occupants of the two highest of the six realms of the *desire realm*, whose experiences are blissful and whose bodies are made of light; the result of *virtuous karma*. Occupants of the *form and formless realms* are also "gods." *See also* samsara.

grasping. Here referring to the ninth of the twelve links of *dependent arising*, a powerful form of *attachment* that arises during the *death process*; sometimes used as a synonym for attachment.

great compassion. *See* compassion.

great thousand of three thousand world systems (Sanskrit: trisahasramahasahasram lokadhatu; Tibetan: stong gsum gyi stong chen po'i 'jig rten gyi khams). Well known in Buddhist literature, the world referred to includes four continents, the sun and moon, Sumeru (king of mountains), the desire realm gods, and the first of the form realms of Brahma. "Three thousand world systems" refers to the three categories of such worlds—a thousand basic world systems (with the four continents, etc.) called "the small thousand," a thousand of those (or a million such world systems) called "the middling thousand," and a thousand of those (or a billion world systems) called "the great thousand." The last of the three categories, "the great thousand of three thousand world systems," thus includes a billion world systems.

gross body and gross mind. The gross body is the blood, bones, sense organs, and so forth that make up the body of a human being (and most animals), and serves as the basis of the gross *mind*: the *five sense consciousnesses*. *See also* extremely subtle body and extremely subtle mind; mental consciousness; subtle body; subtle mind.

guru (Sanskrit; heavy with knowledge). Lama (Tibetan). A person's spiritual teacher. *See also* guru devotion.

guru buddha. One's *guru* seen in the aspect of a *buddha*. *See also* guru devotion; guru yidam.

guru devotion. Confidence that the *guru* is a *buddha*, the *deity*, expressed in thought and action, formalized in such practices as *Guru Puja* and other deity practices.

Guru Puja (Sanskrit). Offering to the Guru; in Tibetan, *Lama Chöpa*. A practice popular among *Geluk*pas in which the central figure of devotion is Lama (one's guru) Losang (Tsongkhapa) Thubwang (*Shakyamuni Buddha*) Dorje Chang (Vajradhara, the tantric aspect of Shakyamuni Buddha), written by *Panchen Lama Losang Chökyi Gyaltsen*. *See also* guru devotion.

Guru Three Rare Sublime Ones. *Buddha*, *Dharma*, and *Sangha* personified in the *guru*. *See also* refuge.

guru yidam. In tantra, the guru and the deity seen as one.

Guyhasamaja. A male *deity*, the personification of purified *anger*. *See also* Vajrayana.

gyaling (Tibetan). A Tibetan wind instrument like an oboe, mainly played during *pujas*.

happiness. The result of *virtuous karma*. *See also* karma; motivation; suffering.

hell. *See* lower realms.

Heruka. Heruka Chakrasamvara. A male *deity*, the personification of purified *attachment*. *See also* Vajrayana; Vajrayogini.

highest tantra. The fourth and supreme class of *tantra*, consisting of *generation* and *completion stages*. *See also* initiation; lower tantras; tantra; Vajrayana.

His Holiness the Dalai Lama. The current Dalai Lama, Tenzin Gyatso, born in 1935, is the fourteenth in this line of reincarnated *lamas*, revered as the manifestation of the Compassion Buddha; the spiritual and, until 2011 when he resigned, political head of Tibet.

hungry ghost (Sanskrit: preta). *See* lower realms.

ignorance. Basic ignorance, root ignorance. The *delusion* that grasps at everything, including the self and the five aggregates, as *existing from its own side*, gives rise to *attachment* and all the other delusions, is the root cause of the *sufferings* of *samsara*, and is eradicated by realizing *emptiness*. *See also* dependent arising; illusion; liberation; meditation.

illusion. Everything is said to be like an illusion—not an illusion but *like* an illusion: it does not exist from its own side but nevertheless does function. *See also* dependent arising; emptiness; ignorance.

illusory body. A *subtle body* made of *wind* that resembles a *deity*; cause of the deity's body. *See also* highest tantra; three bodies of a buddha; yogi and yogini.

imprints. Karmic seeds, or potentials, left in the *mind* when actions of body, speech, and mind are done, which ripen as future experiences. *See also* karma.

indestructible drop. The conjoined red and white *drop* with its red and white halves, the size of a tiny bean, that is received from the parents and mixes with the extremely subtle mind at the time of conception, and abides throughout life in the very center of the heart *chakra*. *See also* extremely subtle body and extremely subtle mind.

inherent existence. *See* existing from its own side.

initiation. Empowerment. The transmission from a *guru* to a disciple of the practice of a particular *deity*, which empowers the disciple to engage in that deity's *sadhana*. *See also* samaya; Vajrayana.

intermediate state (Tibetan: bardo). A state of existence that a person takes the moment their extremely subtle mind leaves the *indestructible drop* at the heart *chakra* at death until taking another life in *samsara*, lasting anywhere from a moment to forty-nine days; said to be similar in experience to a dream. The intermediate-state body is subtle and has no resistance to matter and is similar in appearance to the body of the next life. *See also* death process; extremely subtle body and extremely subtle mind; reincarnation.

karma (Sanskrit). Compounded action, action, intention. The intention (mental action), underpinned by a *motivation*, to think or do or say something that impels an action of body or speech, which leaves *imprints* or seeds in the mind that, unless eliminated, will result in the future as (1) a type of rebirth in *samsara*, (2) the habit to keep thinking or doing or saying it, (3) an experience similar to it, (4) an environmental result. Used loosely to refer to the natural law of cause and effect—that *negative karma* produces *suffering* and *virtuous karma* produces *happiness*—that plays out in the minds and lives of all *sentient beings*. *See also* negative karma; purification; reincarnation; virtuous karma.

karmic appearances. The way things, people, events, and so on appear to *sentient beings*—as pleasant, unpleasant, etc.—according to their past *karma*; here in particular referring to the appearances at the time of death.

Khunu Lama Rinpoche (1894–1977). A lay lama renowned for his *bodhichitta*.

Kirti Tsenshab Rinpoche (1926–2006). A scholar and *yogi* who lived in Dharamsala, India; one of the author's *gurus*.

Kopan Monastery. The monastery established in 1970 by the author and *Lama Yeshe*, in Nepal, five miles northeast of Kathmandu, where now some 350 monks study the full curriculum of the main *Geluk* monastic universities, such as Sera Je, one of the colleges of *Sera Monastery*, with which it is affiliated. Its sister monastery of 350 nuns nearby, Kachoe Ghakyil, follows the same course of study, with a newly established branch of twenty nuns in Sarnath, India. Kopan also holds courses throughout the year for visitors from other countries, including the annual November course, the first of which was taught by the author in 1970.

lama. *See* guru.

Lama Tsongkhapa (1357–1419). Scholar, *yogi*, and teacher, founder of the *Geluk* tradition of Tibetan Buddhism; author of many texts, including *Lamrim Chenmo*.

Lama Yeshe (1935–84). Lama Thubten Yeshe; the *guru* of the author. Born in Tibet and educated since childhood at the Je college of *Sera Monastery* in Lhasa; escaped into exile in 1959 and settled in Kathmandu, Nepal, in 1967; founded, with the author, the *FPMT* in 1975 after they started teaching Dharma to people from the West at *Kopan Monastery* in 1970.

lamrim (Tibetan; graded path). Path to *enlightenment*. Buddha's sutra teachings, based on *Lamp for the Path* by Atisha (982–1054), presented as a course of study and practice according to three levels of capability: (1) lower-capacity beings, motivated by the wish to not be reborn in the *lower realms*; (2) middle-capacity beings, motivated by the wish to not be reborn in *samsara*; and (3) higher-capacity beings, motivated by the wish to become a *buddha*. Practitioners of the *Lesser Vehicle* practice the first two levels; those of the *Mahayana* practice all three. See also *Lamrim Chenmo*.

Lamrim Chenmo (Tibetan; *The Great Treatise on the Stages of the Path*). The most extensive of *Lama Tsongkhapa*'s commentaries on the *lamrim*.

Land of Medicine Buddha. An *FPMT* retreat center in Soquel, California.

Lawudo Lama. The author is the recognized reincarnation of the first

Lawudo Lama (1864–1945), Kunsang Yeshe, a meditator in the Solo Khumbu region of Nepal.

Lesser Vehicle (Sanskrit: Hinayana). The path that leads to *liberation* from *suffering* and its causes, often referred to as the path of individual liberation. *See also* arhat; lamrim; Mahayana; Perfection Vehicle; Vajrayana.

liberation (Sanskrit: nirvana). Liberation from *samsara*; liberation from *suffering* and its causes. Achieved when the *delusions* and their *imprints*, the obstacles to liberation, have been removed from the *mind*, thus eliminating the causes of *samsara*; the goal of the *Lesser Vehicle* practitioner. *See also* arhat; emptiness.

Ling Rinpoche (1903–83). The senior tutor of *His Holiness the Dalai Lama* and one of the author's *gurus*.

long-life vase. A container of blessed substances used in rituals for extending life.

lower realms. Three realms of rebirth among the six of the *desire realm*: those of (1) the animals, (2) the spirits (often referred to as hungry ghosts, or pretas, one type of spirit), and (3) the hell beings. Each is the result of *negative karma* and each is characterized by its own particular *sufferings*. The vast majority of all sentient beings are said to exist in the lower realms. *See also* reincarnation; samsara.

lower tantras. The first three of the four classes of *tantra*—the action, performance, and yoga tantras. *See also* highest tantra; Vajrayana.

Mahayana (Sanskrit; Great Vehicle). The path of the *bodhisattva*, the goal of which is the *enlightenment* of a *buddha*; includes *Perfection Vehicle* and *Vajrayana*.

mantra. A series of Sanskrit words and/or syllables, some of which are recited in conjunction with the practice of a particular *deity* that are the verbal expression of the qualities of that deity.

meditation. In Tibetan, *gom*, to familiarize. A process of familiarizing the mind with (1) that which is virtuous and (2) that which is true. There are two types of formal meditation techniques (taught in the *Mahayana* as the fifth and sixth of the *six perfections*): the goal of the first, calm abiding, is to gain single-pointed *concentration*; and the goal of the second, special insight (or wisdom), is to gain a *realization* of *emptiness*, which is induced by the concentrated mind precisely and logically analyzing, for example, *dependent arising*. In

Vajrayana, concentration by the *yogi or yogini* on themselves as the *deity* is combined with insight into emptiness. Realizations of any of the points of the path to *enlightenment* can be gained by combining concentration and analysis.

mental continuum. Mindstream. The *beginningless* and endless continuity of *mind* of individual beings.

mental consciousness. The various conceptual states of *mind*—*mental factors*—as well as *subtle mind* and extremely subtle mind. *See also* extremely subtle body and extremely subtle mind; five sense consciousnesses; mental continuum.

mental factors. States of *mind* such as *attachment, anger,* love, intention, *concentration,* etc., that are divided into the three categories of positive, negative, and neutral. A person has thousands of such states of mind, although traditionally fifty-one are mentioned. *See also* five aggregates; five sense consciousnesses; mental consciousness.

mind. Consciousness. Defined as that which is formless, or clear, and which can cognize or know; includes both *mental consciousness* and the *five sense consciousnesses. See also* beginningless; extremely subtle body and extremely subtle mind; gross body and gross mind; mental continuum; sentient being; subtle body; subtle mind.

motivation. Usually used to refer to the attitude that underpins an intention to think or do or say something. A negative motivation causes the *karma* to be nonvirtuous and the result of *suffering;* a positive motivation causes the karma to be virtuous and the result of happiness. *See also* negative karma; virtuous karma.

mudras (Sanskrit). In tantra, hand gestures, each of which has a meaning.

Nagarjuna. The Indian scholar and tantric adept who around the start of the first millennium elucidated the actual meaning of Buddha's teachings on *emptiness.*

negative action. *See* negative karma.

negative karma. Negative action, negative karmas, nonvirtuous action, nonvirtuous *karma.* With *delusions,* the main cause of *suffering. See also* purification.

nirmanakaya (Sanskrit). *See* three bodies of a buddha.

nirvana (Sanskrit). *See* liberation.

nonvirtuous thought. A *delusion*, such as anger, jealousy, arrogance, etc. *See* karma; mental factors; motivation.

Nyingma (Tibetan). The oldest of the four traditions of Tibetan Buddhism (the others being Kagyü, Sakya, and *Geluk*), which traces its teachings back to Guru Rinpoche *Padmasambhava*.

omniscience. *See* enlightenment.

Padmasambhava. Guru Rinpoche. Invited to Tibet from India by the Tibetan king Trisong Detsen in the mid-eighth century; revered among Tibetans as the founder of Buddhism in Tibet.

Panchen Lama Losang Chökyi Gyaltsen (1570–1662). The fourth (or first, depending on numbering) Panchen Lama, author of many key texts, including the *Guru Puja*.

Perfection Vehicle. The *Mahayana* sutra teachings. *See also* Lesser Vehicle; Vajrayana.

phowa (Tibetan; transference of consciousness). A practice done by a *lama* after the person has stopped breathing, or by the practitioner themselves beforehand, that helps their consciousness take rebirth in a *pure land*.

pratyekabuddha (Sanskrit). A type of Hinayana *arhat*. *See also* Lesser Vehicle.

preta. *See* lower realms.

protectors. Beings—worldly or enlightened—who protect Buddhism and its practitioners.

puja (Sanskrit). A religious ceremony.

pure land. Subtle, blissful states of existence associated with various *buddhas*, such as Amitabha, where there is no suffering and often where one can achieve enlightenment. *See also* Amitabha's pure land.

purification. The weakening of *negative karmas* and *imprints*, often accomplished by doing practices such as Vajrasattva and the Thirty-Five Buddhas of Confession in conjunction with the four opponent powers: (1) reliance, (2) regret, (3) the remedy, and (4) restraint.

realization. An understanding of any of the points of the path to *enlightenment* gained through the union of the two kinds of *meditation*.

realms. *See* samsara.

rebirth. *See* reincarnation.

refuge. Heartfelt reliance upon the *Three Rare Sublime Ones* for guidance on the path to *enlightenment*.

reincarnation. Rebirth. The natural process of continuous birth and death within the various realms of *samsara* that all *sentient beings*, propelled by the force of their past *karma*, have been going through since *beginningless* time and will go through until they achieve *liberation*. *Buddhas* choose to be reborn in the various realms for the benefit of others, for as long as *suffering* exists.

relics. Things, often pearl-like, that emanate from holy objects such as statues and *stupas* or the cremated bodies of *yogis and yoginis*.

renunciation. The wish to be liberated from *samsara*, based on the understanding that the happiness that comes from *attachment* is in the nature of *suffering*, and that suffering is caused by *karma* and *delusions*.

Rinpoche (Tibetan; precious one). An honorific when addressing or referring to reincarnated lamas and one's own *guru* or other lamas.

root ignorance. *See* ignorance.

sadhana (Sanskrit; method of accomplishment). The step-by-step set of meditations and prayers related to a particular *deity*.

samadhi. *See* concentration.

samaya (Sanskrit). A pledge made to one's *guru* to keep vows and commitments, typically made when receiving an *initiation*. *See also* three sets of vows; Vajrayana.

sambhogakaya (Sanskrit). *See* three bodies of a buddha.

samsara (Sanskrit; cyclic existence). Being caught up in the process of death, the *intermediate state*, and rebirth in the *desire realm* and *form and formless realms* propelled by past *karma*. Also used to refer to the aggregates of a person going from one life to the next in the various realms. *See also* death process; ignorance; liberation; lower realms; reincarnation.

Sangha (Sanskrit; spiritual community). The third of the *Three Rare Sublime Ones*, specifically a group of at least four fully ordained Buddhist monks or nuns; often refers to Buddhist monks and nuns in general.

seeds, karmic. *See* imprints.

sense bases. *See* five sense consciousnesses.

sense consciousness. *See* five sense consciousnesses.

sentient being (Tibetan: *semchen*, "mind-possessor"). Refers to all beings other than *buddhas*.

Sera Monastery. One of the "Three Greats": *Geluk* monastic universities near Lhasa, Tibet; founded in the early fifteenth century by Jamchen Chöje, a disciple of *Lama Tsongkhapa*, and now also established in exile, in South India; the author's monastery.

Shakyamuni Buddha (563–483 BC). The fourth of the one thousand founding *buddhas* of this present world age, Lord Buddha was born a prince of the Shakya clan in northern India, renounced his kingdom, achieved *enlightenment* at the age of thirty-five, and then taught the paths to *liberation* and enlightenment until he passed away at the age of eighty.

shravaka. (Sanskrit; hearer). A practitioner of the *Lesser Vehicle* who strives for individual liberation. *See also* arhat.

six perfections. Final stages of the *bodhisattva* path: (1) generosity, (2) morality, (3) patience, (4) perseverance, (5) *concentration*, and (6) wisdom, or *realization* of *emptiness*.

six sense bases. *See* five sense consciousnesses.

six yogas of Naropa. A *completion stage* series of *highest tantra* practices, which include *phowa*, transference of consciousness.

Song Rinpoche (1905–84). A renowned Tibetan master, one of the author's *gurus*, first invited to teach in the West by *Lama Yeshe* and who advised the author at the time of Lama Yeshe's passing away.

sorrowless state. *See* liberation.

southern continent. According to Buddhist cosmology, our world, Jambudvipa.

spirit. *See* lower realms.

stupa. A reliquary of *relics* of the *buddhas* and other holy beings; representative of the enlightened *mind*.

subtle body. The system of *channels*, *winds*, and red and white *drops* inextricably linked with the *subtle mind*. *See also* death process; extremely subtle body and extremely subtle mind; gross body and gross mind.

subtle mind. The *eighty superstitions* and the *minds* of white appearance, red appearance or red increase, and dark, or black, appearance that occur during the fifth, sixth, and seventh stages of the *death process*.

See also extremely subtle body and extremely subtle mind; gross body and gross mind.

suffering. The various levels of experience of *sentient beings* in the three realms of *samsara*, caused by *karma* and *delusions*: (1) the suffering of suffering, (2) the suffering of change, and (3) pervasive compounded suffering. *See also* ignorance.

sugata (Sanskrit; one gone to bliss). An epithet for a buddha.

Sukhavati. *See* Amitabha's pure land.

sutra (Sanskrit). The *Lesser Vehicle* and *Perfection Vehicle* discourses of Buddha; a scriptural text and the teachings and practices it contains.

tantra (Sanskrit). Secret mantra. The teachings and practices of the *Vajrayana*; a text containing those teachings.

tantric vows. *See* three sets of vows.

ten virtuous actions. The actions of refraining from (1) killing, (2) stealing, (3) sexual misconduct, (4) lying, (5) harsh speech, (6) divisive talk, (7) idle talk, (8) craving, (9) ill will, and (10) wrong views.

thangka (Tibetan). A painting, usually on canvas, usually of deities or the abode of a *deity*, a mandala.

three principal aspects of the path. *Renunciation, bodhichitta,* and *emptiness*.

three bodies of a buddha. (1) The mind of a buddha, or wisdom body (Sanskrit: dharmakaya), and the two forms in which enlightened mind manifests to benefit sentient beings: (2) the enjoyment body (Sanskrit: sambhogakaya) and (3) the emanation body (Sanskrit: nirmanakaya).

three poisons. Attachment, anger, and ignorance, the three main *delusions*.

Three Rare Sublime Ones. *Buddha, Dharma,* and *Sangha,* the three objects of refuge of a Buddhist; the Triple Gem. *See also* Guru Three Rare Sublime Ones.

three sets of vows. Formally taken decisions to refrain from various types of behavior, which are crucial for the development of *realizations* in the three levels of practice: the vows of individual liberation, the vows of the *bodhisattva*, and tantric vows. *See also* Lesser Vehicle; Mahayana; Vajrayana.

throwing karma. The karmic seed that determines the future life, which is triggered at the time of death.

transcendental nondual great bliss-voidness. Within *Vajrayana* practice, the *mind* of great bliss realizing *emptiness*.

true existence. *See* existing from its own side.

Trulshik Rinpoche (1924–2011). A Tibetan lama who lived in Nepal and who in 2010 was appointed head of the *Nyingma* tradition of Tibetan Buddhism; one of the author's *gurus*.

tsa-tsa (Tibetan). A bas-relief image of buddhas, usually small, traditionally made of clay, but these days often made of plaster.

tsok (Tibetan; assemblage). In tantra, a ritual feast offered to the *guru yidam*.

Tushita Retreat Centre. An *FPMT* center near Dharamsala, northern India, where *His Holiness the Dalai Lama* is based and where many Tibetan meditators practice.

twelve deeds of the buddha. There are different versions of the twelve deeds that all buddhas are said to accomplish. Here the version is from *Praise of the Lord, Our Teacher, By Way of His Twelve Deeds* attributed to Nagarjuna. (1) Entering his mother's womb, (2) taking birth in Lumbini, (3) becoming skilled in the arts and playing the sports of youth; (4) taking charge of the kingdom and possessing a female retinue; (5) becoming discouraged with cyclic existence and leaving the householder's life; (6) practicing austerities for six years; (7) going to the Bodhi tree and becoming fully enlightened; (8) turning the wheel of Dharma; (9) subduing the maras, Devadatta, and the six tirthikas; (10) displaying miracles at Sravasti; (11) passing from sorrow in Kushinagara; (12) manifesting *relics* in eight portions.

twenty-five components. Various physical and mental components of a person that gradually cease to function throughout the eight stages of the *death process*: the *five aggregates*, the *five wisdoms*, the four elements, the *six sense bases*, and the *five inner sense objects*.

Vajrayana (Sanskrit). Tantra; secret mantra. The more advanced of the two stages of the *Mahayana* path to enlightenment. *See also* Lesser Vehicle; Perfection Vehicle.

Vajrayogini. A female *deity*, the personification of purified *attachment*. *See also* Heruka; Vajrayana.

virtuous karma. Positive *karma*. An action of body, speech, or *mind* driven by a positive *motivation*, which causes *happiness*.

virtuous thought. Positive thought. A virtuous state of *mind* such as love, *compassion*, etc. *See also* motivation.

vows of individual liberation (Sanskrit: pratimoksha). *See* three sets of vows.

winds. According to Vajrayana, various subtle air energies that flow in the *channels* of the body, which enable the body to function and which are associated with the different levels of *mind*—it is said that "the mind rides on the winds"—and which, with the channels and the *drops*, constitute the *subtle body*. *See also* extremely subtle body and extremely subtle mind; gross body and gross mind.

wisdoms: base-time and result-time. *See* five wisdoms.

yidam. *See* deity; guru yidam.

yogi and yogini (Sanskrit). Accomplished *Vajrayana* male and female meditator, respectively. *See also* meditation.

Index of Practices by Category and Their Numbers

Blessed Substances
inner-offering pill, 61
Kalachakra mandala sand, 61
mani pills, 56, 61
phowa pills, 61
relics of buddhas, 57

Buddhas
Akshobhya. *See* Mitrukpa
Amitabha, 1, 11, 20, 64, 66, 79, 81
Amitayus, 11, 66, 68, 81
Avalokiteshvara. *See* Compassion Buddha
Buddha who protects from the lower realms, 3, 19
Chenrezik. *See* Compassion Buddha
Compassion Buddha, 1, 8, 21, 58, 73, 77, 79, 87
Damtsik Dorje. *See* Samayavajra
Dorje Khadro, 83
Drimé Tsuktor. *See* Stainless Pinnacle
Droden Gyalwa Chö, 16
Kalachakra, 61

Kunrik, 27, 31, 58, 78
Lotus Pinnacle of Amoghapasha, 31. *See also* Pema Tsuktor
Maitreya, 30, 69, 70, 71
Medicine Buddhas, 1, 14, 22, 36, 59, 78, 79, 81, 87
Milarepa, 28
Mitrukpa, 1, 2, 24, 31, 58, 87
Namgyalma, 8, 25, 31, 58, 77
Padmasambhava, 26
Padmoshnisha. *See* Pema Tsuktor
Pema Tsuktor, 23
Ratna Shikhin. *See* Buddha who protects from the lower realms
Rinchen Tsuktorchen. *See* Buddha who protects from the lower realms
Samayavajra, 51
Shakyamuni Buddha, 10, 72
Stainless Beam, 6, 16, 29, 37, 58, 87
Stainless Pinnacle, 6, 31, 58
Thirty-Five Buddhas of Confession, 15, 49, 87

Ushnishavijaya. *See* Namgyalma
Ushnishavimala. *See* Stainless Pinnacle
Vajra Armor, 58
Vairochana. *See* Kunrik
Vajrasattva, 50, 53

Guru, 1, 10, 18, 35, 43, 47, 60, 72, 85

Holy Objects
blessed cord, 8
pictures of gurus, buddhas, 1
prayer wheels, 7
statues, 1, 79, 87
stupas, 6, 37, 79, 87
thangkas, 87
texts, 5
tsa-tsas, 79, 87
written mantras, 2, 3, 4, 58

Mantras
Achala. *See* Mitrukpa
Akshobhya. *See* Mitrukpa
alleviate fear or pain, 17
Amitabha, 1, 20
Avalokiteshvara. *See* Compassion Buddha
Beam of Completely Pure Stainless Light, 6, 16, 29, 37, 58, 87
Buddha who protects from the lower realms, 3, 19
Droden Gyalwa Chö, 16
Chenrezik. *See* Compassion Buddha

Compassion Buddha, 1, 8, 21, 58, 73, 77, 87
five great mantras, 8, 23, 24, 25, 27, 31, 58
four dharmakaya relic mantras, 6, 37, 87
Guru Rinpoche. *See* Padmasambhava
Great Increasing Jewel Fathomless Celestial Mansion Extremely Well-Abiding Secret Holy Mantra, 20
"Just by Seeing," 4
Kunrik, 27, 31, 58
Lotus Pinnacle of Amoghapasha, 23, 31, 58
Maitreya, 30, 58, 69
Medicine Buddha, 1, 22, 58, 81
Milarepa, 28, 58
Mitrukpa, 1, 2, 24, 31, 58
name mantra of His Holiness the Dalai Lama, 18
name mantra of your loved one's guru, 18
Namgyalma, 8, 25, 31, 58, 77
Ornament of Enlightenment, 6, 37, 87
Padmasambhava, 26, 58
Padmoshnisha. *See* Lotus Pinnacle of Amoghapasha
Pema Tsuktor. *See* Lotus Pinnacle of Amoghapasha
Rashmi Vimala Vishuddhaprabha. *See* Beam of Completely Pure Stainless Light
Ratna Shikhin. *See* Buddha

who protects from the lower
   realms
Rinchen Tsuktorchen. *See* Buddha who protects from the lower realms
Secret Relic, 6, 37, 87
Stainless Beam. *See* Beam of Completely Pure Stainless Light
Stainless Pinnacle, 6, 31, 37, 58, 87
ten powerful mantras, 21–30, 58
Ushnishavijaya. *See* Namgyalma
Ushnishavimala. *See* Stainless Pinnacle
Vairochana. *See* Kunrik
Vajra Armor, 58
Vajrasattva, 50, 53
Wish-Granting Wheel. *See* Lotus Pinnacle of Amoghapasha

Meditations
death process, 39
emptiness of death, 45
emptiness of the mind, 46
giving and taking. *See* tonglen
sleep meditations, 40–44
sleep in the guru's lap, 43
sleep in the lion position, 40
sleep process, 41
sleep with bodhichitta, 42
sleep with emptiness, 44
tonglen, 38
using stupas, 37

Miscellaneous Practices
bless the body with or turn a prayer wheel, 7
bless with a stupa, 6
bless the body with a blessed cord, 8
bless the body with a text, 5
bless the body with written mantras, 58
check that the mind has left the body, 74
consult a Tibetan astrologer, 76
give away possessions, 9
hear mantras, 16–31
hear names of buddhas, 14, 15
hear sutras, 32–34
hear teachings, 35
help your love one with their daily practices, 47
lie in the lion position, 55
make holy objects on behalf of your loved one, 87
shout in your loved one's ear the name of their guru, 60
show mantras, 2, 3, 4
show statues, pictures of buddhas, guru, 1
sleep in the lion position, 40
sponsor Dharma activities with your loved one's money, 86
sponsor monasteries, Dharma centers, friends, to perform practices, 59
sprinkle blessed seeds, water, and so forth on your loved one's body, 77

talk about Amitabha's pure land, or heaven, 11
talk about compassion, bodhichitta, 13
talk about your loved one's good qualities, 12
talk about your loved one's guru, or Buddha, or God, 10
throw blessed ashes into the water or wind, 80
tug at the hair at the crown chakra, 75
write a will. *See* give away possessions

Offerings
offer lights in front of the body, 63
offer lights, flowers, and so forth on behalf of your loved one, 84
offer money on behalf of your loved one, 85

Prayers
"A Daily Prayer to Bodhisattva Maitreya," 69
"Dedication" chapter from Shantideva's *Guide to the Bodhisattva Way of Life*, 65
eight prayers to benefit the dead, 64–71
"King of Prayers," 64
"Prayer to Be Reborn in the Blissful Realm of Amitabha Buddha," 66
"Prayer for a Statue of Maitreya," 70
"Prayer for Spontaneous Bliss," 71
"Prayer for the Beginning, Middle, and End of Practice," 67
"Until Buddhahood," 68

Pujas and Practices
Amitabha Buddha phowa, 81
Dorje Khadro burning offering, 83
jangwa, 78
Guru Puja, 72
Medicine Buddha, 36
phowa, 48, 62, 81
sur, 82
your loved one's daily practices, 47

Purification Practices
abbreviated tsok offering, 52
Dorje Khadro burning offering puja, 83
prostrations to the Thirty-Five Buddhas of Confession, 49
Samayavajra, 51
self-initiation, 54
Vajrasattva and the four opponent powers, 50
Vajrasattva tsok offering by Lama Yeshe, 53

Retreats
nyungné fasting retreat, 73

Sutras and Texts
By Wearing, Liberates, 5
Heart Sutra, 33
Lamrim Chenmo, 5
sutra for alleviating pain, 32
Great Noble Sutra on Entering the City of Vaishali. See sutra for alleviating pain
Shitro. See *By Wearing, Liberates*
Takdröl. See *By Wearing, Liberates*
Vajra Cutter Sutra, 34

About the Author

LAMA ZOPA RINPOCHE is one of the most internationally renowned masters of Tibetan Buddhism, working and teaching ceaselessly on almost every continent.

He is the spiritual director and cofounder of the Foundation for the Preservation of the Mahayana Tradition (FPMT), an international network of Buddhist projects, including monasteries in six countries and meditation centers in over thirty; health and nutrition clinics, and clinics specializing in the treatment of leprosy and polio; as well as hospices, schools, publishing activities, and prison outreach projects worldwide. Lama Zopa Rinpoche is the author of numerous books, including *Transforming Problems into Happiness*, *Ultimate Healing*, *The Door to Satisfaction*, *How to Be Happy*, *Wholesome Fear*, *Wisdom Energy*, and *Dear Lama Zopa* from Wisdom Publications, as well as other works from the Lama Yeshe Wisdom Archive. To find out more about the FPMT, contact:

FPMT International Office
1632 SE 11th Avenue
Portland, OR 97214-4702 USA
Tel. 503-808-1588 | Fax 503-808-1589
www.fpmt.org

About the Editor

VENERABLE ROBINA COURTIN was ordained in the late 1970s and has worked full time since then for Lama Thubten Yeshe and Lama Zopa Rinpoche's FPMT. Over the years she has served as editorial director of Wisdom Publications, editor of Mandala Magazine, executive director of Liberation Prison Project, and as a touring teacher of Buddhism. Her life, including her work with prisoners, has been featured in the documentary films *Chasing Buddha* and *Key to Freedom*.

What to Read Next from Wisdom Publications

Lack and Transcendence
The Problem of Death and Life in Psychotherapy, Existentialism, and Buddhism
David R. Loy

Whatever the differences in their methods and goals, psychotherapy, existentialism, and Buddhism are all concerned with the same fundamental issues of life and death—and death-in-life.

Bodhichitta
Practice for a Meaningful Life
Lama Zopa Rinpoche

An accessible, inspiring book on one of the most important topics in Tibetan Buddhism—bodhichitta, or compassion—written by one of its renowned masters who has an international following of thousands.

Four Noble Truths
A Guide to Everyday Life
Lama Zopa Rinpoche

An excellent elucidation of the nature of the mind and its role in creating the happiness we all seek, followed by an in-depth analysis of the four truths.

Dying with Confidence
A Tibetan Buddhist Guide to Preparing for Death
Anyen Rinpoche
Translated by Allison Choying Zangmo

"A powerful guidebook and a source of comfort at life's most crucial moment."—Tulku Thondup Rinpoche, author of *Boundless Healing*

About Wisdom Publications

Wisdom Publications is the leading publisher of classic and contemporary Buddhist books and practical works on mindfulness. To learn more about us or to explore our other books, please visit our website at wisdomexperience.org or contact us at the address below.

> Wisdom Publications
> 199 Elm Street
> Somerville, MA 02144 USA

We are a 501(c)(3) organization, and donations in support of our mission are tax deductible.

Wisdom Publications is affiliated with the Foundation for the Preservation of the Mahayana Tradition (FPMT).